# DICTIONARY *of*
# SCIENCE

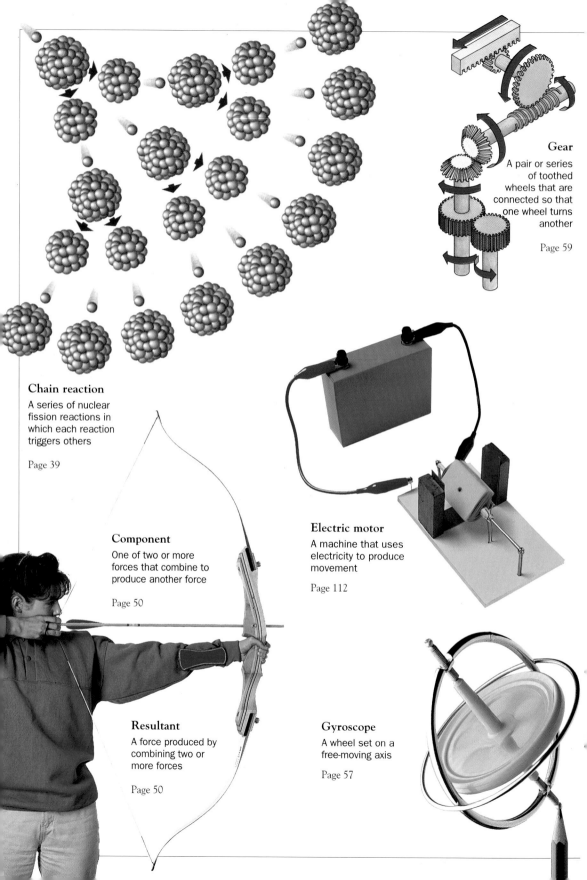

**Gear**
A pair or series of toothed wheels that are connected so that one wheel turns another

Page 59

**Chain reaction**
A series of nuclear fission reactions in which each reaction triggers others

Page 39

**Component**
One of two or more forces that combine to produce another force

Page 50

**Electric motor**
A machine that uses electricity to produce movement

Page 112

**Resultant**
A force produced by combining two or more forces

Page 50

**Gyroscope**
A wheel set on a free-moving axis

Page 57

# DICTIONARY *of* SCIENCE

## Written by Neil Ardley

# www.dk.com

**Project Editor** Stephen Setford

**Art Editors** Christopher Howson
Yaël Freudmann

**Editors** Bridget Hopkinson
Miranda Smith

**Production** Susannah Straughan

**Managing Editor** Helen Parker

**Managing Art Editor** Peter Bailey

**Special Photography** Michael Dunning

**Picture Research** Anne Lyons

**Database Manager** Mina Patria

**Educational Consultants** Jackie Hardie, B.Sc., M.Ed.,
The Latymer School, London

Kimi Hosoume, B.A., Lawrence Hall of Science,
Berkeley, California

**Editorial Consultants** Jack Challoner, B.Sc.
Christopher Cooper, B.Sc.
Michael White, B.Sc

**U.S. Editor** Charles A. Wills
**U.S. Consultant** Harvey B. Loomis

First American Edition, 1994
10 9 8 7 6 5 4 3
Published in the United States by
DK Publishing Inc., 95 Madison Avenue
New York, New York 10016
Copyright © 1994 Dorling Kindersley Limited, London
Text Copyright © 1994 Neil Ardley

Library of Congress Cataloging–in–Publication Data
Ardley, Neil.
    Dictionary of science / Neil Ardley. – – 1st American ed.
        p.   cm.
    Includes index
    ISBN 1–56458–349–X
    1. Science – – Dictionaries, Juvenile.   2. Technology – – Dictionaries, Juvenile.
    [1.  Science – – Dictionaries.   2. Technology – – Dictionaries.]   I. Title.
Q123.A73   1994
500– – dc20                                                                         93–29811
                                                                                            CIP
                                                                                             AC
        Reproduced by Colourscan, Singapore
Printed and bound in China by L.Rex Printing Co., Ltd.

## Warning

This dictionary contains many
photographs of experiments and
demonstrations that show science
in action. These were carried out
under carefully controlled conditions
in a laboratory and a photographic
studio. It is dangerous for readers to
perform these experiments and
demonstrations themselves.

## Safety symbols

Safety signs may be fixed to doors,
cabinets, or other areas of a
laboratory to warn of a nearby
hazard or a hazardous substance.
Each symbol is enclosed in a
triangle and has a yellow
background. Examples include:

 Danger

 Risk of
electric shock
(dangerous
voltage)

 Highly
flammable

 Radioactive

 Laser
radiation

Hazardous equipment and containers
of hazardous materials may also carry
warning symbols. Each symbol is
enclosed within a square (or in a
diamond shape, in the case of
vehicles). Examples include:

 Explosive

 Oxidizing

 Toxic

 Corrosive

Highly
flammable

Harmful
or irritant

Other safety symbols include:

No smoking

Eye protection
must be worn

First aid

## A note on numbers

In science and mathematics, it is usual
to break up large numbers into groups
of three digits, each group being
separated by a space (1 000 000, for
example). But four-digit numbers are
usually written as 1000, 2000, and so
on. However, for ease of reading, this
book keeps to the old convention of
using commas rather than spaces.

500
ARD
1994

**Hammer thrower
(pages 48–49)**

Force and motion are
part of everything we
do. This athlete, for
example, whirls the
hammer around by
using his arms and body
weight to exert a force
on the hammer. We put
our knowledge about
force and motion to use in
machines. More about
force, motion, and
machines on pages 48–61.

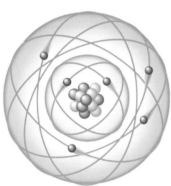

**Carbon atom (pages 34–35)**

Atoms are the "building blocks" of matter.
But atoms are made up of even smaller
particles. This carbon atom, for example,
contains particles called protons, neutrons,
and electrons. When changes occur inside
atoms, huge amounts of energy are released.
More about tiny particles on pages 34–45.

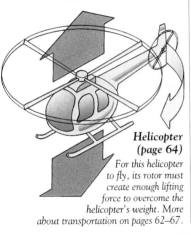

**Helicopter
(page 64)**

For this helicopter
to fly, its rotor must
create enough lifting
force to overcome the
helicopter's weight. More
about transportation on pages 62–67.

# Contents

# ENERGY 68–75

*The different kinds of energy that make actions happen, and how energy can travel from one place to another*

# LIGHT 76–89

*How we see objects, colors, and images, and how we make and use light*

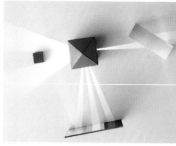

**Light rays (pages 76–77)**
*Light is the only form of energy that we can see. With mirrors and lenses we can bend, reflect, and even split up light rays into different colors. More about light, color, and how we use light in instruments such as cameras, telescopes, and microscopes on pages 76–89.*

# HEAT 90–97

*Why things burn, how everything possesses heat energy, how we measure hot and cold, and how we harness heat in engines and other machines*

# SOUND 98–99

*The nature and properties of sound, and how it can be used to detect unseen objects*

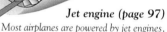

**Jet engine (page 97)**
*Most airplanes are powered by jet engines, which burn fuel to produce heat energy. Whether it is hot or cold, every object has a certain amount of heat energy. By controlling heat energy, we are able to power machines, to keep our homes warm or cool, and even to keep food fresh. More about fire, heat, and their many uses on pages 90–97.*

# MAGNETISM & ELECTRICITY 100–113

*How magnets work, and the Earth's magnetism; the principles of electricity, and how we generate electricity for daily use*

# ELECTRONICS & COMPUTING 114–123

*How electronic parts such as transistors work, and all about computers*

# COMMUNICATIONS 124–131

*The different ways in which we exchange knowledge and information*

**Telephone (page 128)**
*A telephone lets you speak to people on the other side of the world. Books, newspapers, television, radio, and sound recordings entertain us and keep us up to date with world events, while fax machines enable us to send information from place to place instantly. More about the technology that helps us to communicate on pages 124–131.*

**Electrolysis
(page 148)**

In electrolysis, an
electric current is passed
through a substance so
that it splits up into
simpler substances. A
substance that cannot be
split into anything
simpler is an element.
Most materials are
compounds, which are
combinations of two or
more elements. Changes
that result in new
substances being formed
are called chemical
reactions. More about
elements and chemical
reactions on pages
132–149.

**Paper chromatography (page 156)**

This experiment separates out the pigments
in flower petals. Chromatography is a method
of finding out what a substance contains. In
industry, it is used to check
that foods and medicines are
pure. More about chemical
substances and the chemical
industry on pages 150–168.

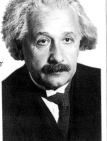

**Albert Einstein (page 179)**
The German-born scientist Albert
Einstein developed the theory of relativity,
which is the basis for most modern
scientific ideas about the
history and structure
of the Universe.
The discoveries
and inventions of
scientists have
transformed the
way people live their
lives. You will find
a list of some of
the world's most
famous scientists,
inventors, and
mathematicians on
pages 178–181.

# How to use this book

This dictionary explains the most important words, terms, and concepts in physics and chemistry and in the technology that puts them to use. It also explains some of the mathematics used in science. It is a thematic dictionary, which means that the words defined in this book are arranged into subject areas, such as "Force." This enables you to find out about a whole subject, as well as to look up individual words. The Contents on pages 5–7 lists the different sections and subjects. If you do not know where to find a word, you can look it up in the index at the back of the book.

### Main illustration
*A large photograph or artwork usually illustrates several related entries. It helps to explain the entries by showing them in action. This photograph of a hammer thrower shows force, centripetal force, gravity, and center of gravity.*

### Cross reference
*A small gray square (▥) after a word shows that the word is an entry or a subentry elsewhere in the dictionary. The "See also" box gives the page number of the entry.*

### Subentries
*A subentry is found in **bold type**. It gives the meaning of a word that is related to a main entry. This subentry explains that the term "center of mass" means the same as center of gravity.*

### Using the index
*The index lists all the entries in alphabetical order and gives their page numbers. If you look up Newton's law of gravitation in the index, for example, it will tell you that the entry is on page 49. The word you want may be a main entry, or it may be a subentry, which is to be found in bold type inside an entry. It may also be an entry in a table.*

---

48 • Force, Motion, & Machines

## Force

A force is invisible, but you can see and feel its effect. Forces push or pull. They cause objects to start or stop moving, change speed or direction, bend, stretch, twist, or change shape. A common force is the Earth's gravity. It pulls us to the ground and gives us weight.

### Force
A push or a pull

If an object is free to move, a force will make it move in a particular direction. But if an object is not free to move, a force may make it stretch or change its shape. When the forces acting upon an object are balanced, the object is in equilibrium ▥.

### Mechanics
The study of the effects of forces upon objects

There are two main branches of mechanics. Dynamics ▥ is the study of forces on objects in motion. Statics ▥ is the study of forces on objects that do not move.

*An athlete's hammer is a heavy weight attached to a wire*

### Center of gravity
The point at which the whole weight of an object balances

You can balance a tray of glasses on one hand if you support it directly beneath its center of gravity. Gravity pulls equally on all parts of the tray around this point. The center of gravity is also called the **center of mass**.

### Centripetal force
The force that keeps an object moving in a circle

If you whirl a weight on a piece of string, its inertia ▥ makes it try to fly off in a straight line. You have to pull on the string to keep the weight moving in a circle. This pull is the centripetal force. Its direction is inward, toward the center of rotation.

### A moving force
*This hammer thrower's muscles produce a strong force to lift the hammer and start it moving.*

### Centripetal force
*The hammer thrower pulls strongly on the wire as he whirls the hammer. This pull is the centripetal force.*

### Centrifuge
A machine that spins a mixture high speed to separate its different components

In a centrifuge, a container holding a mixture ▥ spins around at high speed. This exerts a strong force on the mixture, causing it to separate into its different components The heavier particles of the mixture move outward becau of their greater inertia. There appears to be an outward forc often called **centrifugal force** acting on the particles.

*The hammer's inertia pulls it outward as it spins around*

### Center of gravity
*As he swings the hammer, the hammer thrower leans back to keep his center of gravity above his feet.*

### Annotation and captions
*A headed caption explains what you can see in the picture. This caption tells you how the athlete's center of gravity changes as he whirls the hammer. Details in a picture, such as what happens to the athlete's hammer as he whirls it around, are pointed out by annotation.*

## Explanations

The explanation tells you more about the entry. It can help you to understand the definition. This explanation uses the examples of the Earth, the Moon, and the Sun to help you understand gravitational fields.

## Definitions

The definition is a short, precise description. This definition tells you what a gravitational field is.

## Running heads

For quick reference, the running head shows you which section you are in. This section is Force, Motion, & Machines.

## Entry headings

This entry is about Gravity.

## Units

On page 51, you will find a "Units" box that contains the newton, the unit of force. The dictionary has entries on all the main units. There is also a table of units on page 14. You can also look up abbreviations, such as N for newton, on page 177, where you will find that N also stands for the element nitrogen.

### Gravity

A force of attraction between bodies of matter

There is a force of gravity between you and the Earth. The Earth's gravity pulls on you, giving you weight and keeping you on the ground. At the same time, you pull on the Earth. All bodies of matter ▪ exert a force of gravity. But it is strong only when something has a large mass ▪, such as a planet, moon, or star. Gravity becomes weaker as bodies of matter move farther apart.

### Gravitational field

The region in which a body of matter exerts a force of gravity

The Sun's gravitational field extends far out into space. It pulls on the planets of the solar system, holding them in orbits around the Sun. The field becomes weaker farther away from the Sun. The Earth's gravitational field keeps satellites and the Moon in orbit around the Earth.

When the hammer is released, it flies off because centripetal force no longer holds it back.

### Weight

The force of gravity acting on a body of matter

Your weight is the force of the Earth's gravity pulling on you. So if you move away from the Earth, your weight becomes less. On the Moon, astronauts have only one-sixth of their normal weight, because the Moon's gravity is only a sixth of that of the Earth.

Gravity soon pulls the hammer back to Earth

### Newton meter

An instrument that measures force

A newton meter, or force meter, measures force using a spring. The spring stretches when a force pulls on it, moving a pointer along a scale. This indicates the strength of the force. For example, 1 kilogram (2.2 lb.) pulls on the spring with a force of 10 newtons ▪. A spring balance measures weight in the same way.

### Newton's law of gravitation

The force of gravity between two bodies of matter depends on their mass and the square of the distance between them

If the Moon had twice its mass, the force of gravity between it and the Earth would be twice as great. But if the mass of the Moon stayed the same and it moved twice as near to the Earth, the force of gravity between the two bodies would be four (two squared) times greater. The physicist Isaac Newton ▪ discovered this law, which applies to all bodies of matter.

1 kilogram pulls with a force of about 10 newtons

2 kilograms pull with a force of about 20 newtons

|  Earth | Moon |
| --- | --- |
| Force of gravity = 1 | |
| Mass = 1 | Mass = 1 |
| Force of gravity = 2 | |
| | Mass = 2 |
| Force of gravity = | |
| | Mass = 1 |
| | Moon twice as near |

### See also

Dynamics 55 • Equilibrium 50
Fundamental force 43 • Inertia 54
Mass 23 • Matter 27
Newton 5 • Newton, Isaac 55
's law.
Stat

## UNITS OF FORCE

### Newton (N)

unit of force

One newton of force causes a mass of 1 kilogram to move with an acceleration ▪ of 1 meter per second per second. On earth, a mass of 1 kilogram weighs 9.8 newtons.

### Statics

The study of the forces acting on bodies that do not move

Statics is important in the design of stationary structures such as buildings and bridges. The forces in a structure must balance so that the structure does not move or fall down. Hydrostatics is the study of fluids at rest and objects immersed in fluids. It is used in the design of hydraulic ▪ machines and ships. The force caused by the pressure of a fluid can break up a machine or ship.

## Biographies

On page 55, you will find a biography of Isaac Newton, who first explained gravity. The dictionary contains individual biographies of famous scientists, usually with a picture of them or of apparatus that they used. There is also an alphabetical listing of pioneer scientists on pages 178 through to 181.

### first law

at rest or el at a a force on it

all not acts on it elerate. Then it avel forward, force slows it ll a ball along the m provides the lerates the ball. s forward until t to a stop.

### second law

ccelerates an object is equal to its mass multiplied by its acceleration

The acceleration of an object depends on its mass and the amount of force acting on it. If you hit a small ball with a large amount of force, the ball accelerates rapidly. But if you apply the same force to a heavier ball, the acceleration will be less.

The white billiard ball collides with the red billiard ball

### Isaac Newton

English physicist and mathematician (1642–1727)

Newton took Galileo's observations of force and motion further when he developed his three laws of motion. He also discovered the law of gravitation ▪, which may have been inspired by seeing an apple fall from a tree. Newton made other important discoveries in light ▪ and developed calculus ▪ in mathematics.

### Conservation of momentum

As the two billiard balls collide, the white ball transfers most of its momentum to the red ball. Both move forward, but the red ball travels with a greater velocity.

### Dynamics

The study of forces that cause changes in motion

There are two main branches of dynamics. Hydrodynamics is the study of the motion of fluids, such as water, and the movement in water of objects such as boats. Aerodynamics is the study of the motion of gases, particularly air, and the

### Newton's third law of motion

When two objects act on each other, they experience equal forces in opposite directions

Forces always act in pairs called

### Perpetual motion

Motion that carries on forever without a force to keep it going

A space probe can travel through space forever. There is no air in space, so there is no friction to slow it down. It is impossible for an object to achieve this perpetual motion on Earth. With no force to keep it going, friction with the air or other matter always slows a moving object to a stop.

### Force of friction

Friction between the ball and the table slows the ball to a stop.

Without friction to slow it down, the ball would keep on moving forever

### Momentum

The mass of an object multiplied by its velocity

The momentum of an object depends on its mass and velocity. This means that an object's momentum changes as it accelerates. Momentum can be transferred between objects. When a moving ball collides with a stationary one, for example, the first ball transfers some of its momentum to the second ball. The total momentum of the two balls is the same as the first ball's momentum before the collision. This is called the principle of conservation of momentum.

Continued on next page ►

## Diagrams and other illustrations

A diagram explains a scientific principle or term. This diagram shows how Newton's law of gravitation works. A small photograph or artwork usually illustrates a single entry.

## "See also" boxes

You will find a "See also" box with each subject. This directs you to other entries or subentries that can help you understand the subject better. This "See also" box may lead you to look up Isaac Newton, and a unit called the newton.

# What is science?

If you are sitting in a chair reading this book, how are you able to see its pages? What is the paper made of? How can the pictures be printed with so many colors? What keeps you in the chair? And why don't you fall through the floor? These are the kinds of questions that science seeks to answer. Some of the answers may seem obvious: you don't fall through the floor because it is solid. But this leads to another question: why is it solid? Science is the search for knowledge about the Universe and how it works. It is a search that never ends, because scientists do not settle for the first explanation they find, but always seek better explanations. Scientists try to discover the fundamental reasons why everything is the way it is.

**Laboratory research**
Scientists carry out their work in laboratories, where they can perform experiments under controlled conditions.

## Science – a study of everything!

Studying the whole Universe is a huge task, so it isn't surprising that there are many different branches of science. Physics investigates energy and matter, the material of which everything is made. Chemistry studies the basic substances, or elements, that are found in the Universe, and how they combine to form more complex substances called compounds. The study of plants and animals is called biology. It looks at how they grow, feed, and reproduce, and how they change over long periods of time. The shape and structure of the Earth are studied in geology, while meteorology looks at weather and the Earth's atmosphere. Mathematics – the study of numbers, shapes, and quantities – enables scientists to make measurements and calculations and to understand the results of their experiments and research.

**From frogs to personal stereos**
You may think that there is no connection between a leaping frog and listening to a music tape on a personal stereo – but you would be wrong! The sequence of pictures below shows how a chain of scientific discoveries enables your stereo to work. These began with experiments on dead frogs in 1791.

**1** In 1791, the Italian scientist Luigi Galvani found that the leg of a dead frog twitched when he touched it with two different metals connected together. Galvani thought it was caused by electricity made by the frog. He did not realize that the electricity was produced by a chemical reaction between the metals and chemicals in the frog's nerves and muscles.

**2** Alessandro Volta was an Italian physicist who correctly explained Galvani's discovery. He used it in 1800 to build a device that produced electricity continuously. This "Voltaic pile" consisted of a stack of copper, zinc, and cardboard disks. The cardboard was soaked in a solution of salt or a weak acid, such as vinegar. A chemical reaction occurred between the solution and the two metals, producing a flow of electric current. Volta had made the world's first battery.

— Cardboard disk

— Copper disk fixed to zinc disk

An electric current passes through the wire

The compass needle is deflected by the magnetic field of the current

**3** In 1820, the Danish physicist Hans Oersted moved a compass near to a wire carrying an electric current. The wire caused the magnetized compass needle to swing away from its normal north-south alignment. This showed that magnetism had been produced by the electric current. This effect is now called electromagnetism.

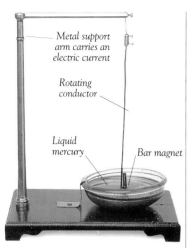

**4** *In 1821, a year after Oersted's discovery of the connection between electricity and magnetism, the English physicist Michael Faraday devised a simple apparatus in which electromagnetism caused a current-carrying wire to rotate around the pole of a magnet. Faraday's apparatus was the first electric motor, although it had no real practical use.*

Metal support arm carries an electric current

Rotating conductor

Liquid mercury

Bar magnet

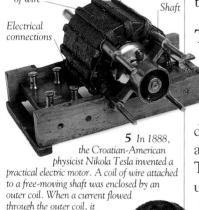

Outer coil of wire

Inner coil

Shaft

Electrical connections

**5** *In 1888, the Croatian-American physicist Nikola Tesla invented a practical electric motor. A coil of wire attached to a free-moving shaft was enclosed by an outer coil. When a current flowed through the outer coil, it produced a changing magnetic field in each coil. The fields pushed and pulled on each other and rotated the shaft.*

### Music machine
*Your personal stereo makes use of the discoveries and inventions listed above. It is powered by batteries, in which chemical reactions create an electric current. The batteries drive an electric motor, which uses electromagnetism to play the tape and send sound to your ears.*

# How science works

Science is not limited to what happens inside a laboratory – it is going on around us all the time. Machines start up and do their tasks because they obey certain scientific laws that control their operations. And if they do break down, it is because other scientific laws stop them from working. These laws were discovered because scientists looked at the world around them and observed events, such as water freezing to form ice. A scientist produces an explanation for such an event. The explanation must then be tested. If it is always true in every test, it can become a scientific law. The law that governs freezing is obeyed constantly at the North and South Poles, and each time you make ice in a freezer.

**Making use of science**
*This scientist is testing solar cells, which use sunlight to produce electricity.*

# Technology – science in action

Life for people today is very different from what it was for people 5,000 years ago. Over the years, scientists have made many discoveries in their search for knowledge. The way in which these discoveries are put to practical use to build machines and to make tasks easier is called technology. Technology greatly changes people's lives. It has helped us to grow more food, for example, and to make our homes more comfortable. Thanks to technology, we have fast, safe transportation systems that carry people and products from place to place with ease – even into space. Technology also enables us to communicate with other people over long distances. Advances in medicine help us to live longer and healthier lives. New drugs and machines, for example, can prevent and cure many illnesses and diseases. However, science has also brought us deadlier weapons and pollution that harms the environment. But science is in the service of us all, and we can use it for good or for ill.

# The practice of science

All scientists work with great care, using their hands and their brains, as well as complex equipment. Many carry out research and try to make discoveries and inventions. Others check machines and materials to make sure that they are safe and work efficiently.

Newton meter reads 4 newtons

**Weighing the wood**
*Eight blocks of wood are made so that they all have the same volume. Each block is weighed on a newton meter. The weight in newtons (N) is carefully recorded.*

Oak block (4.0 N)

Spruce (2.5 N)  Balsa (0.5 N)  Pine (2.5 N)  Mahogany (3.0 N)  Ash (3.7 N)  Birch (3.8 N)  Douglas Fir (3.3 N)

## Laboratory

A place where scientists work

Scientists carry out experiments and analysis in a laboratory. It contains **apparatus**, the equipment needed for scientific work.

**Laboratory experiments**
*All the factors that might affect the results are carefully controlled.*

## Experiment

A practical scientific test

An experiment tests a prediction or a hypothesis ■. The result is evidence that may support or disprove the idea. An experiment must have a **control** in order for its results to be valid. A test of a new medicine, for example, needs a control test in which everything is the same except that the medicine is not used. If the test gives better results than the control, then the new medicine is effective.

## Variable

A factor in an experiment that can change and affect the result

When you change the length of a pendulum ■ string, you also change the time that the pendulum takes to swing back and forth. Both these changing quantities are variables. An **independent variable** is a factor that causes a change in the result of an experiment. In this case, the length of the string is an independent variable. A **dependent variable** is the result that you observe changing – in this case, the time of the swing. A **control variable** is one that may affect the result of the experiment, but that must be kept the same in order to be sure that the result is caused by changing the independent variable. The mass of the pendulum bob or the thickness of the string could possibly affect the time of the swing, so they are control variables for the pendulum experiment. A **fair test** is an experiment or investigation in which all the variables except one are kept the same, so that the result has only one possible cause.

The displaced water flows out of the beaker, down the spout, and into the pan of the newton balance

Newton balance

The reading on the balance increases as more water flows into the pan

**Testing ideas**
*This experiment tests the principle of flotation,*
*which states that the weight of water displaced by a floating object is equal to the weight of the object (see page 51). The results of this experiment support the principle. When the oak is floating properly, for example, the balance reads 4 newtons.*

## Empirical

Known as a result of experience

Empirical knowledge is gained by doing experiments or making observations, rather than from theory.

## Scale

The marking of units on a measuring instrument

Many scientific measuring instruments use a pointer that moves over a dial marked with a scale of units. A thermometer  is marked along the side with a scale of degrees. The actual marks along the scale are called **graduations**.

*Scale*

*The reading on the newton meter falls as the wood enters the water*

*The oak block displaces water as it enters the beaker*

## Accuracy

How exact a result is

A result or measurement that is correct is said to be accurate. An instrument or machine that gives accurate results works with **precision**. In fact, every result has a certain amount of **error**, which is a lack of accuracy. For example, a result may be given as 500 ± 15 (500 plus or minus 15), which means that it lies somewhere between 485 and 515. A result that is not very accurate is an **approximate** result.

## Unit

A basic amount

A scientific experiment usually involves measuring something, such as the length of an object. Most measurements must be expressed as a number and a unit: a number on its own would be useless. For example, if the length of the object is said to be 10, no-one will know whether the object is 10 centimeters or 10 inches long. Most measurements are made by reading the number of units from a scale. The actual size of a unit is called a **standard**. Making or setting a measuring instrument so that it measures in units of the correct size is called **calibration**. Science uses an international set of units called SI units ▨.

*Floating the wood*
*The wooden blocks are immersed in the water in the glass beaker until they float, and the weight of the water displaced is measured on the newton balance.*

*Each of the remaining blocks gives a similar result to the oak when floated in water – the weight of the water displaced always equals the weight of the block*

## Analysis

Finding out what things contain, and why events happen

Chemical analysis ▨ identifies the elements that make up a substance. It includes checking the purity of a substance. Analysis also means solving problems and finding out what causes them. This can be done by thinking and discussion, as well as by calculation, observation, and experiment.

*Calipers with a vernier divided into 0.02-millimeter graduations*

### See also

Chemical analysis 156 • Hypothesis 18
Pendulum 56 • SI unit 14
Thermometer 92

## Analog

A way of expressing one quantity in terms of another quantity

A watch with hands and a mercury thermometer are both analog instruments. They both display measurements in terms of length. The clock shows time by the distance that the hands move, while the thermometer shows temperature by the length of the column of mercury inside it. A **digital** instrument shows a measurement directly as a number. A digital watch, for example, shows the time as a number on a display.

## Vernier

A very accurate form of scale

A measuring instrument with a scale often gives a reading that lies between two graduations on the scale. A vernier removes the guesswork in this measurement. It enables the final reading to be made on a set of subdivisions alongside the main scale.

*Ball bearing*

*The reading on the main scale shows just over 1.2 centimeters*

*The vernier reads 0.076 centimeters*

*Using a vernier*
*A reading is taken on the vernier where one of its graduations lines up with a graduation on the main scale. The vernier reading is added to the reading on the main scale. The diameter of this steel ball bearing is 1.276 centimeters.*

# Measurement

The system of SI units is used for measurement in science throughout the world. These pages explain the main SI units and how they relate to each other. In some parts of the world, the imperial system of measurement is still used.

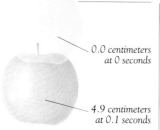

0.0 centimeters
at 0 seconds

4.9 centimeters
at 0.1 seconds

**Falling apple**
*From these photographs, we can work out that the falling apple accelerates at 9.8 meters per second per second. An accurate balance measures its mass as 102 grams (0.102 kilograms).*

19.6 centimeters
at 0.2 seconds

**Basic and derived units**
*We can measure the force that pulls the apple to the ground by multiplying its mass (0.102 kilograms) by its acceleration (9.8 meters per second per second). The calculation gives a result of 1 kilogram meter per second per second. This combination of basic SI units is awkward to use, so a derived unit, called the newton, is used to measure force. A newton equals a force of 1 kilogram meter per second per second, so the force pulling on the apple is 1 newton.*

44.1 centimeters
at 0.3 seconds

## SI unit

An international unit of measurement used in science

SI stands for *Système International*, which is French for "international system." The system of SI units has been agreed for international use, so that scientists around the world can all record the results of their experiments and make their calculations using the same units. One example of an SI unit is the **meter**. This is the SI unit of length, which equals the distance that light travels in 1/299,792,458 of a second through a vacuum. Light is used as a standard because it has a constant speed.

## USCS UNITS

**Length**
1 mile = 1,760 yards
1 yard = 3 feet
1 foot = 12 inches

**Volume**
1 gallon = 8 pints

**Mass**
1 pound = 16 ounces
1 ton = 2,000 pounds

## Imperial or USCS unit

A unit of measurement still in common use in some countries

Imperial units include the pound, mile, and gallon. Unlike SI units, imperial units have no scientific standards. Calculations with imperial units are more complex than with SI units. In the USA, this system is called the **United States Customary Systems** (USCS). USCS gallons and tons are smaller than the equivalent imperial units used elsewhere.

## SI UNITS

### Basic SI units

| Quantity | Unit | Symbol |
|---|---|---|
| Length | Meter | m |
| Mass | Kilogram | kg |
| Time | Second | s |
| Electric current | Ampere | A |
| Temperature | Kelvin | K |
| Light intensity | Candela | cd |
| Amount of substance | Mole | mol |

**Basic SI units and derived SI units**
*The seven basic SI units have scientific standards that define the size of the units with great precision. The meter and its standard are given in the entry above on SI unit. Other basic units and derived units also have their own entries elsewhere in the dictionary.*

### Derived SI units

| Quantity | Unit | Symbol |
|---|---|---|
| Area | Square meter | $m^2$ |
| Volume | Cubic meter | $m^3$ |
| Frequency | Hertz | Hz |
| Force | Newton | N |
| Pressure | Pascal | Pa |
| Energy | Joule | J |
| Power | Watt | W |
| Electric potential | Volt | V |
| Electrical resistance | Ohm | Ω |
| Electric charge | Coulomb | C |
| Radioactivity | Becquerel | Bq |

*All derived units are related to the basic SI units.*

# DECIMAL MULTIPLES AND SUBMULTIPLES

## Decimal multiple

| Name | Symbol | Multiple |
|------|--------|----------|
| tera | T | x 1,000,000,000,000 $(10^{12})$ |
| giga | G | x 1,000,000,000 $(10^9)$ |
| mega | M | x 1,000,000 $(10^6)$ |
| kilo | k | x 1,000 $(10^3)$ |
| hecto | h | x 100 $(10^2)$ |
| deca | da | x 10 |

## Decimal submultiple

| Name | Symbol | Submultiple |
|------|--------|-------------|
| deci | d | ÷ 10 |
| centi | c | ÷ 100 $(10^{-2})$ |
| milli | m | ÷ 1,000 $(10^{-3})$ |
| micro | μ | ÷ 1,000,000 $(10^{-6})$ |
| nano | n | ÷ 1,000,000,000 $(10^{-9})$ |
| pico | p | ÷ 1,000,000,000,000 $(10^{-12})$ |

## Using multiples and submultiples

*Multiples and submultiples allow one unit to be used whatever the amount measured. For example, 1 kilogram (1 kg) is 1,000 grams, and 1 milligram (1 mg) is one-thousandth of a gram. Large masses are measured in kilograms, and small masses in milligrams, as shown on the right.*

*Jumbo jet 386,000,000 grams or 386,000 kilograms*

*Liter of liquid 1,000 grams or 1 kilogram*

*Bee hummingbird 1.6 grams*

*Human hair 0.01 grams or 10 milligrams*

# CONVERSION FACTORS

## SI units to imperial/USCS units

### Length
| | |
|---|---|
| 1 kilometer (km) | = 0.6214 mile |
| 1 meter (m) | = 1.0936 yards |
| 1 meter (m) | = 3.2808 feet |
| 1 centimeter (cm) | = 0.3937 inch |

### Area
| | |
|---|---|
| 1 square kilometer (km²) | = 0.3861 square mile |
| 1 hectare (ha) | = 2.47 acres |
| *1 hectare = 10,000 square meters* | |
| 1 square meter (m²) | = 10.76 square feet |
| 1 square centimeter (cm²) | = 0.155 square inch |

### Volume
| | |
|---|---|
| 1 cubic meter (m³) | = 35.31 cubic feet |
| 1 liter (l) | = 0.22 gallon |
| 1 liter (l) | = 1.76 pints |
| *1 liter = 1,000 cubic centimeters* | |
| 1 cubic centimeter (cm³) | = 0.061 cubic inch |

### Mass
| | |
|---|---|
| 1 tonne (t) | = 0.9842 ton |
| *1 tonne = 1,000 kilograms* | |
| 1 kilogram (kg) | = 2.2046 pounds |
| 1 gram (g) | = 0.0353 ounce |

### US Measures
| | |
|---|---|
| 1 liter (l) | = 0.264 gallon |
| 1 liter (l) | = 2.11 pints |
| 1 tonne (t) | = 1.1023 tons |

## Imperial/USCS units to SI units

### Length
| | |
|---|---|
| 1 mile (mi.) | = 1.6093 kilometers |
| 1 yard (yd.) | = 0.9144 meter |
| 1 foot (ft.) | = 30.48 centimeters |
| 1 inch (in.) | = 25.4 millimeters |

### Area
| | |
|---|---|
| 1 square mile (sq. mi.) | = 2.59 square kilometers |
| 1 acre | = 0.4047 hectare |
| *1 acre = 4,840 square yards* | |
| 1 square foot (sq. ft.) | = 0.0929 square meter |
| 1 square inch (sq. in.) | = 6.452 square centimeters |

### Volume
| | |
|---|---|
| 1 cubic foot (cu. ft.) | = 0.0283 cubic meter |
| 1 gallon (gal.) | = 4.546 liters |
| 1 pint (pt.) | = 0.568 liter |
| *1 pint = 34.68 cubic inches* | |
| 1 cubic inch (cu. in.) | = 16.39 cubic centimeters |

### Mass
| | |
|---|---|
| 1 ton | = 1.0161 tonnes |
| *1 ton = 2,240 pounds* | |
| 1 pound (lb.) | = 0.4536 kilogram |
| 1 ounce (oz.) | = 28.35 grams |

### US Measures
| | |
|---|---|
| 1 gallon | = 3.785 liters |
| 1 pint (*28.88 cu. in.*) | = 0.473 liter |
| 1 ton (*2,000 lb.*) | = 0.9072 tonne |

Example: to find out what 16.5 inches equals in millimeters, simply multiply 16.5 by 25.4, to give 419.1mm or 41.91 cm

## Temperature

To convert °Celsius or Centigrade to °Fahrenheit multiply by 9, divide by 5, and add 32
To convert °Fahrenheit to °Celsius or Centigrade subtract 32, multiply by 5, and divide by 9
To convert °Celsius or Centigrade to kelvins add 273.15

# Data collection

Scientists make measurements and collect results as they work. They often display this information as graphs and charts, which help the scientists to understand the results of their research.

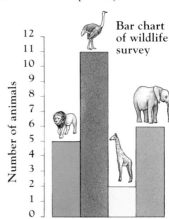

**Wildlife survey**
*Helicopters are sometimes used to collect valuable data about the distribution of wildlife. This helicopter is being used to count ostriches in a part of Africa.*

## Data

Information obtained during an investigation

Data may be a set of numbers, such as daily measurements of the temperature, or other information, such as descriptions of the weather: cloudy, sunny, rainy, and so on. Graphs and charts present data in ways that make it easier to understand.

## Graph

A diagram showing how one quantity varies in relation to another quantity

Most graphs have two **axes** (singular **axis**). These are two straight lines that meet at a point called the **origin** and form a right angle. Each axis is marked with a scale that indicates the amount of a quantity, such as temperature or time. You mark points on the graph using coordinates. Each point shows the values of both quantities, such as the temperature on a particular day. Joining up the points gives a line that shows how the quantities change. A graph can also have three axes, showing how three quantities relate.

**Graph of daily temperatures**

*Coordinates are 3,10*

## Coordinates

A set of numbers that gives the position of a point on a graph

A graph with axes at right angles uses **Cartesian coordinates**. A point on a graph has two or three coordinates. Each is a number that gives the distance of the point from an axis. This number is a measurement of a quantity, such as the number of degrees of temperature.

*Using data*
*The data in this table can be plotted on a graph. For example, the coordinates of the point that marks the temperature on the first day are 1, 20. When the points are joined up, it is easy to see how the temperature rose and fell over the period when data was collected.*

| DAILY TEMPERATURE (°C) | | | |
|---|---|---|---|
| Day 1 | 20 | Day 6 | 12 |
| Day 2 | 18 | Day 7 | 15 |
| Day 3 | 10 | Day 8 | 8 |
| Day 4 | 15 | Day 9 | 5 |
| Day 5 | 22 | Day 10 | 1 |

## Bar chart

A chart that shows data as columns

A bar chart has two axes. The vertical axis is marked with a scale. Different quantities are shown as columns. The height of each column shows the amount of each quantity. A **histogram** is a bar chart in which both axes have scales. The area of the column, rather than its height, gives the amount of the quantity.

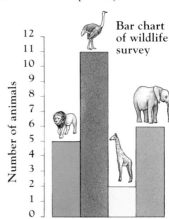

**Bar chart of wildlife survey**

# Permutation

An arrangement of a group of items

The permutations of A and B are AB and BA. The permutations of any two out of A, B, and C are: AB, BA, AC, CA, BC, and CB. Each permutation must have the same number of items.

***Animal pictogram***
*Each image represents one animal recorded in a survey.*

# Set

A group of similar things

A wildlife survey may show that there are sets of four- and two-legged animals. They are part of a **universal set**, an overall set that contains all other sets. Here, the universal set is the set of all animals. A set within another set is a **subset**. Elephants are in a set of four-legged animals with trunks – a subset of the set of four-legged animals. A **Venn diagram** shows how sets relate to each other. A member of a set is an **element**.

*Universal set of animals*

*Subset of four-legged animals with trunks*

*Set of all two-legged animals*

*Set of all four-legged animals*

**Venn diagram of wildlife survey**

# Average

The total of several items divided by the number of items

An average is also called a **mean**. To work out the average daily temperature from the data in the table on page 16, add up all the temperatures and divide the total by the number of days. The calculation is: $126 \div 10 = 12.6°C$. A **median** is the middle number in a group of numbers arranged in ascending order. The median of the temperatures in the table is 13.5 (halfway between 12 and 15, the middle two numbers). A **mode** is the number which occurs most often in a group of numbers. The mode of daily temperatures is 15.

# Frequency

The number of times a particular measurement occurs in a group of measurements

A group of 20 people has 6 people under 5 ft. 6 in. (1.7 m) in height, 12 people between 5 ft. 6 in. and 6 ft. (1.8 m), and 2 over 6 ft. tall. The frequencies of these groups are 6, 12, and 2. The **distribution** is the range of frequencies that occurs, and is shown by a bar chart.

# Matrix

A table of numbers arranged in rows and columns

A matrix is a compact way of writing down information or results. It is easy to use and to store, especially in a computer.

# Pictogram

A chart that presents data in the form of pictures

A pictogram is similar to a bar chart, but instead of using columns and a scale, it shows data using groups of pictures or symbols. The number of pictures in each group shows the size of that group.

# Pie chart

A chart that presents data as slices of a circle

Each quantity is shown as a sector ■ of a circle, like a slice cut out of a pie. The amount of each quantity is given by the area of the sector. It clearly shows the proportions of quantities.

*Elephants*  *Ostriches*

*Lions*  *Giraffes*

**Pie chart of wildlife survey**

# Statistics

The analysis of data

We can use statistics to examine large collections of data, such as a census of a country's population. It can tell us, for example, how much the population has increased or decreased and how it is likely to change in future years.

## See also

Sector 175

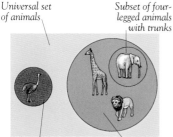

# Scientific method

Scientists first make observations of events. Their observations lead to explanations of why things happen, and to laws that govern how they work. But before any scientific idea can be accepted, it must be tested thoroughly to show that it is correct.

## Observation

**Scientific information that is gained by using all the senses**

You may observe, for example, that a stone speeds up as it falls to the ground. This observation could lead you to make an **inference**, which is a statement based on an observation. The inference might be that a force is acting on the stone as it falls. From this inference, you may come up with a hypothesis about the nature of the force. To test the hypothesis you will need to carry out experiments and make more observations. A **correlation** is a link between observations or variables ■. For example, the greater the force acting on an object, the more it accelerates.

## Hypothesis

**A suggested explanation that can be tested**

A hypothesis is tested by doing experiments to check whether the explanation always works. If it does, the hypothesis becomes a **theory**, which is the best explanation that can be offered. The kinetic theory ■, for example, states that all gases contain tiny moving particles. We cannot see these particles, but the kinetic theory does explain how gases behave. A **theorem** is a mathematical truth. One example is Pythagoras' theorem ■.

*The longer the screwdriver, the less effort is needed to open the can*

**Observations and inferences**
*You may observe that it is easier to open a paint can with a long screwdriver than with a short screwdriver. From this you can infer that the longer the implement is, the less effort you need to open the can.*

## Law of science

**A statement or explanation that always appears to be true**

When a theory is used successfully, it becomes a law of science. This explains and predicts exactly what happens whenever a certain kind of action occurs. Newton's laws of gravitation ■ and of motion ■ explain how a stone falls to the ground when dropped. They can state exactly how much force and motion are involved each time a stone falls. However, a law of science may be superseded or may need to be changed. Einstein's ■ theory of relativity ■ is found to be more accurate than Newton's laws. A law of science is also called a **scientific principle**.

## Formula

**A way of representing something using letters and numbers**

Laws of science and facts may be represented by a formula ■. Newton's second law of motion has the formula $F = ma$. This shows how a certain amount of force $F$ is needed to make an object of mass $m$ move with an acceleration of $a$. The force is always equal to the object's mass multiplied by the acceleration that occurs. A chemical formula ■ is a way of showing what a substance is made of.

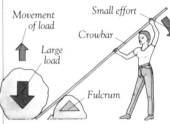

*Movement of load*  *Small effort*

*Large load*  *Crowbar*

*Fulcrum*

**Simple lever**
*When you open a can with a screwdriver, the screwdriver acts as a lever in the same way as a crowbar. A lever uses a small effort to lift a large load. The effort is farther from the fulcrum than the load.*

## Constant

**A quantity that does not change**

A formula may include a constant, such as pi ■ or the speed of light ■. The constant shows how other quantities in the formula relate to each other. Energy ($E$) and mass ($m$) are linked by the formula $E = mc^2$, where the constant $c^2$ equals the speed of light squared. Because $c$ has a very large value, the formula shows that a little mass can produce a lot of energy. The word constant also means "unchanging." A **coefficient** is a constant that is different for different materials.

## Symbol

A letter or group of letters that represents something

Symbols are used in formulas. Every constant has a particular symbol. The speed of light is $c$, and pi is always shown as the Greek letter $\pi$, for example. Each chemical element has its own chemical symbol ▩.

## Vector

A quantity that has a particular direction

Force is a vector quantity. When you push something, you exert a certain amount of force in a particular direction. A **scalar** is a quantity that has magnitude, or amount, but no specific direction. Temperature is a scalar.

## Cycle

An operation that returns to its starting point and may begin again

A playground ride goes through a cycle of movements, and each to-and-fro swing of a pendulum is a cycle. The length of time taken by one cycle is called a **period**. The rate at which a cycle is repeated is its **frequency**.

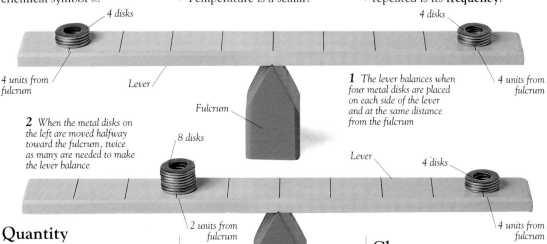

*4 disks*

*4 disks*

*4 units from fulcrum*

*Lever*

*Fulcrum*

**1** *The lever balances when four metal disks are placed on each side of the lever and at the same distance from the fulcrum*

*4 units from fulcrum*

**2** *When the metal disks on the left are moved halfway toward the fulcrum, twice as many are needed to make the lever balance*

*8 disks*

*Lever*

*4 disks*

*2 units from fulcrum*

*Fulcrum*

*4 units from fulcrum*

## Quantity

An amount that can be measured

A quantity, such as a number of degrees of temperature or a volume of water, can be measured with accurate instruments. If it is more than zero on a measurement scale, it is said to be **positive**. A **negative** quantity is less than zero, or an amount by which a quantity decreases. A quantity can also mean the thing that is measured, such as temperature itself.

## Uniform

Unchanging

A car that moves with uniform velocity does not change its speed or its direction.

## Conservation

Remaining the same

A quantity that remains the same during a process is conserved. Mass ▩, for example, is conserved during a chemical reaction ▩.

### From an observation to a law

*Observing that it is easier to open the lid of a can with a long screwdriver than with a short one could lead to the experiment above, which tests a theory about levers. It shows that when a lever balances, the amount of force multiplied by its distance from the fulcrum is the same on each arm of the lever. If the distance halves, the force doubles. This is always true of every lever, and so is a scientific law.*

## Chaos

A branch of science that studies very complex systems

The way that the weather changes may seem to be unpredictable and random. But scientists believe that such complicated events must follow some underlying pattern or order. Chaos studies complex events and systems and tries to find explanations for chaotic behavior. A **fractal** is a computer-generated image of great complexity, which is a visual representation of chaos.

***Never-ending image***
*You can enlarge any part of this swirling fractal again and again, but you will still get a pattern that is just as complex.*

# Physics

What keeps an airplane in the air or makes a stone fall to the ground when you drop it? And why is wood solid but water able to flow? Physics aims to discover the reasons that explain how the world works. This research leads to many new inventions.

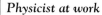

## Physics

The branch of science that studies matter and energy

Physicists investigate the nature of matter ▪, seeking to discover the basic particles of which everything is made. They also study force and motion, and forms of energy ▪, including heat, light, and electricity.

## Biophysics

The study of the physics of living things

Biophysicists investigate the physical changes that happen in people and other living things. They discover how the various parts of the body work and how energy, such as heat and light, affects living things. Biophysics is also used to help find the causes of illness and disease. **Health physics** studies the effects of nuclear radiation ▪, especially in nuclear power stations.

## Geophysics

The study of the processes that go on in the Earth

Geophysicists investigate such things as the weather, the Earth's magnetism, and the movement of rocks and water. Their work helps us to understand and predict earthquakes and the eruption of volcanoes. Geophysics is used to find underground oil deposits.

## Astrophysics

The study of processes that go on in planets and stars and in space

Astrophysicists use telescopes and other instruments to discover what happens inside stars. They determine how stars form and why they shine, and how they group together in huge galaxies.

## Physical change

A change in a physical property

When a substance is heated, it becomes hotter and may melt or boil. Melting and boiling are examples of physical changes. A physical change, unlike a chemical change ▪, does not alter the composition of a substance.

*Physicist at work*
*This scientist is examining equipment that uses powerful beams of laser light to weld atoms together, releasing energy.*

## Physical property

The physical nature of an object

The temperature and size of an object, and whether it is a solid, liquid or gas, are examples of its physical properties. An object's physical properties do not depend on its chemical composition.

## Solid-state physics

The branch of physics that investigates solids

A prominent aspect of solid-state physics is the development of solid electronic components, such as transistors and microchips, which are important in computers and telecommunications.

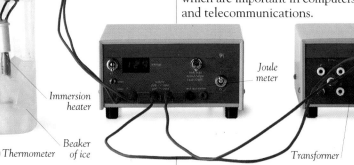

*Immersion heater*

*Joule meter*

*Thermometer*    *Beaker of ice*    *Transformer*

**Ice to water – a physical change**
*A physical change occurs as the heater above melts ice to water. A joule meter measures the amount of heat energy used to melt the ice, and the thermometer shows that the temperature in the beaker stays the same as this change takes place.*

### See also
Chemical change 21
Chemical property 21 • Energy 68
Matter 23 • Nuclear radiation 37

# Chemistry

Metals, wood, water, ceramics, plastics, sugar, salt – these are just a few of the many materials that we use each day of our lives. Chemistry tries to find out what materials are made of and how to make new and useful materials.

## Chemistry

The branch of science that studies the composition of substances

Every substance ▪ contains elements ▪. Chemists discover which elements are present in a substance and the way in which these elements combine together to form the substance. There are two main branches of chemistry. **Inorganic chemistry** studies the elements and all substances that do not contain the element carbon. **Organic chemistry** studies carbon-containing substances.

## Physical chemistry

The branch of chemistry that measures how substances form or change

Physical chemists measure physical properties ▪, such as how much heat or electricity a substance can produce. This work is important in industry – in manufacturing engines and batteries, for example.

## Biochemistry

The study of the chemistry of living things

Animals and plants are made up of chemical substances. These are constantly changing from one substance to another in order to sustain life. Biochemists study all these substances and the chemical changes that go on inside living things. Their discoveries lead to important advances in medicine.

*Chemical change*
*This laboratory experiment shows how a chemical change occurs when copper and concentrated nitric acid come into contact with each other. Copper nitrate forms as a solution in the flask, while nitrogen dioxide gas is produced and fills the gas jar.*

*Concentrated nitric acid*

*Controlled by the tap, the acid is carefully released into the flask*

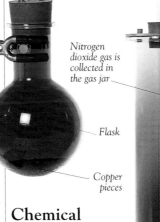

*Nitrogen dioxide gas is collected in the gas jar*

*Flask*

*Copper pieces*

## Chemical change

A change in the composition of a substance

A chemical change, such as burning, causes a substance to become a new substance with different chemical properties. Fuels such as wood or coal change as they burn, taking in and giving off other substances and forming ash.

*Searching for gold*
*This engraving shows an alchemist at work during the 15th century.*

## Alchemy

An early form of chemistry

People practiced alchemy during the Middle Ages. Alchemists tried to find ways of turning common metals into gold, and of giving people everlasting life. They did not succeed, but the alchemists developed some methods used in chemistry, such as distillation ▪.

## Chemical property

A way in which a substance affects other substances

Two substances may react ▪ together to form new substances. Their chemical properties affect the kind of reaction that occurs. A substance may be an acid ▪, for example. Acidity is a property that enables a substance to dissolve certain metals and form new substances called salts.

## Geochemistry

The study of the composition of the Earth

Geochemists investigate which kinds of minerals make up the Earth's rocks and determine how such minerals were formed.

### See also

Acid 149 • Chemical reaction 144
Distillation 27 • Element 132
Physical property 20 • Substance 138

# Formulas

A formula shows how basic quantities relate to one another, whichever system of units you use. These are some of the most important formulas in science.

## Boyle's law

$pV$ = constant

  $p$ = pressure of gas
  $V$ = volume of gas

*Only at constant temperature*

## Charles' law

$\frac{V}{T}$ = constant

  $V$ = volume of gas
  $T$ = absolute temperature of gas

*Only at constant pressure*

## Pressure law

$\frac{p}{T}$ = constant

  $p$ = pressure of gas
  $T$ = absolute temperature of gas

*Only at constant volume*

## Equations of motion

$v = u + at$
$s = ut + \frac{1}{2}at^2$
$v^2 = u^2 + 2as$

  $v$ = final velocity
  $u$ = initial velocity
  $a$ = acceleration
  $t$ = time taken
  $s$ = distance traveled

## Newton's second law of motion

$F = ma$

  $F$ = force
  $m$ = mass
  $a$ = acceleration

## Mass-energy equation
(Relativity)

$E = mc^2$

  $E$ = energy
  $m$ = mass
  $c$ = speed of light

## Newton's law of gravitation

$F = Gm_1m_2/s^2$

  $F$ = force
  $G$ = gravitational constant
  $m$ = mass
  $s$ = distance

## Gravitational potential energy

$W = mgh$

  $W$ = potential energy
  $m$ = mass
  $g$ = gravitational field strength
  $h$ = height

## Kinetic energy

$W = \frac{1}{2}mv^2$

  $W$ = kinetic energy
  $m$ = mass
  $v$ = velocity

## Work

$W = Fs$

  $W$ = work
  $F$ = force
  $s$ = distance moved

## Lenses and mirrors

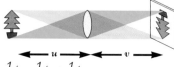

$1/f = 1/u + 1/v$

  $f$ = focal length
  $u$ = distance to object
  $v$ = distance to image

## Static electricity

$Q = CV$

  $Q$ = charge
  $C$ = capacitance
  $V$ = potential difference

## Current electricity

$V = IR$

  $V$ = potential difference
  $I$ = current
  $R$ = resistance

## Resistance of a circuit

*Series circuit*
$R = R_1 + R_2$

  $R$ = total resistance
  $R_1$ = separate resistance
  $R_2$ = separate resistance

*Parallel circuit*

$\frac{1}{R} = \frac{1}{R_1} + \frac{1}{R_2}$

## Electrical power

$P = IV$

  $P$ = power
  $I$ = current
  $V$ = potential difference

## Electric charge

$Q = It$

  $Q$ = charge
  $I$ = current
  $t$ = time

# Matter

We are surrounded by matter – from raindrops and tiny specks of dust, to animals, plants, rocks, stars, huge planets, and even air. All the objects and materials in the Universe, including ourselves, are forms of matter.

## Matter

Anything that occupies a space

All matter is made up of very tiny **particles**, such as atoms ▪. They link together in a variety of ways to give the many different types of matter we see around us. Matter can change into energy ▪, and energy can change into matter.

*The left-hand pan holds a glass object with a mass of 200 grams*

## Mass

The amount of matter in an object

An object's mass depends on how many atoms it contains and on the masses of the individual atoms. Mass is different from weight ▪, which is the pull of gravity ▪ on an object. Astronauts on the Moon have the same mass as they do on Earth, because they still contain the same atoms. But they weigh less on the Moon, because the force of gravity is weaker.

### See also

Atom 34 • Conservation of mass 145
Energy 68 • Gravity 49
Substance 138 • Weight 49

*When the pointer is vertical, the masses on each pan are equal*

*The bar is level because gravity pulls equally on each pan*

## Balance

An instrument that measures mass

A simple balance consists of a horizontal bar with a pan hanging from each end. The object or quantity of substance ▪ to be measured is placed on one pan, and units of mass are placed on the other. The bar is level when the masses on the pans are equal, because gravity pulls on each pan with equal force.

## Density

The mass of an object divided by its volume

A model aircraft made of metal is heavier than the same model made of balsa wood. This is because the metal is more dense than the balsa wood. Both models have the same volume, but the atoms of metal have a greater mass than the atoms of wood. The metal aircraft also contains more atoms, packed tightly together. **Relative density**, or **specific gravity**, is the density of a particular substance compared with the density of water. The relative density of gold is 19.3. This means that it is 19.3 times denser than water.

## MEASURING MASS

### Kilogram (kg)

The SI unit of mass, equal to the mass of a cylinder of platinum alloy kept at Sèvres in France

A kilogram is equal to 1,000 **grams** (g) and a gram is equal to 1,000 **milligrams** (mg). A **tonne** (t), or **metric ton**, is equal to 1,000 kilograms (kg).

*Basic balance*
*This simple balance shows that the glass object and the pile of paint have the same mass. The glass object takes up less space than the pile of paint because it has a greater density.*

*In the right-hand pan is a pile of powder paint with a mass of 200 grams*

## Hydrometer

An instrument that measures the density of a liquid

The hydrometer floats higher in liquids of high density and lower in liquids of low density. Density is read where the scale on the stem meets the surface of the liquid.

*Relative density of water is 1*

*Relative density of oil is 0.91*

*Oil and water*
*The hydrometer floats higher in water than in oil, because water is more dense.*

# States of matter

Matter can be a solid, a liquid, or a gas. These are called the three states of matter. Most substances can exist in all three states, depending on the temperature. For example, when you put ice cubes in a drink, take a shower, or steam some vegetables, you are using water in each of its three states. The cold ice is a solid, the warm shower water is a liquid, and the steam is a gas.

## State of matter

The physical form of a substance

A substance may take the form of a solid (symbol s), a liquid (symbol l), or a gas (symbol g). Each of these three states of matter is also called a **phase**. A **fluid** is any substance that flows. It can be either a liquid or a gas. The boundary between two states of matter is called an **interface**.

Changes of state

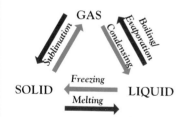

## Freezing

The change of a liquid to a solid

When a liquid cools, the forces between its particles grow stronger until it freezes. A pure substance freezes at a fixed temperature called its **freezing point**, or **freezing temperature**. Water, for example, freezes at 32°F (0°C). Freezing point is normally given for standard atmospheric ▪ pressure ▪. It is the same as the melting point.

## Solid

Matter in a form that has a definite shape and volume

The particles (molecules ▪, atoms ▪, or ions ▪) of most solids are packed tightly together in orderly patterns, similar to the way apples or oranges are often stacked in shops. Strong forces ▪ between the particles hold them in place. The particles vibrate but cannot move from their positions. This gives the solid a fixed shape and volume ▪.

*Particles of a solid*
*In most solids, strong forces hold the particles firmly in precise patterns, giving the solid a rigid shape.*

## Antifreeze

A substance that lowers the freezing point of water

During very cold weather, motorists often add an antifreeze, such as ethylene glycol (ethane-1,2-diol), to the water in the radiator of the car engine. This prevents the water from freezing. A liquid's freezing point can usually be lowered by dissolving a substance in the liquid.

## Melting

The change of a solid to a liquid

When a solid is heated ▪, its particles vibrate faster and faster. They partly overcome the forces holding them in place, so the solid melts. A pure substance melts at a fixed temperature known as its **melting point**, or its **melting temperature**. Melting point is normally given for standard atmospheric pressure. It is the same as the substance's freezing point. Melting is also called **fusion**.

*One substance, three states*
*When solid ice is heated, it changes first to liquid water and then to gaseous steam. These are the three states of water.*

As the ice cubes melt, liquid water forms at the bottom of the jar

# Gas

Matter in a form that has no definite shape or volume

Gas particles are spaced far apart. The forces between them are not strong enough to hold them in place, so they move freely and rapidly in all directions. This means that a gas has no fixed shape or volume. It expands to fill any container it is put into.

*Particles of a gas*
*The fast-moving particles of a gas are free to travel in any direction.*

*Steam escapes at the water's surface and condenses in the cool air above*

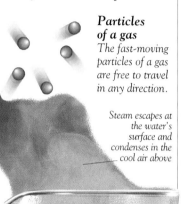

# Boiling

The change of a liquid to a gas

When a liquid is heated, the particles vibrate faster and faster. Eventually they break free of the forces between them and the liquid boils. The temperature at which a pure substance boils is its **boiling point**, or its **boiling temperature**. The boiling point depends on the pressure of the surrounding air. Water boils at 212°F (100°C) at sea level, but its boiling point is much less in high mountain regions, where the air pressure is lower. Boiling point is normally given for standard atmospheric pressure.

# Liquid

Matter in a form that has a definite volume but no fixed shape

Liquid particles are farther apart than solid particles. The forces between the particles are weaker than those in a solid. The liquid particles vibrate and are able to move short distances. This allows the liquid to flow and take the shape of its container.

*Particles of a liquid*
*A liquid's particles can move short distances, enabling the liquid to flow and take the shape of any container.*

*As the water boils, bubbles of steam form throughout the liquid*

## See also

Atmosphere 53 • Atom 34
Force 48 • Heat 68
Ion 144 • Latent heat 26
Molecule 138 • Pressure 52
Vapor 26 • Volume 174

# Sublimation

The change of a solid to a gas, or a gas to a solid

Some solids sublime when they are heated. This means that they change directly to a gas without first melting and becoming a liquid. An example is solid carbon dioxide, which is also called **dry ice**. When cooled, the gas turns right back to a solid.

# Condensation

The change of a gas to a liquid

As a gas cools, its particles move more slowly and the forces between them grow stronger. The gas then condenses to a liquid. Condensation occurs at or below the substance's boiling point. Oxygen, for example, condenses at −297°F (−183°C). It condenses at a higher temperature if the pressure on it is increased.

*The boiling sea*
*As hot lava from a volcano flows into the sea, the water boils. The steam condenses into clouds of tiny water droplets.*

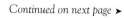

*Continued on next page* ➤

# Evaporation

The change of a liquid to a gas below the boiling point

On a sunny day, a puddle of rainwater will slowly disappear as it is warmed by the Sun's heat. When a liquid ▪ gets warmer, some particles at its surface vibrate fast enough to escape and form a gas ▪ called a vapor. Its pressure ▪ is the **vapor pressure**. Evaporation stops when the vapor can no longer absorb particles from the liquid. It is then a **saturated vapor**.

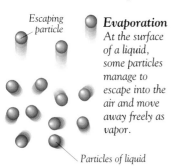

*Escaping particle*

***Evaporation***
*At the surface of a liquid, some particles manage to escape into the air and move away freely as vapor.*

*Particles of liquid*

# Vapor

A type of gas

A vapor is a gas that is below its **critical temperature**. This is the highest temperature at which a gas can be changed into a liquid by pressure alone. Above this temperature, it must first be cooled and then compressed. **Liquefaction** is the manufacture of gases in liquid form, such as producing liquid oxygen from air.

# Volatility

The ability to evaporate easily

A **volatile** liquid, such as petrol, evaporates quickly.

# Vacuum

A complete absence of matter

It is impossible to obtain a true vacuum. Pumping air out of a container can produce a near vacuum. However, a little air will always remain inside the container. The space between stars is almost a total vacuum.

# Latent heat

Heat taken in or given out when a substance changes its state

When a solid ▪ melts ▪ to a liquid, heat energy ▪ is taken in. On the other hand, if a liquid freezes ▪ to a solid, the same amount of heat is given out. This energy is the **latent heat of fusion**. The heat needed to change a liquid to a gas, or a gas to a liquid, is the **latent heat of vaporization**. While these changes of state are happening, the temperature of the substance stays the same. The heat taken in or given out is used to weaken or strengthen the forces between the particles.

***Melting an iceberg***
*Icebergs sometimes float hundreds of miles from the cold polar regions into warmer waters before they melt. This is because it takes a lot of heat to change such a huge mass of solid ice into liquid water.*

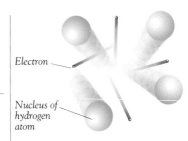

*Electron*

*Nucleus of hydrogen atom*

***Plasma in the Sun***
*The intense heat inside the Sun makes electrons break away from the nuclei of hydrogen atoms to form plasma.*

# Plasma

Matter in the form of electrically charged atomic particles

A plasma forms when a gas becomes so hot that electrons ▪ break away from atoms ▪. Plasma forms in the Sun and in stars and lightning. It is produced artificially inside thermonuclear reactors ▪ and in the gas-filled tubes of neon lights. Plasma is a good conductor of electricity.

# Absorption

The taking up of one substance by another

Absorption occurs when one substance completely absorbs another, like the way a sponge soaks up water. In **adsorption**, the second substance collects at only the surface of the first. A gas mask, for example, removes poisonous gases from the air by passing the air through a layer of charcoal. The charcoal adsorbs the poisonous gases at its surface and leaves the air safe to breathe. Absorption also means the taking up of energy such as light ▪.

## See also

Atom 34 • Electron 34 • Freezing 24
Gas 25 • Heat energy 68
Light 76 • Liquid 25 • Melting 24
Nucleus 35 • Pressure 52
Solid 24 • Thermonuclear reactor 40

# Mixtures

Only a few of the materials that we come across in our daily lives are made of just one substance. Most are mixtures. Almost all the foods we eat are mixtures of chemical compounds. It is this mix of different substances in our food that gives it so many different flavors.

*Water in the mixture boils at 212°F (100°C)*

## Miscible

Able to mix completely

Miscible liquids, such as alcohol and water, mix to form a single liquid. **Immiscible** liquids, such as vinegar and oil, do not mix but form separate layers.

*Hot water vapor enters the condenser*

*Vapor forms as water in the mixture boils*

*Water is led off from the outer tube*

## Mixture

A material made of substances that are not combined together chemically

Most materials are either compounds ■ or mixtures. A compound contains particles of elements ■ combined strongly together. A mixture contains particles of compounds or elements mingled loosely together. The substances in a mixture can be easily separated.

*The vapor condenses to a liquid as it touches the cool glass walls inside the condenser*

*Separating a mixture*
*Pure water can be distilled from a solution of sodium dichromate by heating the mixture and cooling its vapor in a Liebig condenser.*

## Distillation

A method of separating a pure liquid from a mixture

Heating a mixture containing a liquid causes the liquid to boil and form a vapor ■. The vapor goes into a condenser, where it cools to form a pure liquid. **Fractionation**, or **fractional distillation**, is a way of separating liquids with different boiling points ■. Each liquid is boiled off at a different temperature and its vapor condensed separately.

## Filtration

A method of separating a mixture made of solid particles in a liquid

The mixture is passed through a **filter** (1). The filter contains small holes. The liquid passes through the holes, but the solid particles are held back. The separated liquid is called the **filtrate**, and the separated solid is called the **residue** (2).

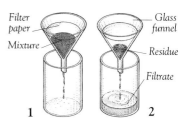

*Filter paper*          *Glass funnel*
*Mixture*               *Residue*
                        *Filtrate*
**1**                   **2**

## Condenser

A piece of equipment for changing a vapor into a liquid

A condenser ■ is a device that cools vapor so it will change to liquid. In a **Liebig condenser**, named for the chemist Justus von Liebig ■, cold water flowing through an outer tube cools the vapor in an inside tube.

*Cold water is fed into the condenser's outer tube*

*Pure water runs down the tube and collects in the flask*

### See also

Boiling point 25 • Condensation 25
Compound 138 • Element 132
Liebig 180 • Vapor 26

# Solutions & colloids

Stirring sugar into a hot drink is an easy way of making a solution. The sugar disappears, but it still exists: it has dissolved in the water. A colloid is a slightly different kind of mixture of two substances. Solutions and colloids are very common. Seawater is a solution of salt in water, while milk is a colloid of fat in water.

*Dissolving*
*When dropped in water, potassium permanganate crystals leave purple trails as they dissolve.*

*Potassium permanganate diffuses into the water and forms a solution*

## Solution

A uniform mixture of one substance dissolved in another

The substance that dissolves is called the **solute**. The substance it dissolves in is called the **solvent**. The solute breaks down into tiny particles (such as ions ▪ or molecules ▪) that mix completely with the particles of solvent. Solutions may be formed in liquids, solids, or gases by dissolving other liquids, solids, or gases in them. **A solid solution is** a solution of one solid in another, as in some alloys ▪.

## Concentration

The strength of a solution

A strong, or **concentrated**, solution contains a large amount of solute compared with the volume of solvent. A weak, or **dilute**, solution contains a small amount of solute. The maximum amount of a substance that can dissolve in 1 liter of solvent at a given temperature is known as its **solubility**. A solution that contains this maximum amount is called a **saturated solution**.

## Diffusion

The natural mingling of two or more substances to form a mixture or solution

Two gases diffuse or mix together when they meet because the moving molecules of each gas quickly intermingle. When solids or liquids dissolve, they form solutions by diffusion. The ions or molecules of solute slowly diffuse with those of the solvent, giving a solution of even concentration.

**1** *Distilled water and pigment are mixed together thoroughly*

**2** *The water and pigment are ground together*

*The mixture of pigment and water is a suspension*

*Grinder*

## Soluble

Able to dissolve and form a solution

Salt, for example, is soluble in water. If one substance will not dissolve in another substance, it is said to be **insoluble** in that substance. Salt is insoluble in cooking oil.

## Suspension

A liquid containing small solid particles that easily separate out

The particles in a suspension, such as muddy water, are larger than those in a solution or a colloid. The Earth's gravity ▪ eventually makes them settle and separate out from the liquid.

*Making a colloid*
*An emulsion is a colloid of two liquids. Emulsion paint can be made by mixing liquid egg yolk, water, and pigment.*

## Slurry

A suspension containing a large amount of solid material

Cement and water mixed into a runny paste is a kind of slurry.

## TYPES OF COLLOID

| Name of colloid | Particles | Main substance | Example |
|---|---|---|---|
| Solid sol | Solid | Solid | Stained glass (metal in glass) |
| Gel | Liquid | Solid | Jelly (water in gelatin) |
| Solid foam | Gas | Solid | Pumice (air in rock) |
| Sol | Solid | Liquid | Blood (cells in plasma) |
| Emulsion | Liquid | Liquid | Milk (fat in water) |
| Foam | Gas | Liquid | Whipped cream (air in cream) |
| Aerosol | Solid | Gas | Smoke (ash in air) |
| Aerosol | Liquid | Gas | Fog and mist (water in air) |

*Background picture: clouds of smoke*

# Colloid

A mixture containing tiny particles of one substance scattered evenly throughout another

A colloid is also known as a **dispersion**. Colloid particles can be gas bubbles, liquid droplets, or solid particles. They are larger than the solute particles in a solution. They are held in the main substance because they are too small to be separated by the Earth's gravity.

Egg yolk · Suspension of pigment in water

*When the paint dries, the pigment binds to the painting*

**3** *The yolk is added to form an emulsion with the water*

# Electrophoresis

An electrical method of separating solid particles from a liquid in a colloid

Placing electrodes ▪ in a colloid and passing an electric current through it causes solid particles to move toward one electrode. **Genetic fingerprinting** uses electrophoresis to separate fragments of the substance DNA, which is found in all living things. The separated fragments appear as a striped pattern. Each person's DNA produces a different pattern, so genetic fingerprinting can be used to identify people, using samples of their skin, hair, or blood.

# Dialysis

A method of separating solid particles from a liquid in a colloid using a porous barrier

A semipermeable membrane allows the tiny liquid particles to pass through, but not the larger solid particles, which remain behind. Hospitals use dialysis machines to purify the blood of people with kidney problems.

## See also

Alloy 166 • Electrode 148

Gravity 49 • Ion 144

Molecule 138 • Pressure 52

# Osmosis

The flow of liquid from one solution to another through a porous barrier

Osmosis happens when two solutions of different strengths are separated by a semipermeable membrane (1). Solvent flows through holes in the membrane. The net flow is from the weaker solution to the stronger solution. The volume of each solution changes as the solvent flows through the membrane (2). The pressure ▪ of this flow of solvent is called **osmotic pressure**. The solvent flow reaches equilibrium when the strengths of the two solutions are equal.

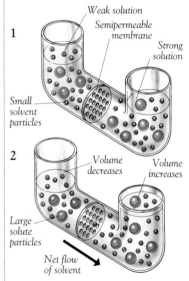

**1**

Weak solution

Semipermeable membrane

Strong solution

Small solvent particles

**2**

Volume decreases

Volume increases

Large solute particles

Net flow of solvent

**Osmotic flow**
*The semipermeable membrane allows solvent particles (red) to pass through, but not larger particles of solute (green).*

# Semipermeable membrane

A porous barrier containing very small holes

A semipermeable membrane works rather like a sieve. The tiny holes in the membrane prevent large particles of a dissolved substance from passing through. Smaller particles of solvent pass through with ease.

# Air & water

We could not survive without air and water. Our bodies are made up largely of water, and each day we breathe in and out thousands of liters of air. Air and water are the most common substances on Earth. They are used in many industrial processes.

## Air

The mixture of gases that surrounds the Earth

Air contains mainly the gases nitrogen and oxygen, with small amounts of argon and other noble gases ▨, and carbon dioxide. The proportions of these gases in air are the same anywhere around the world. Air also contains water vapor, dust, and polluting gases, which vary in amount from place to place. When air is cooled to −328°F (−200°C), most of the gases condense, forming a blue liquid called **liquid air**.

— Nitrogen (white) makes up 78% of air

— Oxygen (orange) makes up 21% of air

— Argon (red) makes up 0.93% of air

— Carbon dioxide (black) makes up 0.03% of air

*The content of air*
*These colored balls are mixed together in the same proportions as the gases that make up air.*

## Water

The liquid in oceans, rivers, lakes and rain

Water is a compound ▨ of the elements hydrogen and oxygen. Each molecule ▨ of water contains two atoms of hydrogen and one of oxygen, so its chemical formula is $H_2O$. Seawater is a solution ▨ of various salts ▨, mainly common salt (sodium chloride), in water. Fresh water may contain dissolved substances from the rocks and soil over which it has flowed. **Distilled water** is water made pure by distillation ▨.

## Heavy water

Water containing heavy hydrogen

Heavy water contains heavy hydrogen, or deuterium, instead of normal hydrogen. Deuterium is an isotope ▨ of hydrogen that is heavier, or has a greater atomic mass ▨, than normal hydrogen. It is present in normal water in small amounts. Some nuclear reactors ▨ use heavy water as a moderator ▨.

## Ice

The solid form of water

Pure water freezes to ice at 32°F (0°C). Dissolving a compound such as salt in water lowers its freezing point ▨, so the sea does not freeze in winter unless it is very cold. Ice expands slightly as it forms, which explains why water pipes burst in freezing weather. Ice cubes float in a cold drink because ice is less dense than water.

## Water vapor

A form of water that is usually present in the air

When water is exposed to the air, it evaporates ▨. Some of the molecules of water escape into the air as a vapor ▨. The pressure ▨ exerted by the escaping molecules is the **vapor pressure**. When the vapor pressure becomes the same as the pressure of the air, the water boils. Water vapor condenses to form water droplets in rain, fog, and mist. Water vapor may be absent from air in very dry places or when the air is very cold.

## Steam

The gaseous form of water

Steam is an invisible gas. The clouds you see above boiling water are not steam, but water drops that form when invisible steam condenses in the cooler air. Pure water normally boils to form steam at 212°F (100°C). Dissolving a substance in water raises the water's boiling point ▨.

*Clouds of "steam"*
*Geysers are jets of boiling water and steam that erupt when water below the Earth's surface is heated at high pressure.*

*Tight-fitting glass lid*

*Substance being dried*

*Desiccant*

# Desiccator

Apparatus for removing moisture from a substance or keeping it dry

A desiccator is airtight and contains a substance called a **desiccant**, or **dehydrating agent**. The desiccant absorbs moisture readily. **Silica gel** (a porous form of silica) and concentrated sulfuric acid are often used as desiccants.

# Hydrate

A compound containing water

In a hydrate, water combines with other compounds or elements. Many crystals ■ are hydrates containing **water of crystallization**. This means that water molecules are bound to the atoms in the crystal. Crystals of copper(II) sulfate are hydrates, but heating them removes the water.

*1 Heating the blue solution evaporates the water to give blue crystals*

*Changing copper(II) sulfate*
*Heating blue copper(II) sulfate solution makes the water evaporate to give a hydrate of blue crystals (1). Further heating drives off the water of crystallization, leaving white anhydrous copper(II) sulfate (2). Adding water (3) gives the blue hydrate again (4).*

# Water softening

The removal of dissolved metal compounds from tap water

**Hard water** contains ions ■ of calcium and other metals. These ions enter the water supply and produce hard deposits in kettles and pipes. **Soft water** does not contain these ions. Water can be softened using an **ion-exchange resin**, which replaces the ions in a solution with other ions. In water softening, harmless sodium ions replace the ions of calcium and other metals.

# Efflorescence

The natural loss of water from a substance

When some crystals are exposed to the air, they lose their water of crystallization by evaporation and become powdery. Sal soda (sodium carbonate) is an example.

# Anhydrous

Not containing water

Solids that have lost their water of crystallization are anhydrous. Liquids, such as pure ethanol, can also be anhydrous. Anhydrous copper(II) sulfate can be used to test for the presence of water.

*2 Eventually the blue crystals turn into a white powder*

# Deliquescence

The natural absorption of water by a solid substance

A **deliquescent** substance, such as calcium chloride, takes up water vapor from the air. It first becomes damp and then changes to a liquid, forming a very concentrated solution. A **hygroscopic** substance also takes up water but does not become a liquid. Table salt contains hygroscopic substances to stop it from becoming damp and "caking."

*Dropper*

*3 Water is added to the white powder*

*4 The white powder turns blue*

# Dehydration

The process of removing water from a substance

Dehydration may be carried out by gently heating a substance or by drying it in a desiccator.

# Properties of matter

No two substances are exactly alike, because their particles link together in different ways. A solid may be hard or soft, for example, and a liquid may be either sticky or able to flow well. And some materials are easier to stretch than others. Such characteristics are called the properties of matter. Many substances are useful because of their particular properties.

## Elasticity

The ability of a solid to regain its original shape and size after it has been squeezed or stretched

For example, if you stretch a rubber band and let it go, it quickly regains its shape. When the force applied to an elastic substance reaches a certain strength, the substance loses its elasticity and may break. The size of this force is called the **elastic limit**.

## Hooke's law

The change in size or shape of an elastic substance depends on the force producing the change

A force pulling on an elastic substance stretches it a certain amount. Double the force will stretch it twice as much. Hooke's law is true only within the elastic limit. It is sometimes written as: "the strain is proportional to the stress." The **strain** is the change in size divided by the original size. The **stress** is the force applied to a unit area of the elastic substance. The law was first stated by Robert Hooke ■.

### Bouncing ball
*This rubber ball is very elastic. When it hits the ground it is squeezed out of shape, but it regains its shape immediately and bounces upward.*

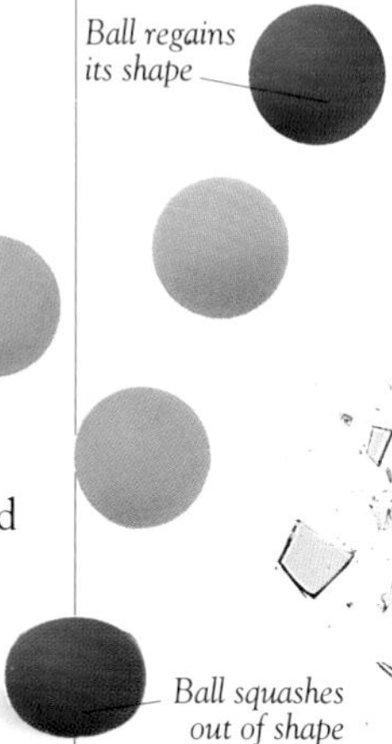

*Ball regains its shape*

*Ball squashes out of shape*

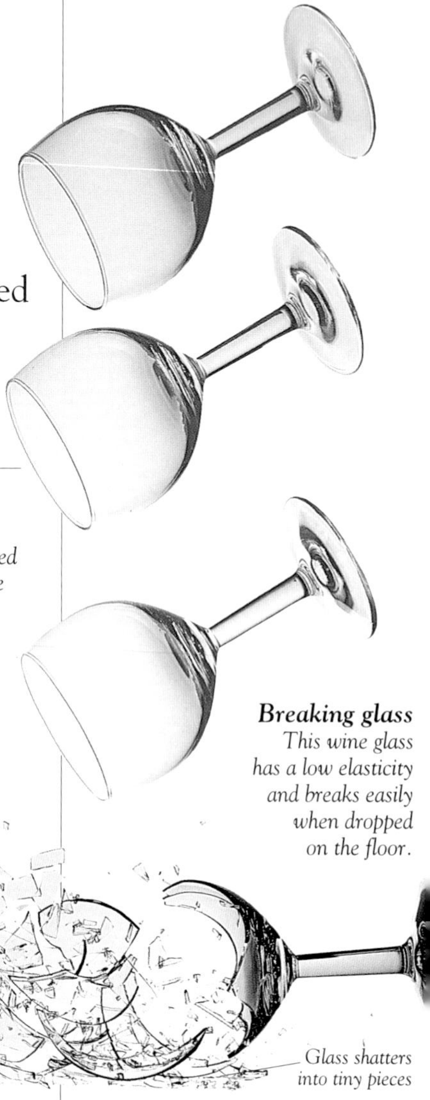

### Breaking glass
*This wine glass has a low elasticity and breaks easily when dropped on the floor.*

*Glass shatters into tiny pieces*

## Young's modulus

A measure of the elasticity of a solid substance

Young's ■ modulus is the stress divided by the strain when an elastic object changes shape.

### See also

Electric current 104 • Force 48
Hooke 180 • Molecule 138
Piezoelectricty 109 • Resistance 105
Young 181

## Tensile strength

The ability of a solid substance to resist being pulled apart

The tensile strength of a solid substance is its strength under **tension**, a force that acts to stretch it. Tensile strength is measured as the amount of force needed to pull a substance apart. Steel wire has a high tensile strength. A substance such as concrete is weak under tension but strong under **compression** – a force that acts to squeeze it.

# Strain gauge

An instrument that measures the load placed on an object

A strain gauge detects a load electrically. It contains either a wire that stretches and changes its electrical resistance ■, or a piezoelectric ■ crystal that produces an electric current ■ as it changes shape. Strain gauges measure the loads placed on vehicles or supported by buildings and bridges.

# Ductility

The ability of a solid to be stretched into shape without breaking

Most metals are **ductile**. Gold, for example, can be stretched out to make very fine wire.

# Malleability

The ability of a solid to be beaten or pressed into shape without breaking

Metals are **malleable** substances. Aluminum, for example, can be rolled out into thin sheets to make kitchen foil. Some metals are malleable only when heated.

*Malleable clay*
*When modeling clay falls on the ground, it changes shape without breaking into smaller lumps.*

## MOHS' SCALE

| Mineral | Hardness |
| --- | --- |
| Talc | 1 (softest) |
| Gypsum | 2 |
| Calcite | 3 |
| Fluorite | 4 |
| Apatite | 5 |
| Feldspar | 6 |
| Quartz | 7 |
| Topaz | 8 |
| Corundum | 9 |
| Diamond | 10 (hardest) |

*Background picture: surface of a diamond*

# Adhesion

The force of attraction between molecules of different substances

Adhesion makes two substances stick together. A raindrop clings to a window pane because of adhesion.

# Cohesion

The force of attraction between molecules of the same substance

Cohesion makes all the molecules ■ of a substance pull on each other. It holds together a piece of solid or an amount of liquid and is responsible for surface tension.

# Viscosity

The ability of a liquid to resist flowing

A **viscous** liquid, such as syrup, has a high viscosity and flows slowly. A liquid with low viscosity, such as water, flows easily. A **thixotropic** liquid, such as nondrip paint, becomes less viscous and flows better when it is shaken or stirred.

*Flowing water*
*Water is a liquid with low viscosity, so it spreads out into a puddle when it is poured on the floor.*

# Hardness

The ability of a solid substance to resist scratching

The hardness of a substance is often measured on **Mohs' scale** (left). This scale compares it with the hardness of ten common minerals rated from 1 to 10. Measured on Mohs' scale, a fingernail has a hardness of 2.5 and a penknife blade 6.5.

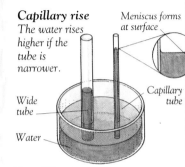

*Capillary rise*
*The water rises higher if the tube is narrower.*

Meniscus forms at surface

Wide tube

Water

Capillary tube

# Capillarity

The rise or fall of a liquid in a narrow, open-ended tube

When a narrow, open-ended **capillary tube** is placed in water, the water rises up the tube. The surface forms a downward curve called a **meniscus**. Capillarity, or **capillary action**, is the result of adhesion between water and glass, combined with surface tension at the top of the water column. If the same tube is placed in mercury, the mercury in the tube goes down instead of up, forming a meniscus with an upward curve. The cohesion within the mercury is stronger than the adhesion between the mercury and the glass.

*Surface tension tries to pull the tiny water splashes into round drops*

# Surface tension

A force in the surface of a liquid

The molecules at the surface of a liquid, with no liquid above them, are pulled together and down by the cohesion of molecules below them. This produces a force, or tension, across the surface that makes it behave like a stretched elastic skin. Surface tension pulls a drop of liquid into a sphere and makes a bubble round. It also allows tiny insects to walk on a pond's surface without sinking.

# Atoms

Many of the atoms that make up your body were once part of a distant star that exploded long ago. Atoms are the building blocks of everything in the Universe. They are so tiny that a comma contains billions of atoms. But atoms are not the smallest particles that exist. Atoms themselves are made up of even smaller subatomic particles.

## Atom

**The smallest particle of an element**

An atom contains a nucleus of tiny particles called protons and neutrons. These are surrounded by a large amount of space containing even smaller particles called electrons. The electrons move around the nucleus at very high speeds. An atom can be split into these subatomic particles, but it is the smallest part of an element ▪ that can exist on its own.

**Actual atoms**
*This picture of gold (red/yellow) and carbon (green) atoms was taken with a special microscope. The atoms are about a fifty-millionth of a centimeter across.*

## Electron

**A negatively charged particle**

An electron is a tiny particle that moves in a path around the nucleus of an atom. This path is called an **orbit**. An atom's electrons are arranged in **shells**. Each shell contains electrons orbiting at the same distance from the nucleus. Electrons have a negative electric charge ▪. They balance an equal number of protons, which have a positive charge. This makes the whole atom electrically neutral. If an atom gains or loses an electron, its charge is unbalanced and it becomes a charged atom called an ion ▪.

## Proton

**A positively charged particle in the nucleus of an atom**

The number of protons in the nucleus of an atom is the atomic number. This determines the element the atom belongs to. If the atomic number changes, the atom becomes a new element. Protons have a positive charge, and the attraction between the protons and electrons holds the atom together.

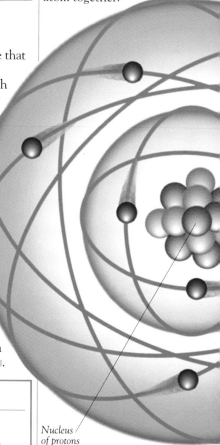

*Nucleus of protons and neutrons*

**Inside a carbon atom**
*This is an atom of carbon–12. It has six electrons (blue) arranged in two shells, one with two electrons and the other with four. The atom's nucleus has six protons (red) – giving carbon an atomic number of 6 – and six neutrons (gray). An isotope's nucleon number is the sum of its protons and neutrons, so this isotope is called carbon–12.*

---

## MEASURING ATOMS

### Atomic number

**The number of protons in the nucleus of each atom of an element**

Every element has a different atomic number. If the number of protons in the nucleus of an atom changes, it becomes a different element. This occurs in radioactivity ▪ and in nuclear reactions ▪.

### Atomic mass

**The mass of an atom relative to the mass of an atom of carbon–12**

Atomic mass is also called **relative atomic mass (RAM)**, or **atomic weight**. It is measured in relation to the mass of an atom of the common carbon isotope carbon–12, which has an atomic mass of 12.

# Neutron

An uncharged particle in the nucleus of an atom

A neutron has no electric charge. The number of neutrons in the nuclei of an element's atoms may vary a little without affecting the identity of the element. An element may exist in several different forms. Each of these has a different number of neutrons in the nuclei of its atoms. Different forms of the same element, and the atoms they contain, are called isotopes.

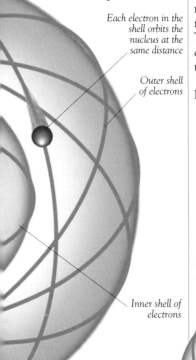

*Each electron in the shell orbits the nucleus at the same distance*

*Outer shell of electrons*

*Inner shell of electrons*

# Nucleus

The central core of an atom, containing protons and neutrons

The nucleus (plural **nuclei**) of an atom is a bundle of protons and neutrons. Each of these particles is about 2,000 times heavier than an electron. This means that almost the entire mass ▦ of an atom is concentrated in its nucleus. The protons in the nucleus make it positively charged.

# Isotope

A form of an element with a different number of neutrons in the nuclei of its atoms than other forms of the same element

Isotopes are different versions of the same element. The isotopes of an element all have the same atomic number, and therefore the same chemical properties ▦. But isotopes may have different physical properties, such as density ▦. An isotope is identified by its **nucleon number**, which is the total number of protons and neutrons, or **nucleons**, in the nuclei of the isotope's atoms. The commonest isotope of carbon has 12 nucleons and is therefore called carbon–12.

**Hydrogen–1**

*One proton in nucleus*

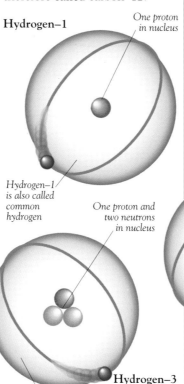

*Hydrogen–1 is also called common hydrogen*

*One proton and two neutrons in nucleus*

**Hydrogen–3**

*Hydrogen–3, or tritium, is the radioactive form of hydrogen*

### The three isotopes of hydrogen
*The nucleus of each hydrogen isotope contains a single proton, plus 0, 1, and 2 neutrons, respectively. A single electron orbits the nucleus of each isotope.*

***Mass spectrometer***
*This scientist is placing a protein sample into a mass spectrometer for analysis.*

# Mass spectroscopy

A method of detecting the different atoms that make up a substance

A **mass spectrometer** bombards a substance with electrons to create ions, or charged atoms. The ions pass through a magnetic field ▦ which bends their paths by different amounts, depending on their mass. The field separates the ions into a pattern called a **mass spectrum**. The mass and charge of the ions can be measured from their position in the spectrum. Scientists can then identify elements and isotopes present in the sample.

**Hydrogen–2**

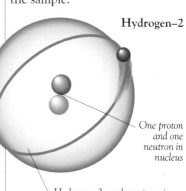

*One proton and one neutron in nucleus*

*Hydrogen–2, or deuterium, is also called heavy hydrogen*

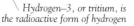

## See also

Chemical property 21 • Density 23
Electric charge 102 • Element 132
Ion 144 • Magnetic field 100
Mass 23 • Matter 23
Nuclear reactions 38 • Radioactivity 36

# Radioactivity

Radioactive substances emit high-energy particles and rays that can damage living things. But radioactivity can also be useful. Safe levels of radiation are used to diagnose and treat illnesses, preserve food, and detect weak points in oil pipes.

## Radioactivity

The emission of high-energy rays or particles by certain elements

The nuclei ▨ of atoms ▨ of radioactive elements ▨ are unstable. This means they break up naturally, releasing nuclear radiation (usually just called radiation). This process is called radioactivity. Radiation consists of alpha, beta, and gamma rays. Alpha rays are the weakest, and gamma rays are the most powerful, although all three types of radiation can be dangerous. When the nucleus of an atom emits alpha or beta rays, it changes, and the atom becomes an atom of a different element. This change is called **decay**. A **radioactive series** is a series of elements formed by the successive decay of one element into another.

## Alpha particle

A particle of two protons and two neutrons emitted by a radioactive element

An alpha particle may be ejected as the nucleus of a radioactive atom decays. It consists of two protons ▨ and two neutrons ▨, which is identical to the nucleus of a helium atom. Because the original nucleus loses two protons, its atomic number ▨ decreases by two. **Alpha rays** are streams of alpha particles.

## Beta particle

An electron or positron emitted by a radioactive element

As an atom decays, a neutron in its nucleus may change into a proton and release an electron. This increases the atomic number by one. A proton may also change into a neutron and release a positively charged electron, or positron ▨. **Beta rays** are streams of beta particles.

## Gamma ray

A high-energy ray emitted by a radioactive element

Gamma rays are a form of electromagnetic radiation ▨. They are similar to X-rays ▨ but have a shorter wavelength ▨. This means that they are able to penetrate most materials. Gamma rays may accompany the emission of alpha or beta particles. They are not often emitted on their own.

### Radioactive decay

*As the nucleus of a radioactive atom decays, it emits alpha or beta rays, and sometimes gamma rays. Alpha rays are weakest and can be blocked by paper. Beta rays pass through paper, but not an aluminum sheet. Gamma rays pass through both, but not through thick lead.*

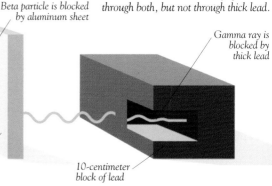

*Decaying nucleus*

*Alpha particle is blocked by paper*

*Beta particle is blocked by aluminum sheet*

*Gamma ray is blocked by thick lead*

*Sheet of paper*

*2-millimeter sheet of aluminum*

*10-centimeter block of lead*

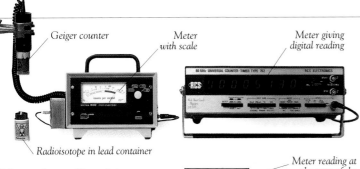

Geiger counter

Meter with scale

Meter giving digital reading

88 MHz UNIVERSAL COUNTER-TIMER TYPE 702    RCS ELECTRONICS

Radioisotope in lead container

## Measuring radioactivity

*This Geiger counter measures the radioactivity coming from the open container. The meter gives an initial reading of 5130.*

## Geiger counter

An instrument that detects and measures radioactivity

A Geiger counter consists of a tube of gas that contains an electrode ■. There is a high voltage between the electrode and the wall of the tube. When radiation enters the tube, the gas forms ions ■. These make pulses of electric current flow between the electrode and the tube. The pulses make clicks in a loudspeaker, or give a reading on a meter. Each particle of radiation produces one pulse, so the strength of the radiation equals the number of pulses. The Geiger counter was invented by the physicist Hans Geiger ■.

## Nuclear radiation

The rays emitted by radioactive substances

Many radioactive elements occur naturally in rocks and minerals. They produce low levels of radioactivity, called **background radiation**, that are not dangerous. **Ionizing radiation** forms ions as it passes through a substance. The particles or rays of radiation strike the atoms in the substance, knocking electrons off them and forming ions. Ionizing radiation is dangerous because it can damage living tissue, but it can be controlled for use in medicine.

Meter reading at the start of the experiment

*5130.0*

After three hours, radioactivity has fallen by a half

*2565.0*

After six hours, the radioactivity is a quarter of the original amount

*1282.5*

## Half-life

*The radioactivity of the radioisotope in the experiment at the top of the page decreases by half every three hours. This means the radioisotope has a half-life of three hours.*

## Radioisotope

A radioactive form of an element

A radioisotope is an isotope ■ that gives out radioactivity. Scientists can make artificial radioisotopes by bombarding an element with neutrons or other particles. These are used as a source of radioactivity in medicine and industry.

## Irradiation

The exposure of a substance to radioactivity

Low levels of radiation can be used to preserve food such as fruit. This is called irradiation. Food is irradiated by exposing it to the rays that come from radioisotopes. Radiation destroys the microorganisms that cause food to decay, without damaging the food or the consumer.

## Half-life

The time taken for a radioactive substance to lose half of its radioactivity

During the period of its half-life, half of the radioactive atoms in any amount of a radioactive substance decay. Over successive half-life periods, radioactivity falls first to a half, then to a quarter, then to an eighth, and so on. Each radioisotope has a particular half-life, which varies from a fraction of a second to millions of years.

## Carbon dating

A method of discovering the age of ancient objects by measuring radioactivity

Living things take in a small amount of the radioisotope carbon–14 from air. When something dies, such as an animal or a tree, the carbon–14 inside it decays at a constant rate. Scientists know that carbon–14 has a half-life of 5,570 years. This makes it possible to determine the age of ancient remains by measuring their present level of radioactivity.

### Carbon count

*Ancient Egyptian mummies are thousands of years old. Scientists can determine their exact age using carbon dating.*

# Nuclear physics

Tremendous energy is involved when changes occur in the centers, or nuclei, of atoms. The energy that sustains life on Earth comes from the Sun, which is powered by this nuclear energy. Scientists have found ways of using nuclear energy to produce electricity, but it can also be used with devastating effect in nuclear weapons.

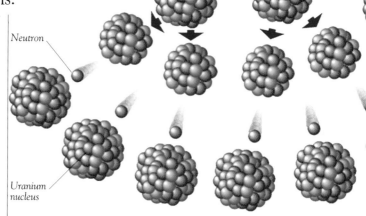

*1 Neutron hits nucleus of uranium atom*

*2 Nucleus splits in two, releasing neutrons*

Neutron

Uranium nucleus

## Nuclear physics

The study of the changes that take place in the nuclei of atoms

Changes in nuclei ▦ are caused by **nuclear reactions**. There are three types of nuclear reaction, called nuclear fission, nuclear fusion, and radioactive decay ▦. In nuclear reactions, the nuclei of atoms ▦ either break up or change, often as a result of being struck by other nuclei or by particles such as neutrons ▦. Because the particles within nuclei are held together by strong forces, nuclear reactions may release a lot of energy ▦. Nuclear power stations use energy from controlled reactions in a nuclear reactor ▦ to generate electricity.

## Transmutation

The change of one element into another element

Nuclear reactions cause the number of protons ▦ in the nuclei of an element's ▦ atoms to change. This changes the identity of the element, so that it becomes a different element with a different atomic number ▦. Artificial elements are made by transmutation. Plutonium, for example, is made by bombarding natural uranium with neutrons in a nuclear reactor.

### Energy from the Sun
*The energy that comes from the Sun is produced by nuclear fusion. The temperature at the center of the Sun is about 14 million °C (25 million °F). Such high temperatures cause the nuclei of hydrogen atoms to collide with one another. As they collide, they change into helium nuclei.*

## Nuclear fission

The splitting of nuclei to release energy

Nuclear fission takes place in certain isotopes ▦ of heavy elements, such as uranium and plutonium. The uranium isotope is **uranium–235** or **U–235**, which has a total of 235 protons and neutrons in the nucleus of each atom. Small amounts of this isotope can be found in naturally occurring uranium. When a nucleus of U–235 is struck by a neutron, it briefly absorbs the neutron but then becomes so unstable that it bursts apart into two smaller nuclei. As it does so, it releases other neutrons and energy in the form of heat ▦. The mass ▦ of the two nuclei is less than the mass of the original nucleus. The mass that is lost becomes energy. Fission occurs in nuclear reactors and in nuclear weapons.

## Chain reaction

*When a neutron collides with a nucleus of uranium–235, a series of fission reactions starts. The chain reaction is very fast and creates high temperatures.*

**3** *Each neutron can strike another nucleus, making it divide and release more neutrons*

**4** *Soon, many nuclei are splitting up at the same time, producing enormous amounts of heat energy*

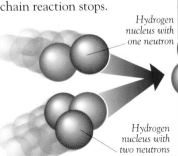

# Chain reaction

A series of fission reactions in which each reaction triggers others

When nuclear fission occurs, a nucleus splits in two and releases neutrons. These neutrons cause other nuclei to split and release more neutrons. As this process continues, more and more neutrons are released, splitting more and more nuclei. Such a buildup of fission reactions is called a chain reaction. It can take place only with a **critical mass** of uranium or plutonium. This is the least amount needed to keep a chain reaction going. Fission starts as neutrons begin to split nuclei. But if the mass of uranium or plutonium is too small, neutrons released by fission escape and the chain reaction stops.

# Nuclear weapons

Very powerful weapons that work by changing the nuclei of atoms

Nuclear weapons are also called **atomic bombs**; they work by nuclear fission or nuclear fusion. In a fission weapon, the chain reaction is not controlled. This means that a great many nuclei are split in a fraction of a second, producing huge amounts of heat in a powerful explosion. A fusion weapon is even more destructive. The fusion reaction has to be triggered by a nuclear fission reaction. Fusion weapons are also called **hydrogen bombs** or **thermonuclear weapons**.

# Nuclear fusion

The combining of nuclei to release energy

Nuclear fusion takes place only with light elements, such as isotopes of the gas hydrogen. Heating hydrogen gas to very high temperatures makes the hydrogen nuclei strike one another with such force that they combine and become nuclei of helium. This fusion releases energy as heat. Nuclear fusion takes place in the Sun, in thermonuclear weapons, and in thermonuclear reactors ▪.

*Fusion reaction*
*When two small hydrogen nuclei collide, they form a larger helium nucleus and release a neutron and heat energy.*

*Hydrogen nucleus with one neutron*

*Hydrogen nucleus with two neutrons*

*Hydrogen nuclei smash together*

*Neutron is released*

*Helium nucleus forms*

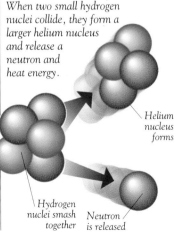

*Nuclear explosion*
*The vast cloud of smoke and flames created by a nuclear weapon is called a mushroom cloud, because of its shape. Nuclear weapons are powerful enough to destroy whole cities. They also create deadly radioactive fallout.*

# Fallout

Radioactive substances that are released by nuclear weapons or power stations and enter the atmosphere before falling to Earth

When a nuclear weapon explodes on the ground or in the air, it releases a huge quantity of radioactive substances. Some of this quickly settles near the place where the explosion occurred, but much of it rises into the air and is carried long distances by the wind before falling to the ground with rain, snow, and fog. The radioactivity of this fallout may be harmful to crops, animals, and people. Accidents at nuclear power stations may also produce fallout.

## See also

Atom 34 • Atomic number 34
Decay 36 • Element 132 • Energy 68
Heat 91 • Isotope 35 • Mass 23
Neutron 35 • Nuclear reactor 40
Nucleus 35 • Proton 34
Thermonuclear reactor 40

# Nuclear power

In some countries, the electricity to light and heat people's homes comes from nuclear power stations. The power stations harness the energy produced by splitting atoms, changing it into electricity.

## Nuclear power

Energy that is generated by changing the nuclei of atoms

Nuclear power is also called **atomic power**. It is produced by nuclear fission ▨ in the reactor of a nuclear power station. The energy is used to boil water and change it into steam. The steam drives turbines that power electricity generators. The electricity travels through a network of wires called a grid, to homes and factories.

## Thermonuclear reactor

A device that produces heat energy by controlled nuclear fusion

Thermonuclear reactors are still in the experimental stage. The **tokamak** design of reactor uses a large, circular tube of hydrogen gas. Electricity flows through the gas to heat it, while powerful magnetic fields keep the hot gas away from the walls of the tube. Nuclear fusion ▨ has occurred, but not in sufficient amounts to make it a useful source of energy.

*Fusion reactor*
*Scientists check the interior of a tokamak reactor at Princeton, NJ.*

## Nuclear reactor

A device that produces energy by controlled nuclear fission

A nuclear reactor is really a large container in which nuclear fuel undergoes fission and releases heat energy. The fuel atoms ▨ naturally fission from time to time, giving off neutrons ▨ that can cause other atoms to fission in a chain reaction ▨. The reactor core has control rods and a moderator to keep the chain reaction going steadily so that heat is produced at an even rate. A **coolant**, which may be a gas or a liquid such as water, circulates through the reactor and heats up. The hot coolant goes to a heat exchanger ▨, which uses heat from the coolant to boil water. Steam from the boiling water drives turbines. A reactor produces intense radiation ▨ and can be used to make radioisotopes ▨. Protective layers, or **shielding**, surround the reactor to stop radiation from escaping.

## Breeder reactor

A kind of nuclear reactor that produces new fuel as it works

A breeder reactor uses fuel that contains plutonium. A layer of uranium surrounds the reactor's core. Neutrons escape from the core and strike the uranium. Some of the uranium changes to plutonium, which can then be extracted and used as fuel. A breeder reactor has no moderator and uses fast-moving neutrons, so it is also called a **fast reactor**.

## Nuclear fuel

A material that undergoes nuclear fission or nuclear fusion

The fuel in most nuclear reactors consists of uranium, often in the form of uranium oxide. It contains a certain amount of the isotope ▨ uranium–235, which undergoes nuclear fission. If the proportion present in natural uranium is not sufficient, the fuel is "enriched," meaning that the proportion of uranium–235 is increased. In the reactor's core, tiny pellets of fuel are enclosed in metal rods.

## Nuclear waste

Waste material that is radioactive

Nuclear waste comes from nuclear reactors, laboratories, industry, and hospitals. It includes used nuclear fuel, which can be reprocessed to make new fuel. Some waste stays radioactive for many years.

*Nuclear waste*
*Protective clothing must be worn to handle radioactive waste. Most waste is buried underground in sealed containers.*

## Melt-down

A serious accident in which the core of a nuclear reactor melts

If the chain reaction inside a nuclear reactor got totally out of control, or the cooling system failed, the core would melt as heat built up. Eventually, the core could explode or burn through the reactor shielding with disastrous results. Partial melt-downs have occurred in accidents at several nuclear power stations.

## Nuclear fission reactor
*This type of reactor is called a pressurized-water reactor because it uses high-pressure water as a coolant. The reactor is housed in a dome with thick concrete walls.*

## Water pressurizer
*The core heats the water coolant to temperatures above 570°F (300°F). The pressurizer ensures that the pressure in the coolant system is so high that the water cannot boil.*

## Steam generators
*The generators act as heat exchangers, using the hot coolant water from the core to boil water in a separate system.*

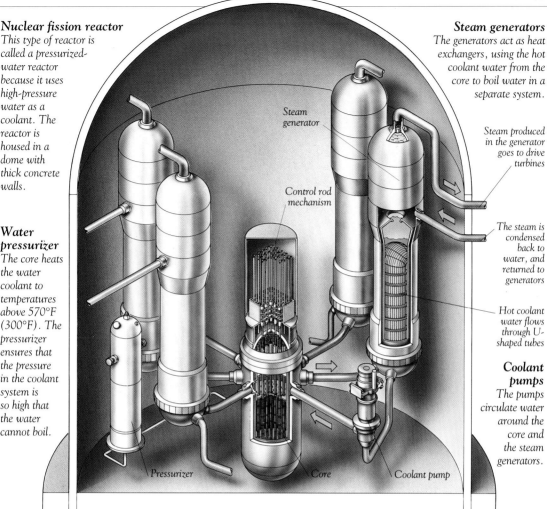

Steam generator

Control rod mechanism

Steam produced in the generator goes to drive turbines

The steam is condensed back to water, and returned to generators

Hot coolant water flows through U-shaped tubes

## Coolant pumps
*The pumps circulate water around the core and the steam generators.*

Pressurizer

Core

Coolant pump

## Control rod

A metal rod used to control the operation of a nuclear reactor

The control rods are inserted into the core of a nuclear reactor. As the rods move in or out of the core, the chain reaction slows down or speeds up accordingly. The rods contain elements, such as boron or cadmium, that absorb neutrons. Lowering the rods into the core absorbs some of the neutrons produced by nuclear fission. This ensures that the chain reaction proceeds steadily. The control rods can also stop the chain reaction and shut down the reactor in an emergency.

## Moderator

A material that helps nuclear fission to proceed in a nuclear reactor

A slow-moving neutron is more likely to cause a fission reaction than is a fast-moving neutron. If a neutron travels too fast, it may bounce off the nucleus of the fuel atom, instead of splitting it and causing another fission reaction. Most reactors need a moderator to keep the chain reaction going. The moderator is present in the core of the reactor and slows down the neutrons produced in the chain reaction. Moderators include ordinary water, heavy water ▦, and graphite.

### Reactor core
*Control rods move in and out of clusters of uranium fuel rods called fuel assemblies (shown as red columns).*

## Core

The central part of a reactor, in which nuclear fission occurs

The core contains nuclear fuel, a coolant, control rods, and often a moderator.

### See also

# Particle physics

One aim of science is to find out what everything in the Universe is made of. Scientists are always searching for smaller and smaller particles, seeking basic particles that make up everything. Their discoveries help us to understand how the Universe began, as well as what its future may be.

## Particle physics

The study of the particles that make up everything in the Universe

All matter ■ is made of atoms ■, which are particles of elements ■. But atoms contain smaller particles called **subatomic particles**. For example, the nucleus ■, or center, of an atom contains neutrons ■ and protons ■. Scientists are now discovering even smaller particles inside subatomic particles. They do this by colliding particles together at high speed, so that new particles are formed. The levels of energy in these collisions may be similar to those present when the Universe began. Particle physics is also called **high-energy physics**.

## Fundamental particle

A particle that is not made up of any smaller particles

Fundamental particles, also called **elementary particles**, are the smallest particles in the Universe. The two main types of fundamental particle are called leptons and quarks.

## Cosmic ray

A particle that comes from space

Cosmic rays are not rays, but fast-moving protons, electrons, and nuclei. They are produced by the Sun and stars and travel through space. Some penetrate the Earth's atmosphere and reach its surface.

## Lepton

A kind of fundamental particle

Leptons include the electron ■ and the **positron**, the electron's antiparticle, which has a positive electric charge ■. Radioactivity ■ produces positrons. Another lepton is the **neutrino**, a particle with no charge and probably no mass ■. Neutrinos come from the Sun and other stars, and can pass right through the Earth.

## Quark

A kind of fundamental particle

Quarks make up larger particles called **hadrons**. The proton and the neutron are both hadrons. Each is made up of three quarks. A quark has either one-third of a unit of negative electric charge (a "down" quark) or two-thirds of a unit of positive charge (an "up" quark). Quarks have never been produced singly, but there is much evidence for their existence.

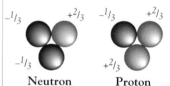

$-1/3$  $+2/3$  $-1/3$  $+2/3$

$-1/3$  $+2/3$

**Neutron**   **Proton**

*Quarks in hadrons*
*A neutron has two down quarks (blue) and one up quark (red), making it neutral. A proton has two up quarks and one down quark, making it positive.*

## Antiparticles

Two particles that have opposite properties to each other

For every particle, there is an antiparticle that has the same mass but an opposite electric charge, or some other opposite property. For example, the electron has a negative charge but its antiparticle, the positron, has a positive charge. **Antimatter** is a kind of matter that consists of antiparticles. Antiparticles can be made in particle accelerators.

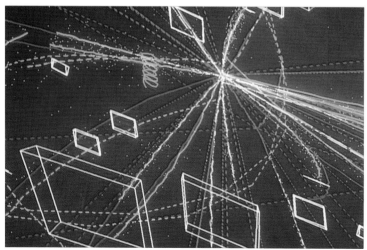

*Particle collisions*
*This computer picture shows an electron-positron collision at CERN, the European Laboratory for Particle Physics near Geneva, Switzerland. The broken and unbroken lines show the tracks of new particles created by the collision.*

# Superstring

A threadlike particle

Some scientists think that all the fundamental particles may be made of very tiny superstrings. The superstrings are like lines, or loops, rather than points. If they exist, they are billions of billions of times smaller than the fundamental particles themselves.

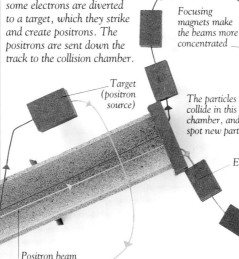

*Electrons and positrons*
*Halfway down the track, some electrons are diverted to a target, which they strike and create positrons. The positrons are sent down the track to the collision chamber.*

*Arc-bending magnets curve the particle beams*

*Focusing magnets make the beams more concentrated*

*Target (positron source)*

*The particles collide in this chamber, and detectors spot new particles*

*Electromagnets guide the particles*

*The straight part of the track is 2 miles (3.2 kilometers) long*

Electron beam

Electron source fires beams of electrons down the track

Positron beam

# Fundamental force

One of the Universe's basic forces

Four fundamental forces ■, or **interactions**, hold everything together. The first of these forces is gravity ■. The second is **electromagnetic force**, which is the force between electrons, atoms, or molecules. The third fundamental force is the **weak nuclear force**, which causes radioactivity. Finally, there is **strong nuclear force**, which holds quarks together inside protons and neutrons, and protons and neutrons together in the nucleus of an atom. Scientists believe that electromagnetic force and weak nuclear force are really versions of the same force, known as the **electroweak force**. The forces occur between particles when they exchange other particles called **bosons**. Bosons include **gluons**, which move between quarks and carry the strong nuclear force.

# Particle accelerator

A machine that accelerates particles to a very high speed

In a particle accelerator, beams of charged particles, such as electrons and protons, are accelerated along a track by electric and magnetic fields. When the beams of particles are moving very fast, they are made to strike other particles, known as targets. In a **collider**, two beams of particles moving in opposite directions collide with each other. The collisions that take place inside a particle accelerator produce new particles. The paths of these particles are recorded by detectors and computers.

*Underground collider*
*CERN's electron-positron collider is housed underground in a circular tunnel 5 miles (8 kilometers) in diameter.*

*How a particle accelerator works*
*This is a model of the Stanford linear accelerator in California. Beams of electrons and positrons are accelerated down a long, straight track. Electromagnets then guide them so that they collide and produce new particles. Some of these new particles exist for less than a billionth of a second.*

# Superconducting super collider (SSC)

The world's largest particle accelerator

The SSC is a planned circular collider 54 miles (87 kilometers) long in Texas. It was designed to detect a particle called the **Higgs' boson** by using superconducting electromagnets to collide two beams of protons. Construction of the SSC was halted in 1993. It is now hoped that the less powerful Large Hadron Collider, to be built in Europe, will detect the Higgs' boson.

# Quantum theory

Quantum theory explains the strange and unpredictable behavior of subatomic particles and the smallest amounts of energy. Thanks to quantum theory, we are able to build machines such as lasers and solar-powered calculators.

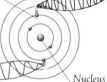

**1** *Electrons leap to higher energy levels as they take in energy*

*Photon of blue light*

**2** *Electrons give out energy as they drop to a lower energy level*

*Photon of red light*

*Nucleus*

*Hot metal*
As this metal bar gets hotter it changes color, because it emits light rays of increasing energy.

## Quantum theory

The theory that energy consists of small units

Energy is made up of very small units of energy called **quanta**. A single unit is called a **quantum**. Because a fraction of a quantum cannot exist, an amount of energy is always equal to a whole number of quanta. In electromagnetic radiation ▪, a form of energy that includes light rays, the amount of energy in each quantum depends on the frequency ▪ of the radiation. This is why heating a metal bar makes it glow first red, then yellow, and finally white. As the temperature rises, the quanta in the light rays gain more energy. This increases the frequencies of the light rays, so that the light changes color.

## Wave-particle duality

The way in which light and other types of electromagnetic radiation act both as waves and as particles

Electromagnetic radiation, such as light, produces effects that are only caused by waves. These effects include interference ▪, which makes colors appear in bubbles. But light also behaves as a stream of particles called photons. Photons cause solar cells to produce electricity. Just as electromagnetic radiation acts as particles, particles such as electrons also act as waves.

## Uncertainty principle

The behavior of particles cannot be predicted exactly

It impossible to measure both the momentum ▪ and the position of a particle, such as an electron, at the same time. This means we can never be certain how a particle will behave, only how it will probably behave. The principle is also called the **indeterminacy principle**.

*Emission of photons*
When atoms gain extra energy, their electrons can jump to higher energy levels (**1**). As the electrons fall back to the original level, they emit photons (**2**).

## Quantum mechanics

An explanation of the behavior of electrons within the atom

Each electron ▪ can orbit the nucleus ▪ of an atom ▪ at different energy levels ▪. Electrons can jump from one level to another when the atom gains energy. The energy supplied can be electricity, light, or heat. When the electrons fall back to their original energy level, the energy is given out. As an electron jumps and falls back, the atom gains and loses one quantum of energy. The amount of energy in the quantum depends on the difference in energy between the two energy levels.

## Photon

A particle of electromagnetic radiation

A photon is a quantum of electromagnetic radiation, which includes radio waves, light rays, and X-rays. Each wave or ray consists of a stream of photons.

*Energy transfer*
When these two children exchange chips, it is similar to the way in which atoms can gain or lose quanta of energy. Like the chips, quanta cannot be reduced to smaller units. They can only be gained or lost in whole numbers.

### See also

Atom 34 • Electromagnetic radiation 74
Electron 34 • Energy level 82
Frequency 71 • Interference 79
Momentum 55 • Nucleus 35

# Discovery of atoms

People first suspected that matter is made up of tiny particles called atoms about 2,400 years ago. But the idea has been found to be true only in the last 200 years. More recently, scientists have found even smaller particles inside the atom itself.

*Heated cathode gives off electrons*

## Democritus

Greek philosopher (c.460–c.370 BC)

Democritus believed that all the many substances that exist are different because they are made of different kinds of tiny particles. He called these particles atoms ▪.

## John Dalton

English chemist (1766–1844)

In 1803, Dalton proposed atomic theory, which states that each element ▪ has its own kind of atom. Compounds form when different kinds of atom link up.

## Antoine Henri Becquerel

French physicist (1852–1908)

Becquerel discovered radioactivity in 1896. He placed a uranium compound on a photographic plate wrapped in dark paper. When he developed the plate, he found that it was fogged, showing that rays from the compound had penetrated the paper. The French chemist Marie Curie ▪ named this process radioactivity ▪.

### See also

***Thomson's cathode ray tube***
*Thomson used electric and magnetic fields to bend cathode rays in this tube of low-pressure gas. Thomson's experiments enabled him to calculate the ratio of the charge on the ray's particles to their mass.*

## Joseph John Thomson

English physicist (1856–1940)

In 1897, Thomson discovered the electron ▪. He studied the rays produced by heating a negative electric terminal, called a cathode. He proved that "cathode rays" are beams of negatively charged particles much smaller than atoms. He called these particles electrons.

## Ernest Rutherford

New Zealand–English physicist (1871–1937)

Rutherford discovered in 1911 that an atom is not a solid particle. He realized that an atom has a heavy centre, or nucleus ▪, surrounded by electrons. He discovered the proton ▪, a positively charged particle within the nucleus, in 1914. Rutherford produced the first nuclear reaction in 1917 by changing nitrogen nuclei into oxygen nuclei. He also named the three kinds of rays produced by radioactive elements: alpha, beta, and gamma rays.

## Niels Bohr

Danish physicist (1885–1962)

Bohr applied to the atom the quantum theory ▪, which was put forward by the German physicist **Max Planck** (1858–1947) in 1900. He combined it with Rutherford's ideas of the structure of the atom, and showed in 1913 that electrons move around the nucleus in different orbits.

## James Chadwick

English physicist (1891–1974)

In 1932, Chadwick discovered the neutron ▪, a particle in the nucleus of an atom that carries no electric charge. The proposal that the neutron and the proton consist of quarks ▪ was made in 1964 by the American physicist **Murray Gell-Mann** (born 1929).

***Chadwick's apparatus***
*Using this apparatus, Chadwick found that when beryllium metal is struck by alpha particles, its nuclei release neutrons.*

## Enrico Fermi

Italian–American physicist (1901–54)

Fermi first produced nuclear fission ▪ in 1934 while bombarding uranium with neutrons. Although Fermi did not realize that fission had occurred, it was proved in 1938 by the Austrian physicist **Lise Meitner** (1878–1968) and the German chemist **Otto Hahn** (1879–1968). Fermi built the first nuclear reactor in the United States in 1942.

# Time & space

We exist in time and space. People, animals, and moving objects move in space as they travel from one place to another. Everything moves in time from one moment to the next. However, at very high speeds, time is actually slowed down.

## Time

The precise measurement of progress from past to future

An event, such as the fall of a stone to the ground, takes a certain amount of time. We measure time in units such as seconds, using clocks and other instruments. Normally, we move in time at a constant rate, and in only one direction – toward the future. We cannot stop or reverse our movement in time. However, relativity explains how this movement may slow down.

## Atomic clock

The most accurate kind of clock

An atomic clock can measure time so accurately that it would be only about a second out after a million years! It detects changes of energy ▪ in atoms ▪ of cesium or certain other elements. These changes take place at an extremely precise rate, which is measured by the clock. Atomic clocks are used to keep other clocks accurate, and in scientific research.

*Bouncing ball in time and space*
*When a ball is bounced at an angle from one person to another, it moves in three dimensions of space – forward, left or right, and up or down – and one dimension of time. This sequence of pictures shows the ball's location in space at each particular point in time.*

## Space

Distance in all directions

We often use the words "space" or "outer space" to mean the empty region between planets and stars. In physics, space is the idea of distance. Space has three **dimensions**, which are three directions at right angles to each other. An object has a particular length, width, and height in space. It can move in three dimensions – forward or backward, left or right, and up or down – to reach a particular position in space. Because everything also moves in time as well as in space, time is the fourth dimension. The four dimensions are called **space-time** or the **space-time continuum**. Everything has a position in space-time, which is its location and the date or time of day.

## Relativity

Two theories that relate matter, space, and time

The special theory of relativity explains that we observe unusual changes happening to an object that travels very fast, such as a tiny particle. Its mass ▪ increases, its length decreases, and time slows down. However, these changes are noticeable only when the object is traveling very fast, at speeds approaching the speed of light ▪, the fastest speed possible. The theory shows that mass (m) and energy (E) are linked by the equation $E = mc^2$, where c is the speed of light. This means that a small amount of mass can be changed into a huge amount of energy, which is what happens in nuclear reactions ▪. The general theory of relativity explains that matter causes space to curve. Huge objects, such as stars, cause light rays ▪ to bend and change their wavelength ▪. Experiments have proved that both theories of relativity are true.

*Explaining relativity*
*When we measure the speed of light, it is always the same. It makes no difference how fast we are moving. This is why time is observed to slow down at very high speeds. We can explain this by using an example of a pulse of laser light fired between two fast-moving spacecraft. This example is often called the "light clock."*

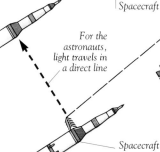

*Spacecraft*

*For the astronauts, light travels in a direct line*

*Spacecraft*

## Albert Einstein

German–American
physicist
(1879–1955)

In 1905, Einstein
explained the
photoelectric
effect ■ and Brownian motion ■.
He published his special theory
of relativity in 1905 and his
general theory of relativity in
1915. Einstein worked out
these theories from two ideas.
One was that the velocity of
light does not change when
either the light source or the
observer moves. The second
was that motion is not absolute.
We cannot say, for example,
that some objects are "really"
at rest and other objects are
"really" moving, only that
things move relatively to each
other. This is why the theories
are called theories of relativity.

## Clock

An instrument that measures time

There are many kinds of clocks,
from huge clocks on display in
public places to small wrist
watches. They all contain a
controlling device that works at
a constant rate. In a mechanical
clock or watch, this is a
pendulum or spring that has a
regular movement. In an
electronic watch, a vibrating
quartz crystal produces a regular
electrical signal, while an electric
clock receives a regular electrical
signal from the household
current. The movement or signal
controls the hands or display of
the clock or watch so that it
keeps good time. A **chronometer**
is a clock that is very accurate
at all temperatures.
Chronometers are
used for
navigation.

## MEASURING TIME

### Second (s)
The SI unit of time

One second equals
9,192,631,770 energy changes
of a cesium atom, measured by
an atomic clock. A **minute**
(min) equals 60 seconds, an
**hour** 60 minutes, and a **day** 24
hours. A **year** is the time it
takes for the Earth to go around
the Sun once (365 days 5 hours
48 minutes and 46 seconds).

*The
spacecraft are
moving forward
at 99% of the
speed of light*

*The spacecraft are shown at
regular intervals of time.
The length of this time
interval is seven times
longer for Earth observers
than for the astronauts.*

*Light travels
at about
186,300 miles
(300,000 kilometers)
per second*

### On Earth
*To the observers on Earth, the spacecraft move
so that the light pulse follows the longer dotted
line, taking seven seconds to travel
from one spacecraft to the other. The
light clock "ticks" once every seven
seconds. To Earth observers,
time aboard the spacecraft is
seven times slower, so the
astronauts age at one-
seventh the rate of
the observers.*

*Pulse of
laser light*

### The spacecraft
*Astronauts on two spacecraft send
a regular pulse of laser light directly
across space from one spacecraft to the
other. The spacecraft are traveling at close to
the speed of light at a constant distance of
186,300 miles (300,000 kilometers). To the
astronauts, the pulse of light takes one second
to travel between them;  the light clock "ticks"
once every second and time is normal.*

### The observer
*The space telescope
observes the fast-moving
spacecraft far away. A pulse
of light can be seen traveling
back and forth between them,
like the regular ticking of a
clock. The telescope relays the
images back to observers on the
Earth below.*

# Force

A force is invisible, but you can see and feel its effect. Forces push or pull. They cause objects to start or stop moving, change speed or direction, bend, stretch, twist, or change shape. A common force is the Earth's gravity. It pulls us to the ground and gives us weight.

## Force

A push or a pull

If an object is free to move, a force will make it move in a particular direction. But if an object is not free to move, a force may make it stretch or change its shape. When the forces acting upon an object are balanced, the object is in equilibrium ▨.

## Mechanics

The study of the effects of forces upon objects

There are two main branches of mechanics. Dynamics ▨ is the study of forces on objects in motion. Statics ▨ is the study of forces on objects that do not move.

*An athlete's hammer is a heavy weight attached to a wire*

## Center of gravity

The point at which the whole weight of an object balances

You can balance a tray of glasses on one hand if you support it directly beneath its center of gravity. Gravity pulls equally on all parts of the tray around this point. The center of gravity is also called the **center of mass**.

## Centripetal force

The force that keeps an object moving in a circle

If you whirl a weight on a piece of string, its inertia ▨ makes it try to fly off in a straight line. You have to pull on the string to keep the weight moving in a circle. This pull is the centripetal force. Its direction is inward, toward the center of rotation.

### A moving force
*This hammer thrower's muscles produce a strong force to lift the hammer and start it moving.*

### Centripetal force
*The hammer thrower pulls strongly on the wire as he whirls the hammer. This pull is the centripetal force.*

*The hammer's inertia pulls it outward as it spins around*

## Centrifuge

A machine that spins a mixture at high speed to separate its different components

In a centrifuge, a container holding a mixture ▨ spins around at high speed. This exerts a strong force on the mixture, causing it to separate into its different components. The heavier particles of the mixture move outward because of their greater inertia. There appears to be an outward force, often called **centrifugal force**, acting on the particles.

### Center of gravity
*As he swings the hammer, the hammer thrower leans back to keep his center of gravity above his feet.*

# Gravity

**A force of attraction between bodies of matter**

There is a force of gravity between you and the Earth. The Earth's gravity pulls on you, giving you weight and keeping you on the ground. At the same time, you pull on the Earth. All bodies of matter ▨ exert a force of gravity. But it is strong only when something has a large mass ▨, such as a planet, moon, or star. Gravity becomes weaker as bodies of matter move farther apart.

# Gravitational field

**The region in which a body of matter exerts a force of gravity**

The Sun's gravitational field extends far out into space. It pulls on the planets of the solar system, holding them in orbits around the Sun. The field becomes weaker farther away from the Sun. The Earth's gravitational field keeps satellites and the Moon in orbit around the Earth.

*When the hammer is released, it flies off because centripetal force no longer holds it back*

# Newton's law of gravitation

**The force of gravity between two bodies of matter depends on their mass and the square of the distance between them**

If the Moon had twice its mass, the force of gravity between it and the Earth would be twice as great. But if the mass of the Moon stayed the same and it moved twice as near to the Earth, the force of gravity between the two bodies would be four (two squared) times greater. The physicist Isaac Newton ▨ discovered this law, which applies to all bodies of matter.

**Earth**       **Moon**
*Force of gravity = 1*    *Mass = 1*

*Force of gravity = 2*    *Mass = 2*

*Force of gravity = 4*    *Mass = 1*
*Moon twice as near*

# Weight

**The force of gravity acting on a body of matter**

Your weight is the force of the Earth's gravity pulling on you. So if you move away from the Earth, your weight becomes less. On the Moon, astronauts have only one-sixth of their normal weight, because the Moon's gravity is only a sixth of that of the Earth.

*Gravity soon pulls the hammer back to Earth*

## Newton meter

**An instrument that measures force**

A newton meter, or **force meter**, measures force using a spring. The spring stretches when a force pulls on it, moving a pointer along a scale. This indicates the strength of the force. For example, 1 kilogram (2.2 lb.) pulls on the spring with a force of 9.8 newtons ▨. A **spring balance** measures weight in the same way.

*1 kilogram pulls with a force of about 10 newtons*

*2 kilograms pull with a force of about 20 newtons*

*Continued on next page ➤*

# Component

One of two or more forces that combine to produce another force

Component forces ■ combine to produce one single force called the resultant. It acts in a different direction from the components. When an archer shoots an arrow, two components in the bowstring combine to give a single force that drives the arrow forward. A single force can also divide into two components. This is a **resolution of forces**.

# Resultant

A force produced by combining two or more forces

If several forces act on an object in different directions, it cannot move in all directions at once. The forces combine to produce a single resultant force, or **net force**, that acts on the object in one direction only. The original forces are components.

*First component acts along the upper half of the bowstring*

**Equal and opposite forces**
*The resultant force acts forward along the arrow and is equal and opposite to the force of the archer's arm pulling back the bowstring.*

# Couple

A pair of equal and opposite forces that cause an object to rotate

When you spin a coin, your finger and thumb apply a couple to the coin. The two forces in a couple act on opposite sides of an object. They push or pull in opposite directions, making the object turn.

**Resultant force**
*The two component forces combine to produce a single resultant force. This force pushes the arrow forward when the archer releases the bowstring.*

**In equilibrium**
*Before the archer releases the arrow, all the forces acting on it balance. The archer, bow, and arrow are in equilibrium.*

# Equilibrium

A state produced when the forces acting upon an object balance

When the forces acting upon an object balance, there is no resultant force to make it change speed ■ or direction. It is in equilibrium. A weight ■ hanging on a string is in equilibrium because the upward pull of the string equals the downward pull of gravity.

*Second component acts along the lower half of the bowstring*

## See also

◄ Continued from previous page

## Moment

The measurement of a force's turning effect

When you push a door, you apply a force at some distance from its hinge, or pivot. This produces a turning effect that opens the door. The turning effect is greater if the force is applied farther away from the pivot. A moment, or **torque**, is the measure of the turning effect. It is the amount of force multiplied by its distance from the pivot.

## Archimedes' principle

The upward force exerted on an object immersed in a fluid (a liquid or a gas) is equal to the weight of fluid displaced

An object placed in a fluid pushes aside, or displaces, some of the fluid. This fluid exerts an **upward force** called upthrust on the object. The weight of fluid displaced by a floating object is equal to the weight of the object. This is the **principle of flotation**.

***The principle of flotation***
*The weight of water displaced by this boat (shown as light blue) equals the weight of the boat.*

*Displaced water*

BM·76

***A greater turning force***
*If you cannot turn a stiff bolt, a longer wrench makes it possible by applying a greater force, or moment, to the bolt.*

## Torsion

The twist produced in an object when forces turn its ends

Torsion occurs in a bar when one end is fixed and the other end turns, or when both ends turn in opposite directions. Cars often have a **torsion bar**, which twists and untwists as the car moves over the road. The torsion bar takes up forces that would cause the car to bump or roll.

## Buoyancy

The upward-acting force on an object immersed in a fluid (a liquid or a gas)

If you place an object in water, the water pushes up on it with a force called **buoyancy**. This **buoyant force**, which makes a rock seem lighter underwater than it is out of water, equals the weight of water displaced by the object. If the displaced water weighs as much as the object, the object floats; otherwise it sinks.

***Buoyancy***
*This boat floats because the upward force of the water is equal to its weight.*

### Newton (N)
The SI unit of force

One newton of force causes a mass of 1 kilogram to move with an acceleration ▣ of 1 meter per second per second. On earth, a mass of 1 kilogram weighs 9.8 newtons.

## Statics

The study of the forces acting on bodies that do not move

Statics is important in the design of stationary structures such as buildings and bridges. The forces in a structure must balance so that the structure does not move or fall down. **Hydrostatics** is the study of fluids at rest and objects immersed in fluids. It is used in the design of hydraulic ▣ machines and ships. The force caused by the pressure of a fluid can break up a machine or ship.

## Archimedes
Greek physicist and mathematician (287–212 BC)

Archimedes is said to have discovered his principle while he was taking a bath. He was so excited he ran naked into the street shouting *"Eureka!"* ("I've found it!"). Archimedes was a famous mathematician and inventor. As well as pioneering hydrostatics, he also studied mechanics ▣. He discovered how moments of forces work and the principle of the lever ▣. Archimedes may well have been the first person to make scientific deductions from observation ▣. This is the basis of all scientific method.

# Pressure

You cannot feel it, but the air around you is pressing on your body with a strong force. At the same time, the weight of your body is pushing down on the ground. Gases, liquids, and solid objects all exert force on surfaces. Pressure is the amount of force pushing on each part of a surface.

## Pressure

The amount of force exerted on a unit area of surface

You exert pressure on something when you apply a force ▨ to it. The amount of pressure depends on the strength of the force, and the surface area ▨ to which you apply the force. Pressure is greater if the area is smaller. A fluid (a liquid or a gas) exerts pressure on its container and on objects immersed in it. For example, when you dive under water, pressure increases with depth as the weight of water pushing on you increases.

## Siphon

A tube that carries liquid from a higher level to a lower level

You make a siphon work by sucking liquid into the tube. The liquid then flows to the lower level because the liquid pressure is greater at the higher end of the tube than that at the lower end.

### Simple siphon
*When this boy takes his thumb off the tube, water will flow into the lower bottle.*

## Pascal's law of fluid pressures

Pressure acts equally throughout a fluid (a liquid or a gas)

If you raise the pressure of a fluid, the pressure increases equally throughout the fluid. When you blow into a balloon, the air inside it expands evenly in all directions. This law was discovered by Blaise Pascal.

### Foot pump
*Pushing the pump with your foot moves a piston inside the cylinder. This pushes more air into the tire, raising the air pressure so that the flat tire becomes firm.*

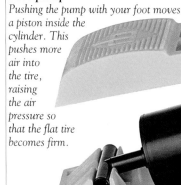

Cylinder

## Compressor

A machine that raises the pressure of a gas

A compressor contains pistons that compress, or squeeze, a gas to deliver it at high pressure. This can be used to power mechanical tools such as drills. A bicycle pump compresses air to force it into a bicycle tire.

## Blaise Pascal
French physicist and mathematician (1623–62)

Pascal was the first scientist to understand that pressure acts equally throughout a fluid. He also showed how air pressure decreases with height by sending a mercury barometer to the top of a mountain. As a young man, Pascal invented a mechanical calculating machine, an early forerunner of the computer ▨.

## Bourdon gauge

An instrument for measuring the pressure of a fluid (a liquid or gas)

The gauge has a curved tube connected to a fluid inside a cylinder. The fluid pressure makes the tube straighten out, moving a pointer along a scale.

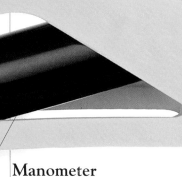

*Pressure gauge*

## Manometer

An instrument for measuring the pressure of a fluid (a liquid or a gas)

A manometer is a U-shaped tube that contains a liquid. It is generally used for measuring gas pressure. Gas is fed into one side of the tube, which pushes the liquid around the U shape. The height of the column of liquid on the other side of the tube indicates the pressure of the gas.

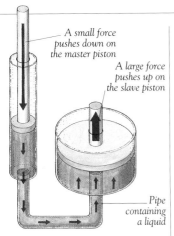

*A small force pushes down on the master piston*

*A large force pushes up on the slave piston*

*Pipe containing a liquid*

**A hydraulic system**
*When the master piston pushes down, it increases the pressure throughout the liquid, which pushes on the slave piston.*

# Hydraulic

Operated by the pressure or movement of a liquid

Machines such as excavators use hydraulic systems to lift heavy loads. A hydraulic system is an efficient way of producing a large force. It usually consists of two pistons, placed inside cylinders. A pipe containing a liquid connects the cylinders.
When you apply a force to the small master piston, it pushes on the liquid, increasing its pressure throughout the system. The liquid pushes on the large slave piston with a stronger force, because the slave piston has a larger surface area. This strong force drives the machine.

*Air pressure increases evenly along the tube*

# Barometer

An instrument for measuring the pressure of the atmosphere

There are two main types of barometer. An **aneroid barometer** consists of a metal box that contains very little air. This makes it sensitive to outside pressure. The box contracts or expands as the pressure of the atmosphere rises or falls. It is linked to a pointer that moves around a scale. A **mercury barometer** consists of a column of mercury inside a glass tube that is sealed at its upper end. The column rises and falls as the air pressure changes.

# Pneumatic

Operated by the force of compressed air

A pneumatic machine contains a compressor. This compresses air to deliver it at high pressure. The compressed air is used to apply a strong force to pistons that power the machine. Pneumatic drills exert a strong force that is used to break up hard materials.

# Valve

A device that allows fluid (a liquid or gas) to flow in one direction only

A simple valve is a hinged flap inside a tube. The valve opens when a fluid flows in one direction, and is pushed shut if the flow reverses.

*Air pressure inflates the tire*

**Tire valve**
*The valve on the bicycle tire lets air into the tire, but stops air flowing back out again.*

*Valve*

# UNITS OF PRESSURE

## Pascal (Pa)

The SI unit of pressure

1 pascal is equal to a force of 1 newton applied to an area of 1 square meter.

## Atmosphere (atm)

A unit approximately equal to air pressure at sea level, used to measure very high pressures

1 atmosphere is equal to 101,325 pascals or 760 millimeters of mercury.

## Millimeter of mercury (mmHg)

A general unit of pressure

A pressure of 1 mmHg is that exerted by a column of mercury 1 millimeter high.

## Millibar (mb)

A unit of atmospheric pressure used in weather forecasting

1 millibar equals 100 pascals. 1 **bar** (1,000 millibars) is the approximate pressure of the atmosphere.

## See also

Altimeter 64 • Computer 117
Force 48 • Surface area 174

# Motion

Motion occurs throughout the Universe, from huge planets that travel through space, to the tiny moving particles that make up matter. Changes in motion cannot take place without force. A moving object needs a force to make it change speed or direction, or slow down and stop.

*Overcoming inertia*
*This boy has to pedal hard to overcome his inertia and start his bicycle moving. Once he is moving, his inertia helps carry him forward.*

*Brakes reduce speed using friction*

## Inertia

The resistance of an object to a change in its motion

Every object has inertia, which causes it to resist a change in its motion. Therefore, a moving object will try to keep moving in a straight line, and a stationary object will try to remain at rest. If you are traveling in a car that stops suddenly, your body's inertia will cause you to keep on moving. Wearing a seatbelt stops this from happening. Inertia depends on mass ▪, so an object with a large mass has a lot of inertia.

## Velocity

The speed and direction of an object

The velocity of a moving object changes if either its speed or its direction changes. For example, if a car travels around a corner at a constant speed, its velocity changes because the car is changing direction. A **uniform velocity** is a velocity that stays the same.

## Friction

A force that opposes motion

Friction occurs where moving objects or surfaces rub together. It acts against the direction of motion, causing objects to slow down or stop. The amount of friction depends on the texture of the surfaces and the force ▪ pressing them together. Rough surfaces create the most friction. Friction gives wheels **traction**, which helps them grip the road.

*Acceleration*
*The cue pushes the white billiard ball, making it accelerate.*

*Decreasing velocity*
*Friction with the billiard table causes the ball to slow down gradually.*

## Speed

The rate at which an object moves

Speed is the measurement of the distance traveled by an object in a certain unit of time. For example, the walking speed of an average person is about 3 miles per hour, or 3 mph (5 kilometers per hour, or 5 kph). A motor vehicle, such as a car or a truck, may travel at a speed of 37 mph (60 kph).

## Acceleration

The rate of change of velocity

When the velocity of an object increases, it is accelerating. Acceleration is a change in velocity over a certain amount of time. When you hit a billiard ball, it accelerates while the cue is pushing it and then travels with a decreasing velocity. When velocity decreases, the rate of change is called **deceleration**.

## Galileo Galilei

Italian physicist and astronomer (1564–1642)

Galileo first stated how force causes acceleration, which he measured by rolling balls down a slope. He also discovered the pendulum ▪ and was the first to use a telescope ▪ to observe stars and planets. He realized that the Earth moves around the Sun, the opposite of what most people then believed.

# Newton's first law of motion

An object remains at rest or continues to travel at a uniform velocity unless a force acts on it

A stationary object will not move unless a force acts on it and makes it accelerate. Then it continues to travel forward, unless another force slows it down. If you roll a ball along the ground, your arm provides the force that accelerates the ball. The ball travels forward until friction slows it to a stop.

# Newton's second law of motion

The force that accelerates an object is equal to its mass multiplied by its acceleration

The acceleration of an object depends on its mass and the amount of force acting on it. If you hit a small ball with a large amount of force, the ball accelerates rapidly. But if you apply the same force to a heavier ball, the acceleration will be less.

*The white billiard ball collides with the red billiard ball*

# Newton's third law of motion

When two objects act on each other, they experience equal forces in opposite directions

Forces always act in pairs called the **action** and **reaction**. When you walk or run, your feet push on the ground (the action). The ground pushes back on your feet with an equal and opposite force (the reaction). This moves you forward.

## Isaac Newton

English physicist and mathematician (1642–1727)

Newton took Galileo's observations of force and motion further when he developed his three laws of motion. He also discovered the law of gravitation ▪, which may have been inspired by seeing an apple fall from a tree. Newton made other important discoveries in light ▪ and developed calculus ▪ in mathematics.

*Conservation of momentum*
*As the two billiard balls collide, the white ball transfers most of its momentum to the red ball. Both balls move forward, but the red ball travels with a greater velocity.*

## Dynamics

The study of forces that cause changes in motion

There are two main branches of dynamics. **Hydrodynamics** is the study of the motion of fluids, such as water, and the movement in water of objects such as boats. **Aerodynamics** is the study of the motion of gases, particularly air, and the movement in air of objects such as aircraft.

# Perpetual motion

Motion that carries on forever without a force to keep it going

A space probe can travel through space forever. There is no air in space, so there is no friction to slow it down. It is impossible for an object to achieve this perpetual motion on Earth. With no force to keep it going, friction with the air or other matter always slows a moving object to a stop.

*Force of friction*
*Friction between the ball and the table slows the ball to a stop.*

*Without friction to slow it down, the ball would keep on moving forever*

# Momentum

The mass of an object multiplied by its velocity

The momentum of an object depends on its mass and velocity. This means that an object's momentum changes as it accelerates. Momentum can be transferred between objects. When a moving ball collides with a stationary one, for example, the first ball transfers some of its momentum to the second ball. The total momentum of the two balls is the same as the first ball's momentum before the collision. This is called the **principle of conservation of momentum**.

## See also

*Continued on next page ▶*

## Oscillation

A repeated back-and-forth movement

A pendulum **oscillates** when it swings to and fro. This means it moves back and forth repeatedly over the same central point. An oscillation can also be a regular change between a maximum and minimum value, as in the voltage of an alternating current ▓ of electricity. A **vibration** is an oscillation, but it usually means a rapid oscillation over a short distance. For example, a guitar string **vibrates** when you pluck it, and atoms vibrate inside a solid.

## Pendulum

A weight that swings back and forth on a fixed string, wire, or rod

You can use a pendulum to keep the time because it swings back and forth in a regular amount of time. The time taken by each swing is called a **period**. Once you set a pendulum swinging, gravity ▓ keeps it moving from side to side. Gravity starts the pendulum moving at the top of its swing, and slows it down again as it rises on the other side. A pendulum will keep swinging until friction ▓ with the air slows it down. A mechanical device powers a clock pendulum.

## Resonance

An increase in the size of oscillations caused by a force applied at an object's natural frequency

When you push a swing in time with its natural rhythm, you build up much bigger swings than you would by pushing it out of rhythm. This is due to resonance, which is an increase in the amplitude ▓, or size, of oscillations. When an object oscillates freely, it does so at its own natural frequency ▓, or rate. Applying a force ▓ at the same frequency increases the size of the oscillations. So timing your pushes on the swing to its natural frequency makes bigger swings.

## Simple harmonic motion

A kind of oscillation

The farther you pull a pendulum to one side before letting it go, the greater its acceleration ▓ toward the central point of its swing. In simple harmonic motion, the force that pulls an oscillating object toward its central point depends on the object's distance from the central point.

## Ballistics

The study of the flight of projectiles

Ballistics investigates the motion of **projectiles**. These are objects, such as bullets and golf balls, that are thrust forward by an initial force, but are unpowered after that. When you fire a bullet from a gun, it flies in a curving path called a **trajectory**. You can use ballistics to find out the **range**, or distance, of the trajectory. This depends on the size, shape, and weight of the projectile and on the forces acting on it. The force that starts the projectile moving, the angle at which it is fired, wind, and gravity all affect its trajectory.

*Pendulum swings*
*The period of a pendulum is the time it takes to make one swing back and forth. A long swing takes the same time as a short swing. The weight of the pendulum bob makes no difference to the period, but the length of the pendulum string does. A pendulum with a long string swings more slowly than a pendulum with a short string.*

◄ Continued from previous page

The skydiver stretches out his arms to increase his air resistance

**Skydiver**
*The terminal velocity of this skydiver is about 124 mph (200 kph).*

# Terminal velocity

The uniform velocity achieved by an object falling through a fluid (a liquid or a gas)

When the skydiver above falls through the air, gravity pulls him downward. He accelerates as he falls, increasing his **resistance**, or friction, with the air. When his resistance equals the force of gravity, the skydiver stops accelerating. He falls at a steady velocity ▪ called terminal velocity.

# Turbulence

The rough flow of a fluid (a liquid or a gas)

A river is **turbulent** when its water is rough and swirling. The turbulence can be caused by strong currents flowing within the river or by friction with the river's banks and rocks on the bottom. A boat traveling upstream creates friction with the water flowing past it, causing turbulence in its wake. Air turbulence affects lift ▪ in aircraft, giving a bumpy flight.

## See also

Acceleration 54
Alternating current 104
Amplitude 71 • Diameter 175
Force 48 • Frequency 71 • Friction 54
Gravity 49 • Lift 62 • Velocity 54

# Streamline flow

The smooth flow of a fluid (a liquid or a gas)

A fluid flows smoothly if it creates low friction between itself and the surfaces it comes into contact with. An object with a **streamlined** shape can move easily through a fluid. For example, air flows smoothly around a car that has a pointed nose and curved, polished sides.

# Gyroscope

A wheel set on a free-moving axis

A toy gyroscope is a simple kind of gyroscope. When the wheel is set spinning, the gyroscope is able to resist forces, such as gravity, that act on its axis. This enables the gyroscope to balance. A **gyrocompass** contains a gyroscope that keeps pointing north once it has been set in that direction.

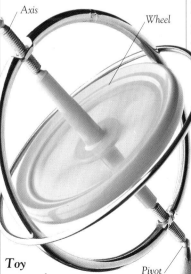

Axis

Wheel

**Toy gyroscope**
Pivot
*This gyroscope resists gravity and balances on a pivot when it spins quickly. When it slows down, gravity will make it fall off.*

**Spinning skater**
*Angular momentum enables this ice skater to spin very quickly.*

# Angular momentum

The momentum of a rotating object

The twirling ice skater above can suddenly speed up by pulling in his arms. This is due to angular momentum, which depends on the diameter ▪ and velocity of a spinning object. Once the skater is spinning, his angular momentum does not change. So when he reduces his diameter, his velocity must increase.

# Precession

A sideways movement by the axis of a spinning object

When you spin a gyroscope and balance it on a pivot, its shaft, or axis, circles slowly. This movement is called precession. It happens because gravity tries to tilt the axis of the gyroscope. When precession occurs, the axis of the spinning object moves at right angles to any force that tries to tilt it. If one end of the axis is fixed, the other end moves in a circle. Precession enables you to balance when you ride a bicycle. Turning the front wheel slightly causes precession, so that the wheel stays upright.

# Machines

Machines enable us do many things that we could not do on our own. They are able to increase the force that we apply to a task, and exert more force than our muscles ever could. They can also work faster than human beings.

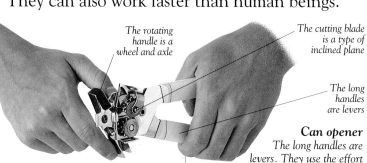

The rotating handle is a wheel and axle

The cutting blade is a type of inclined plane

The long handles are levers

**Can opener**
*The long handles are levers. They use the effort of the left hand to produce a large force so that the blade cuts into the can. The other handle is a wheel and axle. It changes the effort of the right hand into a strong force that rotates the can.*

## Simple machine

A device that changes a force applied to it

A force ■ called the **effort** is applied to one part of the simple machine. Another part of the machine then moves to overcome a resisting force called the **load**. It may raise a heavy weight, for example. A simple machine often magnifies the force applied to it, so that a small effort can move a large load. Simple machines include the lever, inclined plane, screw, gear, wheel and axle, and pulley ■.

## Force ratio

The force produced by a simple machine divided by the force applied to it

A simple machine with a force ratio of 5 magnifies the force applied to it by five times. This means that it can move a load of 50 newtons ■ using an effort of only 10 newtons. Force ratio is also called **mechanical advantage**. The **distance ratio** or **velocity ratio** is the distance moved by the effort divided by the distance moved by the load.

## Lever

A bar that turns on a pivot in order to exert a force

Effort is applied to one part of the bar, which is supported on a pivot or **fulcrum** (a picture of a simple lever appears on page 18). Another part of the bar then moves to raise or overcome a load. In a **first-class lever**, such as a crowbar, the fulcrum lies between the effort and load. A wheelbarrow is a **second-class lever**. The load (what is carried) lies between the effort and fulcrum (the wheel). A hammer is a **third-class lever** when it is used to knock nails in wood. The effort is between the fulcrum (the wrist) and the load (the resistance of the wood). Levers can be used in pairs. Scissors are a pair of first-class levers joined at the fulcrum.

## Inclined plane

A slope that reduces the effort needed to move something

A ramp is an example of an inclined plane. Pushing a cart up a ramp to a higher level is easier than lifting the cart vertically. The cart moves a greater distance along the ramp, but less force is required to move it. A **wedge** is a moving inclined plane that pushes an object with more force than the effort needed to move the wedge. Cutting blades make use of the wedge. An axe's wedge-shaped blade makes it possible to split logs of wood with little effort.

## Screw

A shaft with a spiral groove

The spiral groove is a **screw thread**. It is really a type of inclined plane wrapped around a shaft. Turning the screw makes the thread move the whole screw forward or backward with more force than the turning effort. You cannot drive a nail into wood by turning it; but when you turn a screw, its spiral groove forces the whole screw into the wood.

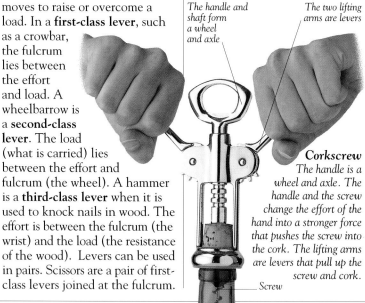

The handle and shaft form a wheel and axle

The two lifting arms are levers

**Corkscrew**
*The handle is a wheel and axle. The handle and the screw change the effort of the hand into a stronger force that pushes the screw into the cork. The lifting arms are levers that pull up the screw and cork.*

Screw

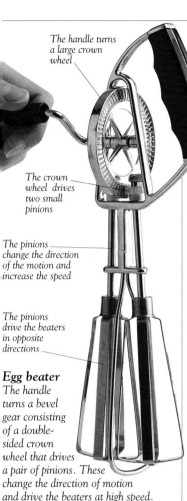

*The handle turns a large crown wheel*

*The crown wheel drives two small pinions*

*The pinions change the direction of the motion and increase the speed*

*The pinions drive the beaters in opposite directions*

**Egg beater**
*The handle turns a bevel gear consisting of a double-sided crown wheel that drives a pair of pinions. These change the direction of motion and drive the beaters at high speed.*

# Wheel and axle

**A rotating device that exerts a force at its center when the outer part is turned, and vice versa**

When a wheel is fixed to a central shaft called an axle, it forms a machine that transmits and magnifies force. The steering wheel of a car is a type of wheel and axle. The driver's hands turn the wheel, causing the shaft to turn with a greater force and operate the steering mechanism. When you pedal a bicycle, you use a wheel and axle in a different way. The bicycle chain turns the axle of the rear wheel, so that the wheel's rim turns with less force but travels a greater distance, moving you along. Other wheel and axle examples are the winch ▨ and turbine.

# Turbine

**A motor in which a set of blades rotates when struck by a moving stream of liquid or gas**

A turbine is a form of wheel and axle. The moving liquid or gas, which is usually water, steam, or air, exerts a turning force on the blades. The shaft of the turbine turns with a greater force than the force exerted on the blades. Turbines are often used to drive electric generators ▨.

# Gear

**A pair or series of toothed wheels that are connected so that one wheel turns another**

Gears transmit force and motion. The wheels are usually of different sizes and mesh together, or are connected by a chain. A large wheel causes a small wheel to turn with less force but greater speed. A small wheel makes a large wheel turn with more force but less speed. Gears can also change the direction of the motion they transmit. Each wheel is called a **gear wheel** or **cog**. A **pinion** is a small gear wheel that drives or is turned by a larger wheel. A **gear train** is a set of several gear wheels.

# Bevel gear

**A pair of wheels with sloping teeth that mesh at an angle to each other**

A bevel gear changes the direction of rotation. The pair of wheels is also called a **crown and pinion**.

# Worm gear

**A toothed wheel that meshes with a shaft bearing a screw thread**

A worm gear changes the direction of motion and greatly alters force or speed.

## See also

Electric generator 110
Force 48 • Newton 51
Pulley 60 • Winch 60

# Spur gear

**A pair of toothed wheels that mesh together and turn in the same plane**

A spur gear regulates the speed or force of motion and reverses its direction.

# Rack and pinion

**A toothed wheel (the pinion) that meshes with a straight-toothed bar (the rack)**

The rack and pinion is a form of gear that changes circular (rotary) motion into straight (linear) motion, and vice versa. The pinion rotates while the rack moves in a straight line. A rack and pinion is often used in the focusing mechanism of microscopes.

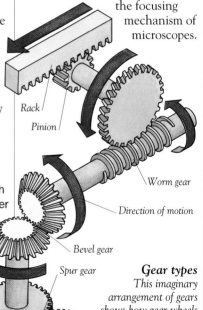

*Rack*

*Pinion*

*Worm gear*

*Direction of motion*

*Bevel gear*

*Spur gear*

***Gear types***
*This imaginary arrangement of gears shows how gear wheels work together to change the direction of the motion transmitted by a machine. The size of the gear wheels affects the speed and force of this motion.*

Continued on next page ➤

The free end of the rope is pulled to raise the load

Single-pulley system

Double-pulley system

Four-part block and tackle

10-newton load

One pulley wheel at each end

20-newton load

Two pulley wheels at each end

40-newton load

## Pulley

**A grooved wheel, or set of wheels, around which a rope passes in order to move a load**

Pulleys can be mounted in wooden or metal frames called blocks. Various combinations of blocks and rope, called tackles, are used to reduce the effort ■ it takes to move a load. In general, the more pulleys used, the less effort is needed, but the shorter the distance the load travels. Also called pulleys are the metal wheels that turn, or are turned by, belts in car engines.

## Lubrication

**The use of oil or grease to make parts of machines move easily**

Oil or grease is a **lubricant**. It spreads out in a thin film over the surface of the moving parts. This stops them from rubbing directly against other parts and reduces the friction between them.

## Bearing

**A support for a rotating wheel or shaft**

A bearing lies between a rotating part and the frame on which it is mounted. For example, the bearing may be between the wheel of a roller skate and the axle. The bearing allows the wheel to rotate with little friction ■. A **ball bearing** consists of steel balls enclosed in a metal case.

*Ball bearing*
*The steel balls are able to roll within the casing, keeping friction to a minimum.*

## Crank

**A device that changes to-and-fro (reciprocal) motion to circular (rotary) motion, or vice versa**

A crank consists of a driving rod linked to a rotating arm or wheel by a connecting rod that is hinged at both ends. As the driving rod moves to and fro (or up and down), the connecting rod moves the arm or wheel in a circle. A piston engine uses a crank to produce rotary motion. The rotating arm or wheel may also drive the rod to and fro.

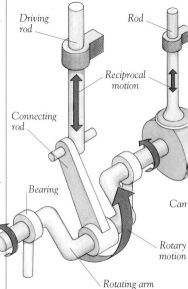

Driving rod

Rod

Reciprocal motion

Connecting rod

Bearing

Cam

Rotary motion

Rotating arm

## Cam

**A device that changes circular (rotary) motion to to-and-fro (reciprocal) motion**

A cam is often a wheel of irregular shape or one mounted off-center on a shaft. With each turn of the shaft, the cam bumps against a rod, moving the rod to and fro or up and down. Cams operate fuel valves in a gasoline engine ■.

*Pulleys in action*
*In the single-pulley system at right, a given force lifts the 1-N load a certain distance. With two pulleys, the same force lifts 2 N, but only half as far. The same force applied to the four-part tackle lifts a 4-N force a quarter of the distance.*

## Winch

**A device for moving heavy loads attached to a rope or wire**

The rope or wire runs over a drum which is turned by a long handle to wind in the rope or wire and move the load ■. The handle and drum form a wheel and axle ■ that makes it easier to move the load. A winch may use gears ■ to reduce the effort even more.

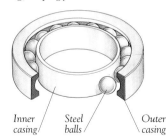

Inner casing

Steel balls

Outer casing

### See also

Effort 58 • Friction 54 • Gear 59
Load 58 • Newton 51
Gasoline engine 67 • Wheel and axle

◄ Continued from previous page

# Automatic machines

Many machines are able to work on their own — from automatic doors and traffic lights to robots and aircraft that guide themselves through the sky. These automatic machines perform complex operations. Some can even measure their own performance.

*Tools can be fitted to carry out a variety of tasks*

## Automation

The use of automatic machines to perform tasks previously done by people

Automation is greatly changing the home, shop, office, and factory as automatic machines take over many routine tasks and manufacturing work.

## Servomechanism

A device for increasing the power used to operate a machine

A machine's control system may not be strong enough on its own to operate the machine. The control system instead instructs a powerful servomechanism, which in turn operates the machine. The braking system of a car may contain a servomechanism. It boosts the force with which the driver presses the brake pedal and quickly stops the car.

## Governor

A feedback device that controls the speed of a machine

A governor can keep an engine running at a constant speed. If the engine speeds up, the governor reduces the supply of fuel to the engine and its speed falls. If the engine slows down, the governor increases the fuel supply to speed up the engine.

**Robot arm**
*Robots like this can be used in factories to perform difficult or dangerous tasks quickly and efficiently.*

## Robot

A machine that can carry out complex tasks automatically

Most industrial robots consist of a mechanical arm that can move in many directions. Attached to the end is a device that carries out a task such as welding ▦ or spraying paint. A computer ▦ instructs the robot to perform a set of actions, often in response to signals from the robot's sensors. These can detect many things, including the position of objects the robot is working on.

### See also
Computer 117 • Welding 166

## Feedback

A process that enables an automatic machine to operate under its own control

Sensors in the machine measure its performance. The results are fed back into the machine's control system and are used to adjust its performance. The autopilot guidance system of an aircraft uses feedback. Sensors measure the position of the aircraft. If it travels off course, the sensors instruct the guidance system to bring the aircraft back onto the correct flight path.

## Sensor

A device that detects the presence of something

Sensors detect such things as heat, pressure, magnetic fields, movement, speed, vibration, and smoke. They may also measure these things. Most sensors send out an electric signal to operate a controlling or warning system.

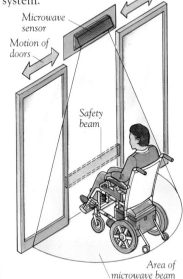

Microwave sensor

Motion of doors

Safety beam

Area of microwave beam

**Automatic doors**
*The sensor above the doors projects a microwave beam toward the floor. When a person moves into the beam, an electronic signal is sent to open the doors. The doors close after the person has passed through the safety beam.*

# Flight

Aircraft can fly because they get support from the air around them. Airplanes and helicopters use wings and rotors to produce this support, while balloons and airships can float in the air.

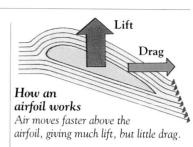

**How an airfoil works**
*Air moves faster above the airfoil, giving much lift, but little drag.*

## Lift

An upward force acting on an aircraft

Airplane wings and helicopter rotors ■ produce lift. Balloons and airships get lift because they contain gases that are less dense ■ than air. A flying aircraft ascends when the upward pull of its lift is greater than the downward pull of its weight ■. It descends when the lift decreases and becomes less than its weight.

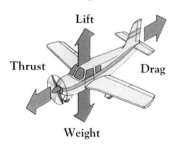

**Forces acting on a flying aircraft**
*When lift equals weight, and thrust equals drag, the aircraft is in level flight.*

## Thrust

A forward force acting on an aircraft

The jet engines or propellers of an airplane produce thrust to drive the airplane forward. In a helicopter, the main rotor produces thrust.

## Drag

A backward force acting on an aircraft

Drag is the natural resistance or friction ■ of the air as an aircraft flies forward. Drag increases as the aircraft flies faster. In order to overcome drag, the aircraft needs thrust from its engines. A streamlined shape reduces drag. There is no drag when the aircraft is stationary.

## Elevator

A horizontal hinged section on the tailplane of an airplane

The elevators control the pitch of the airplane. They move up to lower the tail and raise the nose as the airplane climbs. They move down to raise the tail and lower the nose as it descends.

### Climbing
*The pilot raises the elevators to lower the tail and raise the nose, giving the airplane more lift as it climbs.*

**Ready for take-off**
*The propeller gives the airplane thrust and drives it along the runway. The wings produce lift as they move through the air. The airplane takes off when it has gained enough lift to overcome its weight.*

## Airfoil

A structure, such as a wing, that is shaped to give lift as air flows over it

An airfoil is usually curved on top and flat underneath. Its shape causes air passing over a wing to travel faster than the air passing below the wing. The pressure of a fluid, such as air, is reduced as it moves. The faster air moves, the lower is its pressure. This is **Bernoulli's effect**. It means that the air above the wing has a lower pressure that the air below it. The difference in pressure pushes up the wing and produces lift. The moving air also creates some drag.

*Rudder*

**Using the rudder**
*The airplane may be rocked by air turbulence or strong winds as it climbs, so the pilot uses the rudder to steady the nose of the airplane.*

## Rudder

A vertical hinged section on the tail fin of an airplane

The pilot uses the rudder to control the airplane as it banks to make a turn. Moving the rudder to the left or right produces a sideways force ■ that turns the nose of the airplane. A boat is steered by turning a rudder at the back of the boat.

*Raised elevator*

*Propeller*

*Tail fin*

*Tailplane*

# Flaps

Extending sections on the front and back edges of a wing

The flaps extend when an airplane takes off and lands. They alter the airfoil shape to give the airplane more lift at slow speeds. The flaps retract during flight to reduce drag. A **spoiler** is a flap on top of the wing that is raised to increase drag – for example, during landing.

### Banking right
*Lift on the left wing increases and pulls it up, banking the airplane to the right.*

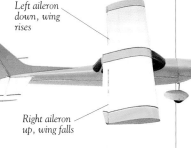

*Left aileron down, wing rises*

*Right aileron up, wing falls*

# Pitch

The movement of an airplane in which the nose rises or falls, and the tail falls or rises

The pilot raises or lowers the elevators on the airplane's tailplane to control pitch. Adjusting the airplane's pitch helps to increase or decrease lift.

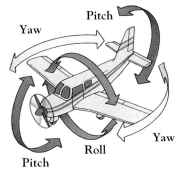

Pitch

Yaw

Pitch

Roll

Yaw

### An airplane's basic movements
*A pilot can use the controls to make the airplane perform three basic movements called pitch, roll, and yaw.*

### Descending
*The pilot moves the elevators down, and the airplane begins to descend.*

*Elevators down, tail rises*

*Right aileron down, wing rises*

*Left aileron up, wing falls*

### Banking left
*Lift on the right wing increases and pulls it up, banking the airplane to the left.*

# Aileron

A hinged section in the back of a wing

An airplane has to bank or tilt its wings in order to turn smoothly. The ailerons on one wing move up, reducing lift. Ailerons on the other wing move down, increasing lift. The difference in lift tilts the wings and turns the airplane. A pilot may lower both ailerons at once to increase lift at low speeds.

# Yaw

The horizontal movement of an airplane to the left or the right

The pilot uses the airplane's rudder to control yaw and steer to the left or the right.

# Roll

The movement of an airplane as one wing rises and the other falls

The pilot raises or lowers the ailerons on the wings to control the roll of the airplane.

# Stall

A loss of lift that can cause an aircraft to crash

An airplane stalls if it flies too slowly, or if it flies at too steep an angle. The airplane's wings lose lift and it begins to fall. A pilot can recover from a stall by lowering the nose and letting the airplane build up enough speed in a dive to gain extra lift. The pilot can also get out of a stall by increasing the thrust from the engines.

# Delta wing

A triangular wing

Some supersonic ■ aircraft have delta wings. The triangular shape cuts through the air more smoothly than long, straight wings. Delta wings produce a lot of lift but little drag, enabling the airplane to fly very fast.

### Delta-winged spacecraft
*The Space Shuttle's delta wings keep drag to a minimum as it re-enters the Earth's atmosphere at very high speed.*

Continued on next page ➤

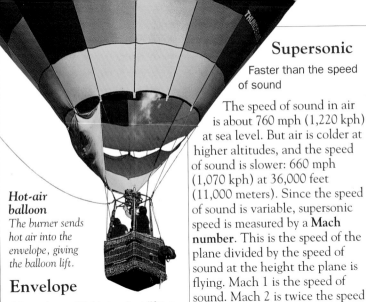

## Hot-air balloon
*The burner sends hot air into the envelope, giving the balloon lift.*

## Envelope

A large bag of light gas that lifts a balloon or airship

The envelope of a hot-air balloon is open at the base and contains air heated by a burner beneath the envelope. The envelope of an airship is sealed and contains helium gas. Hot air and helium are less dense than cool air. This gives the envelope lift ▪, and makes the balloon or airship rise.

## Black box

A device that records the important details of an aircraft's flight

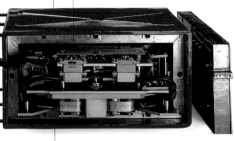

*Front view*   *Inside view*

The black box is also called a **flight recorder**. It records the performance of the engines and the aircraft's other main systems. It also records the crew's voices. After a crash, the black box is recovered and the recording is played back to find out what went wrong.

## Supersonic

Faster than the speed of sound

The speed of sound in air is about 760 mph (1,220 kph) at sea level. But air is colder at higher altitudes, and the speed of sound is slower: 660 mph (1,070 kph) at 36,000 feet (11,000 meters). Since the speed of sound is variable, supersonic speed is measured by a **Mach number**. This is the speed of the plane divided by the speed of sound at the height the plane is flying. Mach 1 is the speed of sound. Mach 2 is twice the speed of sound. **Subsonic** flight is flight at less than Mach 1. (Ernst Mach was an Austrian physicist who studied the behavior of sound.)

## Sonic boom

The loud bang heard when an aircraft flying faster than sound passes overhead

As a supersonic aircraft flies, it produces a wave ▪ of very high pressure in the air. This is called a **shock wave**. It travels away from the airplane and can be heard below as a loud "boom."

*Red black box*
*The "black" box is brightly colored to help locate it after a crash. A strong casing protects it from damage.*

### See also
Airfoil 62 • Barometer 53 • Lift 62
Radar 74 • Thrust 62 • Wave 71

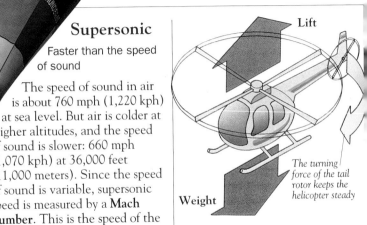

Lift

Weight

*The turning force of the tail rotor keeps the helicopter steady*

*Forces acting on a helicopter*
*The helicopter takes off when the lift produced by the main rotor is greater than the helicopter's weight. The tail rotor can move the tail to the left or the right.*

## Rotor

A set of rotating blades

Most helicopters have a large main rotor above the cabin and a small tail rotor. The main rotor blades have an airfoil ▪ shape and generate lift as they spin, supporting the helicopter in the air. The pilot tilts the rotor to produce thrust ▪ in any direction. This enables the helicopter to fly forward, backward, or even sideways. The tail rotor keeps the helicopter steady. Without a tail rotor, the helicopter would spin in the opposite direction from the main rotor blades. The pilot can control the tail rotor to swing the tail round to the left or the right.

## Altimeter

An instrument that measures how high an aircraft is flying

The **altitude** of an aircraft is its height above the ground or sea. A radar ▪ altimeter works by bouncing radio signals off the ground or sea below. An aneroid altimeter works in the same way as an aneroid barometer ▪. It measures the surrounding air pressure, which decreases as an aircraft flies higher.

# Water transport

Boats and ships are among the oldest and most important forms of transport. Modern boats and ships are able to move safely and rapidly through, under, or even over the water.

**See also**

Airfoil 62 • Buoyancy 51
Density 23 • Elevator 62 • Force 48
Lift 62 • Pressure 52 • Thrust 62

## Propeller

A set of rotating blades that drives a boat, ship, or submarine

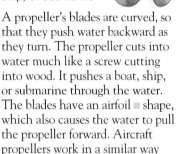

A propeller's blades are curved, so that they push water backward as they turn. The propeller cuts into water much like a screw cutting into wood. It pushes a boat, ship, or submarine through the water. The blades have an airfoil ■ shape, which also causes the water to pull the propeller forward. Aircraft propellers work in a similar way to a boat's propellers, but their airfoil shape produces most of the thrust ■ that powers the aircraft.

## Hydrofoil

A submerged wing under a boat

A hydrofoil has the shape of an airfoil. Hydrofoils give lift ■ as they move through water in the same way that wings generate lift in air. They raise the boat's hull clear of the water, so it can travel at high speed. Any boat carried on submerged wings is also called a hydrofoil.

## Hydroplane

A horizontal fin on the side of a submarine

A submarine has hydroplanes on each side of the hull. They work rather like the elevators ■ of an airplane swiveling to deflect the flow of water and lowering or raising the nose of the submarine. A hydroplane is also a fast boat that skims over the water's surface.

## Stabilizer

A device that helps to stop a ship rolling in large waves

A stabilizer may consist of big tanks of oil or water inside the hull. As the ship begins to roll to one side, water or oil flows to the other side of the boat to stop the roll. A stabilizer can also be a pair of large horizontal fins projecting from the ship's hull beneath the water's surface. As the ship begins to roll, the fins swivel to produce a force ■ that counteracts the roll.

## Load line

A mark on a ship's hull that shows how much it may safely be loaded

The load line is also called the **Plimsoll line**. It shows how deep the ship may settle in the water as it is loaded. For safety, the load line must not go beneath the water. The mark has six levels for different kinds of water and seasons. This is because the density ■ of water varies. Salt water is denser than fresh water, and cold water is denser than warm water. The denser the water, the higher the ship floats.

## Air cushion

A layer of high-pressure air that supports a Hovercraft

A Hovercraft rests on a cushion of air produced by fans that pump air underneath the craft. The air cushion is held in by a flexible wall called a **skirt**. The pressure ■ of the air cushion raises the Hovercraft just above the water. Powerful propellers drive the craft forward.

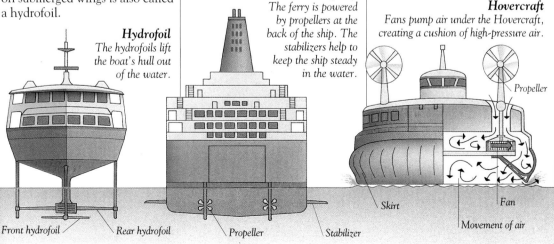

*Hydrofoil*
The hydrofoils lift the boat's hull out of the water.

*Car ferry*
The ferry is powered by propellers at the back of the ship. The stabilizers help to keep the ship steady in the water.

*Hovercraft*
Fans pump air under the Hovercraft, creating a cushion of high-pressure air.

Propeller

Front hydrofoil    Rear hydrofoil    Propeller    Stabilizer    Skirt    Fan

Movement of air

# Cars

Although there are some cars that are powered by electric motors, most modern cars work in the same way as the first cars invented over a century ago. Burning fuel makes pistons in a heat engine move to and fro. Gears and other parts enable the pistons to drive the wheels.

## Fuel injection

A system that injects gasoline into the cylinders of a gasoline engine

Pistons normally suck gas into the cylinders as they move down. But if gas is injected directly in exactly the right quantities, the fuel burns more efficiently.

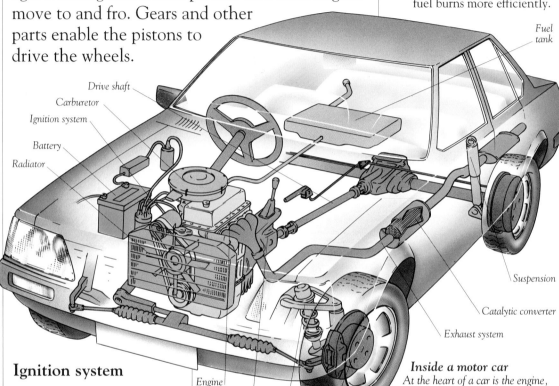

Drive shaft
Carburetor
Ignition system
Battery
Radiator
Fuel tank
Suspension
Catalytic converter
Exhaust system
Engine
Gearbox and clutch
Suspension
Disk brake

### Inside a motor car

*At the heart of a car is the engine, which provides the power to make the car move. The engine must be cooled, because it generates a lot of heat, and it produces waste gases, which are fed out through the exhaust. But the car could not work without electricity, which is supplied by the car's battery.*

## Ignition system

The mechanism in a car that ignites the fuel in a gasoline engine

A car's battery provides electric current at low voltage for the ignition system. The current goes to the **coil**, which works like a transformer ▪ and increases the voltage to several thousand volts. The **distributor** then sends the high-voltage current to each cylinder. There it produces a spark in the **spark plug**, which ignites the gas in the cylinder.

### See also

Catalyst 145 • Compressor 52
Crank 60 • Four-stroke engine 96
Gear 59 • Transformer 110 • Turbine 59

## Radiator

A device that is part of the system that cools a car's engine

In most car engines, a pump pushes cooling water through passages to remove the heat that is generated. The water absorbs heat and flows to the radiator, where it loses its heat to air coming through the radiator grill and flowing over the radiator's surface. The cool water is then pumped back to the engine. Some cars have fans that blow air over the engine to cool it.

## Carburetor

A device that controls the mixture of gas and air going to the engine

A mixture of gas droplets and air goes from the carburetor to the cylinders. The car's **accelerator** pedal is linked to the carburetor and controls the amount of gas in the mixture. Increasing this amount makes the engine run faster. The **choke** allows more gas through to start the engine.

# Gasoline engine

An engine that burns gas as a fuel

A gasoline engine contains several **cylinders**. These are tubes that are closed at one end. In each cylinder is a **piston**, a device shaped like an inverted cup that slides up and down. A valve at the top of each cylinder lets gas and air into the space above the piston. This space contains a spark plug, through which a strong electric current flows to make a spark. The spark ignites the gas, which explodes and forces the piston down the cylinder. A **diesel engine** uses diesel fuel and has no spark plug. The fuel is sprayed into the cylinders, where the air is so hot that it ignites.

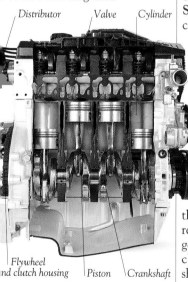

*Distributor    Valve    Cylinder*

*Flywheel and clutch housing    Piston    Crankshaft*

### Four-cylinder engine
*Many engines contain four cylinders. Two of the pistons move up as the other two move down.*

# Turbocharger

A device that boosts the power of a car engine

A turbocharger raises the pressure of the air being fed to the engine cylinders and causes the fuel to burn with more power. It contains a compressor ▓ driven by a turbine ▓ in the exhaust system.

# Brake

A device that slows and stops a car

Brakes work by friction. **Disk brakes** contain a pair of pads that press against a disk fixed to the wheel. **Drum brakes** contain curved brake shoes that press against the inside of a drum attached to the wheel.

# Suspension

A system that protects the body of a car from the movement of the wheels

Car wheels jolt as they move over bumps in a road, but the suspension ensures a smooth ride. Springs in the suspension move up and down, cushioning the body of the car from the jolt of the wheels. **Shock absorbers**, or **dampers**, control the springs and stop the wheels from bouncing after a bump. **Independent suspension** allows one side of a car to roll over a bump without affecting the other side.

# Clutch

A device that sends power to the wheels of a car

Pressing on the clutch pedal disconnects the engine from the wheels. Releasing the pedal reconnects the engine and power goes to the wheels again. The clutch is used in starting the car, shifting gear ▓, and stopping.

# Crankshaft

A shaft driven by pistons in an engine

The crankshaft contains a set of cranks ▓, each driven by a connecting rod linked to a piston. As the pistons move to and fro in the cylinders, the cranks rotate and turn the crankshaft. The **flywheel** is a heavy disk fixed to the crankshaft. It smooths out the jerky movement of the pistons so that the crankshaft turns evenly.

# Exhaust

A system of pipes that carries waste gases away from the engine

The burning fuel in the cylinders produces waste gases and loud bangs. The gases go through a **silencer**, or **muffler**, which contains a set of plates with holes. As the gases flow through the holes, they lose force and the banging sound lessens. The waste gases contain polluting gases and may also be passed through a **catalytic converter**. This changes some of the gases into other gases that are harmless or less harmful.

# Gearbox

A device that changes the amount of power going to a car's wheels

The crankshaft turns a set of gear wheels in the gearbox, which then turn a **drive shaft** to power the wheels of the car. Shifting gears connects gear wheels of different sizes, so that the engine can work faster or slower as the car moves. Low gears give more power for starting or for climbing hills, and high gears allow the car to travel faster. The **differential** is a set of gear wheels in the drive shaft. It allows the drive wheels to turn at different rates as the car goes around corners.

*High-gear wheels    Reverse-gear wheels*

*High-gear wheels    Reverse-gear wheels*

**Shifting gears**    *Low-gear wheels*
*The gearbox contains four or five gears, and reverse gear. In high gear, the gear wheels are closer in size, and the car can travel faster.*

# Energy

Every kind of action – such as playing games, operating machines, manufacturing materials, and cooking food – needs energy to make it happen. Different kinds of energy make different things happen. Almost all the energy on Earth comes from the hot interior of the Sun.

## Energy

The ability to cause an action

There are several different kinds of energy. Whenever anything happens, one kind of energy is present, and it changes to another kind. As you read these words, light energy is changing to electrical energy inside your eyes.

## Potential energy

Energy that is stored

An object gains potential energy as it is raised, squeezed, or stretched. It stores this energy until the object is released. Pulling back the string of a bow gives the string potential energy. The energy is transferred to an arrow when the string is released. As the arrow moves, the potential energy changes to kinetic energy.

## Kinetic energy

Energy of a moving object

Firing an arrow from a bow gives the arrow kinetic energy as it begins to move. An object also has kinetic energy when it rotates or vibrates. It loses its kinetic energy as it slows down.

## Solar energy

Heat and light energy from the Sun

Solar panels on roofs can capture heat from the Sun and use it to heat water. Many calculators run on solar cells, which turn sunlight into electric current.

## Law of conservation of energy

The total amount of energy in a system stays constant

A system is anything that contains or uses energy. The light and heat energy produced by a flashlight bulb equal the electrical energy from the battery ▦. Energy cannot be created or destroyed; it can only change from one form to another. This law is not true for the production of nuclear energy, in which mass changes to energy.

## Nuclear energy

Energy produced by activity inside the nucleus of an atom

The nucleus ▦ of an atom ▦ releases energy if it breaks apart, as in nuclear fission ▦, or combines with another nucleus, as in nuclear fusion ▦. The nucleus loses a little mass, which changes into energy. The Sun and nuclear power ▦ stations produce nuclear energy, which is also called **atomic energy**.

## Radiant energy

Energy that travels out from its source

Radiant energy is electromagnetic radiation ▦, such as light and heat rays. It radiates in all directions from its source, such as the Sun or a fire. Radiant energy can pass through empty space and through some materials. For example, light passes through clear glass.

## Chemical energy

Energy stored in chemical compounds

Growing food requires light ▦ and heat ▦. In the process, chemical reactions ▦ occur, and chemical compounds ▦ form as the energy changes into chemical energy. The compounds store the energy until they undergo further chemical reactions. The chemical energy then changes into heat, light, or electricity. When we eat food, our bodies change the chemical energy into heat to warm our bodies and kinetic energy to make them work.

*Trees use light energy to make chemical compounds that store chemical energy*

*Chemical energy stored in wood is released as heat energy when wood is burned*

## Heat energy

The energy inside an object or substance

Everything has heat energy, whether it is hot or cold. An object has more heat when hot, and less when cold. Heat is the energy of the moving particles, such as molecules ▦, that make up matter. Heat can travel from one object to another as heat rays, which are a form of radiant energy.

## Light energy
### Energy detected by the eye

Lamps and flashlights work by changing electricity ▪ or heat into light energy. Light rays, which are a form of electromagnetic radiation, then travel to our eyes. The rays strike the retina in each eye, producing electrical signals that travel along nerves to the brain so that we see.

## Electrical energy
### The energy of electricity

Electrical energy is the energy of moving electrons ▪, as in an electric current that flows through a wire connected to a battery. When we use electricity, electrical energy changes to another form of energy, such as light in a light bulb or kinetic energy in an electric motor.

## Sound energy
### Energy detected by the ear

Sound travels to our ears as sound waves ▪, which are vibrations in the air. The sound energy changes into electrical signals in the inner ear. The signals go along nerves to the brain, and we hear the sound. Sound can also travel through water, metal, and other materials.

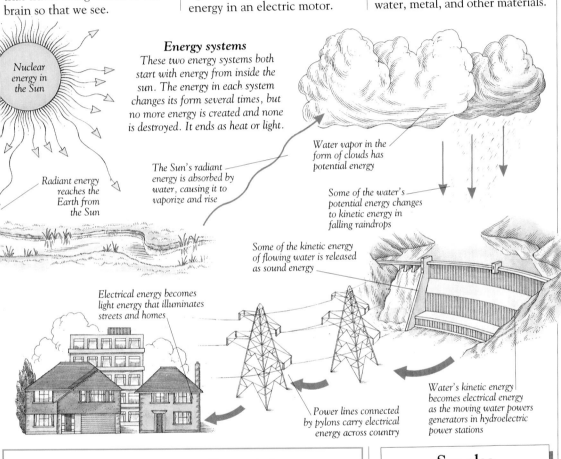

### Energy systems
*These two energy systems both start with energy from inside the sun. The energy in each system changes its form several times, but no more energy is created and none is destroyed. It ends as heat or light.*

Nuclear energy in the Sun

Radiant energy reaches the Earth from the Sun

The Sun's radiant energy is absorbed by water, causing it to vaporize and rise

Water vapor in the form of clouds has potential energy

Some of the water's potential energy changes to kinetic energy in falling raindrops

Some of the kinetic energy of flowing water is released as sound energy

Electrical energy becomes light energy that illuminates streets and homes

Water's kinetic energy becomes electrical energy as the moving water powers generators in hydroelectric power stations

Power lines connected by pylons carry electrical energy across country

## MEASURING ENERGY

### Joule (J)
#### The SI unit of energy

One joule is produced when a force of 1 newton moves 1 meter, or when an electric current of 1 ampere flows through a potential difference ▪ of 1 volt for 1 second. A **kilojoule (kJ)** is 1,000 joules.

### Calorie (Cal or kcal)
#### A unit of energy in food

Energy used to be measured in Calories. One Calorie is equal to 4,187 joules. It is now used to measure the amount of available energy in food. However, these measurements are often given in kilojoules.

### See also

*Continued on next page* ➤

## MEASURING POWER

### Watt (W)

The SI unit of power

One watt is the conversion of 1 joule of energy from one form to another in 1 second. A **kilowatt** (kW) is 1,000 watts. A **megawatt** (MW) is 1,000,000 watts.

### Kilowatt-hour (kWh)

The practical unit of work

A kilowatt-hour is the energy transferred by maintaining the power of 1 kilowatt for 1 hour. A kilowatt-hour is equivalent to 3,600,000 joules.

### James Prescott Joule

English physicist (1818–89)

Joule established the connection between an electric current, the resistance of a wire, and heat generated by the current. This is called Joule's law. By experimenting with paddles churning in water, Joule found that the amount of heat produced is exactly related to the amount of movement. Joule showed that there are different kinds of energy, which can be changed into each other. This led to the law of conservation of energy ■. The joule (J), the SI unit of energy, is named after him.

*Hard work and lots of power*
*A person of mass 49 kilograms (108 lb.) and weight 480 newtons can jump on and off this aerobic step 10 times in 10 seconds. The total distance she moves is about 2 meters. The work done is 480 x 2 = 960 joules. The power is 960 joules ÷ 10 seconds = 96 watts. This is almost the same as the power of a 100-watt light bulb.*

### Work

The transfer of energy

People and machines ■ do work when they move an object. The amount of work done is the energy ■ that is gained by the object. The work (in joules ■) is equal to the force ■ used (in newtons) multiplied by the distance (in meters) that the object moves.

### Power

The rate of doing work, or the rate of transforming energy from one form to another

The power of a machine is the amount of work it does divided by the time it takes to do the work. A powerful machine does a lot of work in a short time. The unit of power is the watt. An alternative unit of power is the **horsepower** (hp), which is equal to 745.7 watts.

### Transducer

A device that converts energy from one form to another

A transducer often converts a non-electrical signal into an electrical one, or vice versa. A loudspeaker ■ is a transducer that changes electricity into sound. Many measuring instruments are transducers. A weighing machine, for example, converts movement of the pan into an electrical signal, which then changes to light in the display.

### Energy conservation

Saving energy

We need energy to heat homes and power machines. We get this energy mainly by burning fuels such as natural gas, oil, and coal. These fuels are in limited supply, and we should conserve the energy sources so that the fuels will last longer. This can be done by making machines and homes more efficient so that they consume less energy. Energy conservation would mean less burning of fossil fuels ■, so it would reduce pollution. The term energy conservation should not be confused with the law of conservation of energy.

*Person weighing 480 newtons*

*Step is 0.2 meters high*

### See also

◀ Continued from previous page

# Waves

There is more to waves than the way in which boats bob up and down on the sea. There are many different types of wave, and all of them carry energy from one place to another. Light waves and sound waves help us communicate.

## See also

Electrical energy 69 • Hertz 72
Kinetic energy 68 • Potential energy 68
Radio waves 74 • Sound waves 98
Wavelength 72

### Making a wave
*If you flick one end of a rope, you can send waves along it. The more you move the rope up and down, the greater the amplitude of the waves will be.*

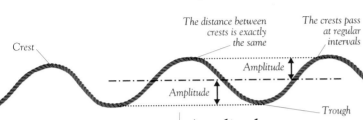

*The distance between crests is exactly the same*

*The crests pass at regular intervals*

Crest

Amplitude

Amplitude

Trough

## Wave

A way of transferring energy through matter and through space

A wave moves along the surface of the sea, making objects move up and down as it passes. The wave carries both kinetic ▨ and potential ▨ energy, and matter is moved to and fro, or displaced. When a sound wave travels through air, the air molecules are displaced. A **wave motion** transfers energy as a regular vibration. A **crest** is the point at which the movement is a maximum in one direction (the highest point in a water wave). A **trough** is the maximum movement in the other. The energy in waves may also be electrical energy ▨ with regular changes of current.

## Amplitude

The maximum amount by which matter moves as a wave passes

Strong winds bring high waves on seas and lakes. The amplitude of a water wave is the height of its crests or the depth of its troughs above or below the normal water level. A greater amplitude means that a wave is transferring more energy. For example, a sound wave with a large amplitude is louder than a sound wave with a small amplitude. The **displacement** is the amount by which matter has moved at any point in a wave. Its greatest value equals the amplitude.

## Frequency

The rate at which the crests of a wave pass

Frequency is the number of complete vibrations of a wave, from one crest to the next, in one second. It is measured in hertz (Hz) ▨. A wave travels at a certain speed, which is equal to the frequency multiplied by the wavelength ▨ of the wave. Audible sound waves ▨ range in frequency from 20 Hz to about 20,000 Hz. FM radio waves ▨ have frequencies of about 100 million hertz .

### Changing frequency
*If you move the rope up and down more slowly, the frequency decreases as the crests and troughs pass at a slower rate.*

Crest

Amplitude

Amplitude

Trough

### Wave power
*The power of waves can be harnessed to produce electricity. As the waves travel along the surface, the water moves up and down. This movement can be used to power electricity generators.*

*Continued on next page ➤*

## Longitudinal wave

A wave in which the vibration is in the same direction as the wave

A sound wave ■ is a longitudinal wave. As the sound wave passes, molecules ■ of air move forward and backward in the same plane as the wave. The molecules repeatedly move together and apart, producing successive regions of high pressure and low pressure called compressions and rarefactions.

## Wavelength

The distance between one crest of a wave and the next

As a wave with a particular frequency passes, the crests are always the same distance apart. This is the wavelength – the distance over which one vibration of energy occurs. Waves with a higher frequency have a shorter wavelength, and those with a lower frequency have a longer wavelength.

## MEASURING WAVES

### Hertz (Hz)

The SI unit of frequency

One hertz is one complete vibration per second. One **kilohertz** (kHz) is 1,000 hertz, and one **megahertz** (MHz) is 1,000,000 hertz. The hertz is named after the German physicist Heinrich Hertz ■.

*Waves on the move*
*A slinky coil can be used to show the two kinds of traveling wave, the longitudinal (above) and the transverse (below).*

*Vibration passing along coil*

Wavelength

*If you shake a slinky coil to and fro lengthwise, the vibrations pass straight along the coil longitudinally*

*If you shake the slinky coil at right angles to the way it is lying, it vibrates at right angles, or transversely*

Wavelength

*Vibration moving along coil*

## Transverse wave

A wave in which the vibration is at right angles to the direction of the wave

Waving a rope produces a transverse wave, and water waves are also transverse. As the wave moves forward, the rope or water moves up and down at right angles to the direction of the wave.

*Direction*

*Energy*

**Waveform**
*This computer graph shows how the energy level of a water wave changes as it travels along.*

*Time*

## Waveform

The shape of a wave

The curve of a water wave shows how a boat bobs up and down as the wave passes. The waveform of a wave shows how the energy changes as the wave passes. An oscilloscope ■ can display the waveform of a sound wave, which determines the tone ■ of the sound. When the waveform is a smooth and regular curve, the wave is a called a **sine wave**. The pure sound of a tuning fork has a sine wave. In a **square wave**, the energy changes suddenly. The sound of a clarinet has a square wave.

## Stationary wave

A wave in which the movement at any point is constant

The ends of a guitar string cannot move up and down, but the middle can. When the string is twanged, waves travel in both directions along it. They are reflected at each end and travel back, interfering with each other and producing a stationary or **standing wave**. At points called **antinodes**, the combining waves are in phase and the amplitude ■ of the stationary wave is greatest. At points called **nodes**, the combining waves are out of phase and the amplitude is zero.

**Making music**
*Blowing at the mouthpiece makes the column of air in this flute vibrate, setting up a stationary wave (blue).*

*The vibrations are greatest at the antinode*

*At the center of the air column is a point of zero vibration, called the node*

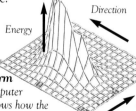

*Top of flute    Mouthpiece*

◄ *Continued from previous page*

# Phase

The degree of movement produced by a wave at any point

As a wave goes from crest to trough and back to crest, its phase is constantly changing. If two waves combine, the difference in their phases is important. The crests of two waves of the same frequency that are "in phase" always arrive together. They produce a combined wave in which the size, or amplitude, is larger. This is the **principle of superposition**. If the crests of one wave always arrive with the troughs of the other wave, then the two waves are "out of phase" and the waves may cancel each other out. Combined light rays  are brighter when they are in phase and darker when they are out of phase. This occurs in interference ▦. Sound waves are louder when in phase, and softer when out of phase.

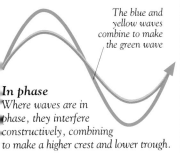

*The blue and yellow waves combine to make the green wave*

**In phase**
*Where waves are in phase, they interfere constructively, combining to make a higher crest and lower trough.*

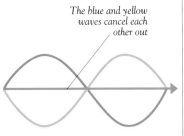

*The blue and yellow waves cancel each other out*

**Out of phase**
*Where waves of the same amplitude are out of phase, they cancel each other out, or interfere destructively, so no wave results.*

**Making waves**
*A thumb and forefinger tapping the surface of water make waves that radiate outward. The waves interfere with each other wherever they overlap.*

# Electromagnetic wave

An electrical and magnetic wave

Light and other forms of electromagnetic radiation ▦ travel as waves. The wave is produced when, for example, an electron ▦ in an atom loses energy and jumps to a lower orbit, or energy level ▦, around the atom's nucleus. This sets off a vibration of electrical energy that travels outward through space in the form of electric and magnetic fields. These fields are at right angles to each other, and to the direction of travel of the wave. When the electromagnetic wave strikes another atom, the fields can cause an electron to jump and gain energy. In this way, an electromagnetic wave carries energy through space.

*Where waves are out of step they interfere destructively*

*Where waves are in step they interfere constructively*

**Spreading out**
*Different kinds of wave behave in similar ways. These water waves are spreading out, or diffracting, after passing through a gap. Light waves also diffract.*

# Electromagnetic radiation

We are bombarded by rays of energy all the time. This is electromagnetic radiation. Your eyes can detect some of these rays, but most of the radiation is invisible. Although some are harmful, all of the rays can be useful to us.

## Electromagnetic radiation

Waves of energy that can travel through space and matter

Electromagnetic radiation comes from the Sun, stars and galaxies, traveling through space to reach us. It can also be made artificially. It consists of electromagnetic waves ■ with a wide range of frequencies ■ and wavelengths ■. In order of increasing frequency (or decreasing wavelength), some of these are: radio waves, microwaves, infrared rays, light ■ rays, ultraviolet rays, X-rays, and gamma rays ■. All electromagnetic radiation travels at the speed of light, and the waves or rays can penetrate materials. The complete range of frequencies of electromagnetic radiation is the **electromagnetic spectrum**.

## Radio waves

Electromagnetic waves that bring us radio and television

Feeding an electrical signal with a certain frequency to a radio transmitter makes it produce a radio wave at the same frequency as the electrical signal. Radio broadcasts use the lower range of radio frequencies, while television ■ broadcasts use the higher range of radio frequencies.

***The electromagnetic spectrum***
*Waves in the electromagnetic spectrum have different frequencies and wavelengths. Each type of radiation occurs across a range of wavelengths. This diagram shows the typical wavelengths, or ranges of wavelength, of the main types of wave, and some examples of their uses.*

## Microwaves

Electromagnetic waves with a short wavelength

Microwaves are produced in a similar way to radio waves but have higher frequencies. They are used for telephone and television links. A **microwave oven** uses microwaves with a frequency of about 2,500 megahertz (MHz) to cook and warm food quickly. A beam of microwaves penetrates the food. The water in the food absorbs the waves and heats up, warming the food.

## Radar

A method of detecting distant objects and finding their positions

Radar is used to track flying aircraft and ships at sea. Radar stands for "radio detection and ranging." A radar system sends out pulses of microwaves. The pulses are reflected from an aircraft or ship and return to the radar system, which measures the time taken for the pulses to return. The time depends on the distance traveled, enabling the radar system to display the position of the aircraft or ship on a screen. Ships use onboard radar for navigation.

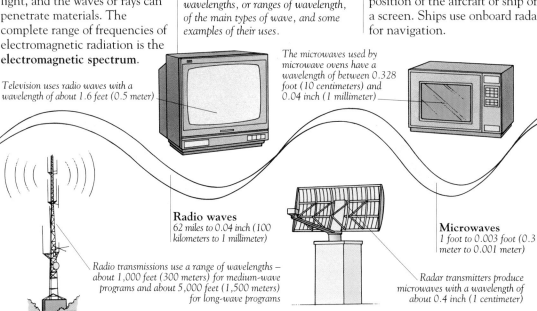

*Television uses radio waves with a wavelength of about 1.6 feet (0.5 meter).*

*The microwaves used by microwave ovens have a wavelength of between 0.328 foot (10 centimeters) and 0.04 inch (1 millimeter).*

**Radio waves**
62 miles to 0.04 inch (100 kilometers to 1 millimeter)

*Radio transmissions use a range of wavelengths – about 1,000 feet (300 meters) for medium-wave programs and about 5,000 feet (1,500 meters) for long-wave programs*

**Microwaves**
1 foot to 0.003 foot (0.3 meter to 0.001 meter)

*Radar transmitters produce microwaves with a wavelength of about 0.4 inch (1 centimeter)*

## X-rays

Electromagnetic radiation with a very high frequency

X-rays can be made in an **X-ray tube**, in which an electron ■ beam strikes a metal target, causing it to emit X-rays. Dentists and doctors use X-rays to take photographs that show your teeth and the bones inside your body. The rays go through your body and form an image on a photographic film or screen. Bones and teeth show up because they block the path of the X-rays. X-rays can be used to treat cancer. Large doses are harmful.

## Window

Part of the electromagnetic spectrum that a material allows to pass

The Earth's atmosphere has a window for radio waves and light rays, which pass easily through air. It blocks most other rays.

## Infrared rays

Electromagnetic rays produced by hot objects

You can feel the heat coming from a hot radiator. When warm and hot objects give off heat by radiation ■, they produce infrared rays. Remote-control keypads for VCRs and television sets use a weak infrared beam to send signals that operate the controls. **Thermography** uses infrared rays to produce pictures that show the warm and cool parts of an object as different colors. It is used in medicine to detect cancer.

## Ultraviolet rays

Electromagnetic radiation with a higher frequency than visible light

Ultraviolet rays come from the sun, and are also produced in fluorescent lamps ■. The rays help your body to produce vitamins, but large doses of ultraviolet rays can damage your skin and eyes. The layer of ozone in the upper atmosphere absorbs most ultraviolet rays, but pollution is damaging this layer and increasing the amount of ultraviolet rays that reach the Earth.

## Wilhelm Roentgen

German physicist (1845–1923)

Wilhelm Roentgen discovered X-rays in 1895. He found that a cathode-ray tube caused a paper coated with a barium compound and positioned some distance away to glow with light. The tube gave out X-rays, which made the compound glow. Roentgen named them X-rays, as "X" means unknown.

## Heinrich Hertz

German physicist (1857–94)

Hertz discovered radio waves in 1888, following the prediction of their existence by James Clerk Maxwell ■. He found that if he created a large spark, it caused a small spark to jump across a gap in a coil of wire some distance away. Radio waves formed by the large spark produced electricity in the coil. Hertz's discovery led to the development of radio broadcasting by Marconi ■. The unit of frequency, the hertz, is named after Heinrich Hertz.

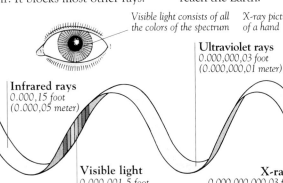

Visible light consists of all the colors of the spectrum

X-ray picture of a hand

**Ultraviolet rays**
0.000,000,03 foot
(0.000,000,01 meter)

**Infrared rays**
0.000,15 foot
(0.000,05 meter)

**Visible light**
0.000,001,5 foot
(0.000,000,5 meter)

**X-rays**
0.000,000,000,03 foot
(0,000,000,000,01 meter)

**Gamma rays**
0.000,000,000,000,3 foot
(0.000,000,000,000,1 meter)

A hot iron emits infrared rays

Ultraviolet rays reach the earth from the sun

A nuclear explosion produces gamma rays

# Light

Light is a form of energy. It travels in waves that have the fastest known speed of anything in the Universe. Life on Earth could not exist without light. Our most important source is the Sun, but we can also produce light using electricity.

## Light

**The form of electromagnetic radiation detected by the eye**

The light you can see is part of a range of electromagnetic radiation ■. It contains wavelengths ■ that your eyes detect as colors ■ ranging through the spectrum. Although light usually acts as waves ■, it is really a stream of tiny packets of energy, or photons ■, which act both as waves and as particles.

## Shadow

**A dark region that forms where an object blocks out light**

Most shadows have two regions – the **umbra** and the **penumbra**. The umbra is the dark central part where the object casting the shadow blocks out all the light rays coming from the light source. The penumbra is the outer part of the shadow. Some of the rays from the light source reach the penumbra, making it less dark than the umbra.

### Splitting light into colors
*A prism bends the wavelengths in white light by different amounts, making them spread out and form a spectrum.*

## Spectrum

**The bands of color formed when white light is split by a prism**

You can create a spectrum by passing a beam of white light through a prism or diffraction grating ■. This separates the different wavelengths in the white light into a spectrum: from red, through orange, yellow, green, and blue, to violet. Red has the longest wavelength and violet the shortest. A prism creates a spectrum by bending wavelengths at different angles. The separation of light into its component colors is called **dispersion**.

### Casting a shadow
*The wooden cube below does not let light pass through. Because light rays travel only in straight lines, there is an area to the left of the cube that cannot be reached by rays from the light box. This is area is the cube's shadow.*

*Shadow cast by the wooden cube*

*The wooden cube blocks out some of the light, creating a shadow behind it*

## Ray

**The straight path along which light travels**

Light rays always travel out from a light source in straight lines. The direction of light rays can be changed by a shiny or transparent substance, such as glass or water, that reflects or refracts light.

## Prism

**A transparent, triangular block that splits light into a spectrum**

A prism splits a beam of white light into a spectrum by separating out its different wavelengths. The glass prism bends each wavelength at a different angle as it passes from glass to air, or air to glass. For example, violet rays bend more than red rays. This bending is called refraction.

### Good and bad reflectors
*A mirror reflects light sharply because light rays bounce off its smooth surface at the same angle. A white surface reflects light rays well but spreads them out. A dark surface absorbs most light, reflecting very little.*

## Reflection
**The way in which light rays bounce off surfaces**

You see an object in front of you because light rays are reflected from it. Bright objects reflect more light than dark objects. When parallel light rays strike a smooth surface, such as a mirror ▥, it reflects all the rays at the same angle. This produces a clear image called a reflection. If the surface is uneven, the rays diffuse, or bounce off at different angles. Light rays passing through a dense substance, such as a glass block, may be reflected from its inner surface back into the substance. This is **total internal reflection.**

*Light rays travel out in straight lines from the light source*

*Ray box containing a light bulb*

*Plastic block*

### Refracting block
*Light bends, or is refracted, as it passes from air into a transparent substance such as this plastic block.*

## MEASURING LIGHT
### Speed of light
The speed at which light travels through space, equal to about 186,300 miles (299,792.5 kilometers) per second

Light slows down when it passes through a transparent substance. For example, it has three-quarters of its normal speed in water, and two-thirds in glass. All electromagnetic radiation has the same speed.

## Rainbow
**An arc of colors that appears in the sky when the sun lights up a shower of rain**

You can see a rainbow when the sun is behind you. The sunlight is reflected inside the raindrops, and is also refracted as it passes into and out of the raindrops. Each wavelength in the light is refracted at a different angle, making the light spread out into a spectrum.

## Mirage
**A distant image that appears on or above the ground**

A mirage is caused by a layer of warm air just above the ground. Light rays travel directly from an object to your eyes and also down toward the ground to be refracted up to your eyes by the warm air. You see an inverted image under the object, like a watery reflection. Mirages also occur in cold regions.

### Water in the desert
*In hot places, you sometimes see a mirage that looks like a shimmering pool of water. It is really light from the sky being bent upward by a layer of hot air close to the ground.*

## Refraction
**The way in which light rays bend as they enter and leave a transparent substance**

Refraction occurs when light rays change speed as they move from one substance to another. For example, rays slow down as they pass from air into glass, bending away from the boundary between the two substances. As they leave the glass, the rays speed up and bend toward the boundary. A lens ▥ can bend light rays to a focus ▥ at a single point, forming a clear image.

### See also

*Continued on next page* ➤

## Fluorescence
*The test tube on the right contains a solution of sodium fluorescein. In normal light, the solution is reddish in color, but when a bright flashlight beam is shone through the solution from close range, the fluorescein in the solution glows bright green.*

## Illumination
The amount of light falling on a unit area of surface

An object receiving a lot of light  is said to be brightly lit or highly illuminated. Light passes through a **transparent** material, such as clear glass. A **translucent** material, like frosted glass, passes some light, and an **opaque** material blocks all light.

## Incandescence
The emission of light by a hot substance

When substances get hot, they glow with light, or become **incandescent**. The color of the light given out depends on how hot the substance is. An object glows red at first, and then yellow and white as it gets hotter. A candle gives off light because tiny specks of soot are heated in its flame. Most household light bulbs contain a thin tungsten filament. When an electric current passes through it, the filament becomes so hot that it gives off a bright white light.

## Luminescence
The emission of light without using heat

Luminescence occurs when objects take in energy other than heat and change it into light energy. Luminescent animals, such as glowworms and fireflies, glow because chemical energy in their bodies changes to light energy. A television screen contains luminescent materials that light up when struck by a beam of electrons. There are two main kinds of luminescence. In **phosphorescence**, a substance absorbs energy and later emits it as light. Luminous paints work in this way, storing the energy of daylight and then glowing in the dark. In **fluorescence**, the light is emitted immediately. Bright fluorescent paints take in light of various colors or invisible ultraviolet rays and emit light of just one color. This light is usually much brighter than normal reflected light.

**Luminescent mushrooms**
*These luminescent mushrooms from Indonesia glow with green light at night. Like certain other plants and animals, including fireflies and glowworms, they are able to emit light without producing heat. This is called bioluminescence.*

# MEASURING LIGHT
## Candela (cd)
The SI unit of luminous intensity

A light source of 1 candela is as bright as a **black body** of area 1/60 square centimeter at the temperature of melting platinum. A black body is a perfect absorber and emitter of radiation.

## Lumen (lm)
The SI unit of luminous flux, or flow of light, from a source

A light source of 1 candela produces a total light output of 4 pi (12.568) lumens.

## Lux (lx)
The SI unit of illumination of a surface

1 lux is equal to the brightness of a surface 1 meter from a light source of 1 candela.

## Scattering
The way in which light spreads out when it strikes tiny particles

When the Sun's rays reach the Earth's atmosphere, they strike tiny particles in the air, which make some of the rays scatter and travel in all directions. Specks of dust and water droplets in the air scatter light rays because they reflect them. This is why there is often a haze on a hot sunny day and why it is difficult to see through a mist or fog. Blue light rays passing between molecules of air bend by diffraction and scatter. Much of the blue light is deflected towards the Earth, causing the sky to look blue. If you shine a bright flashlight beam into a glass of slightly milky water, the blue rays are scattered by the tiny particles of fat in the milk.

◄ *Continued from previous page*

# Diffraction

**The way in which light rays bend as they pass the edges of an object**

When light rays pass through a narrow gap, they bend outward from the edges of the gap so that the light spreads out. This is called diffraction and it occurs in all kinds of waves . The gap has to be about the same size as the wavelength . A **diffraction grating** contains rows of very narrow slits or grooves. White light passing through or reflected from the grating spreads out to produce several spectra . Interference between the bent rays produces bands of colors, which are in the reverse order from spectra formed by prisms . The colors you can see in a compact disc are spectra formed by diffraction as light reflects from tiny notches in the disc's surface.

*Interference gives bright colors*

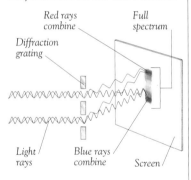

*Diffraction grating*
*White light is a mixture of colors. Every color bends by a different amount as it passes through a diffraction grating. The picture above shows how red and blue each combine to form bright bands at different places on a screen. In this way, white light splits up into a full spectrum.*

# Polarized light

**Light in which the vibrations occur in only one plane**

A source of light, such as the Sun or a light bulb, emits many light rays. Each ray consists of vibrating electric and magnetic fields. Rays of ordinary light vibrate in many different directions, or planes. In polarized light, all the rays vibrate in the same plane. Light can be polarized by passing it through a polarizing material. This allows only rays vibrating in one particular plane to pass. Light is partly polarized as it reflects from a smooth surface. Polarizing sunglasses use polarizing materials to cut out polarized light and remove glare.

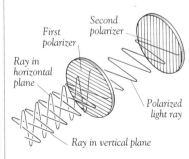

*Polarizing light rays*
*Unpolarized light consists of light rays vibrating in different planes. A polarizer blocks out light vibrating in every plane except one. A second polarizer can be used to cut out this polarized light as well.*

*Colors in a soap bubble*
*The colors that you see in a soap bubble are caused by the interference between rays of light reflected by the bubble.*

# Interference

**The way in which two light rays combine together**

The energy  of a light ray continually rises and falls as it travels, like the motion of a wave. If two waves combine so that they vibrate in step with each other, they are said to be in phase . Rays of light that combine so that they rise and fall together have more energy and are bright. This type of interference is called **constructive interference**. But if the rays combine so that one rises as the other falls, they are said to be out of phase. The combined rays have no energy and are dark. This type of interference is called **destructive interference**. Interference occurs with all types of waves. With light, interference gives a pattern of light and dark bands. Interference also causes the pattern of colors in a soap bubble or film of oil. White light reflects from the inner and outer surfaces of the bubble or film. The two sets of rays then combine to give both types of interference, so that some colors in the light become bright and others dark.

# Color

We see a multicolored world, because our eyes detect colored light reflected from, or produced by, the objects around us. A red rose appears red because it reflects red light into our eyes. White is a mix of colors, and black is an absence of light.

## Color

**The effect of different wavelengths of light upon our eyes**

Our eyes normally detect a range of colors – from red, orange, and yellow, through to green, blue, and violet. We see different colors because light ▪ of each color has a different wavelength ▪. Red has the longest wavelength, and violet the shortest. Some objects, such as traffic lights, emit light of a particular color. Other objects appear colored because they reflect light shining upon them. They absorb some colors and reflect others. Green grass, for example, reflects only green light.

## Additive process

**The process of forming colors by mixing colored light**

Beams of light in the three primary colors of red, green, and blue can be mixed to give other colors, as shown in the picture on the right. This is the additive process. Red and green give yellow, for example, while all three colors mix to give white. Shades such as pink or brown contain different levels of the three primary colors. A color television screen has thousands of tiny dots or strips that light up in red, green, and blue. Our eyes mix these colors so that we see the picture in full color.

**White light**
*When white light shines on this multicolored object, the object reflects all five different colors.*

**Blue light**
*In blue light, red and green look black, and the other colors look blue.*

**Red light**
*In red light, blue and green look black, and the other colors look red.*

**Green light**
*In green light, blue and red look black, and the other colors look green.*

# Filter

A colored film that allows light of only one color to pass through it

A color filter fits over a lamp or camera lens to change the color of the light passing through it. The filter only lets through light of its particular color because it absorbs all the other wavelengths in the white light.

# Primary color

A pure color that cannot be made by mixing other colors

Primary colors mix together to give all the other colors. The primary colors of light, used in the additive process, are red, green, and blue. The primary pigment colors, used in the subtractive process, are yellow, cyan, and magenta.

# Secondary color

A color made by mixing two primary colors

In the additive process, the three secondary colors are yellow, cyan, and magenta. In the subtractive process, they are red, green, and blue.

# Subtractive process

The process of forming colors by mixing colored pigments

A color photograph or picture takes away, or subtracts, colors from the white light shining upon it. A paint, ink, or dye of a certain color absorbs other color wavelengths in the white light and reflects its own color. The three primary colors in the subtractive process are yellow, cyan, and magenta. For example, yellow and magenta mix to give red. Yellow paint subtracts blue wavelengths and reflects red and green, which mix to give yellow. Mixing in magenta also subtracts green, leaving only red.

# Spectroscopy

A method of analysing substances by examining the colors in the light they give out

If you heat a substance, it glows as the elements ▦ in it give out certain wavelengths of light. Salt, for example, glows yellow because it contains the element sodium. A **spectroscope** contains a prism ▦ or a diffraction grating ▦ that separates the light into a spectrum of colored bands. A **spectrometer** measures the positions of the bands in the spectrum, which are different for every element.

# Complementary color

Either of a pair of colors that in the additive process mix to form white, and in the subtractive process mix to form black

Each primary color has a complementary secondary color. Blue is complementary to yellow. Blue and yellow lights mix to form white, but blue and yellow paints form black.

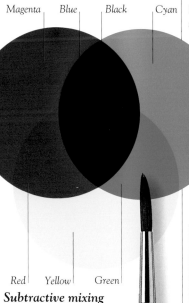

Magenta  Blue  Black  Cyan

Red  Yellow  Green

**Subtractive mixing**
*Mixes of yellow, cyan, and magenta form all other colors in the subtractive process.*

# Emission spectrum

A band of colors produced when light from a substance passes through a spectroscope

When light from a substance is passed through a spectroscope, the light is separated out into a set of colored bands or lines called a spectrum ▦. Sunlight contains many colors and gives a spectrum like a rainbow. A single element gives an emission spectrum that contains only a few colored lines.

*The emission spectrum of a substance consists of a number of colored lines.*

*An absorption spectrum of the same substance shows dark lines on a white light spectrum. The lines are in the same position as those on the substance's emission spectrum.*

# Absorption spectrum

A spectrum produced when white light passes first through a gas and then through a spectroscope

If you pass white light through a gaseous substance, the substance absorbs the same colors as those shown in its emission spectrum. This leaves dark lines in the white light spectrum produced by a spectroscope. The positions of the lines tell you which elements are in the substance.

## See also

# Lasers

The narrow beam of light that comes from a laser can be powerful enough to cut through metal. Lasers have many uses in communications and industry. They are also used in medicine to perform delicate surgical operations.

## Laser

A device that produces a beam of high-energy light

Laser stands for "light amplification by stimulated emission of radiation." Inside a laser is a material called a **lasing medium**. Passing an electric current or light into the medium gives energy to, or excites, its atoms ▪. The excited atoms suddenly give up their extra energy and emit light. One atom emits a light ray, which strikes another atom and causes it to emit another ray, and so on in a rapid cascade of emissions. The rays are all in phase ▪. This means that the waves of energy in the rays are exactly in step, making the light very concentrated. This kind of light is **coherent radiation**. Mirrors reflect the rays, so that the cascade builds up. The light leaves through one of the mirrors, which is partly transparent. Lasers can also emit invisible infrared rays ▪. A **maser** is like a laser, but emits microwaves ▪.

*Laser beam*

*Beam leaves through a half-silvered mirror*

*Lasing medium is a mixture of neon and helium gases*

*Electrodes pass an electric current through the gas*

*Silvered mirror reflects light*

### Inside a laser
*When electricity excites the atoms in the lasing medium, they emit light. The light is reflected between mirrors at either end of the tube, becoming more and more intense. Some of it passes through one of the mirrors, emerging as a laser beam.*

## Energy level

An amount of energy that an atom can have

When an atom takes up energy, such as heat, electricity, or light, electrons ▪ orbiting the nucleus ▪ jump to higher orbits. Electrons can only move in certain orbits, so the atom can only have certain levels of energy. The lowest energy level, when the electrons are nearest to the nucleus, is called the **ground state**. When electrons return to a lower orbit of less energy, they give out a ray of electromagnetic radiation ▪ such as light. The ray's energy depends on the difference in energy between the two levels. The greater the ray's energy, the shorter the wavelength ▪ of the radiation.

## Hologram

A three-dimensional image made with laser light

A hologram is made by lighting an object with a laser. The laser beam is split into two separate beams. One beam, the reference beam, is aimed straight at a photographic plate or film. The other beam, the object beam, is aimed at the object. The plate is struck both by light from the laser and light reflected from the object. A pattern forms on the plate because of interference ▪ between the two beams. The hologram can be seen only when the plate is developed. **Reflection holograms** must be viewed in ordinary light and **transmission holograms** in laser light. The production of holograms is called **holography**.

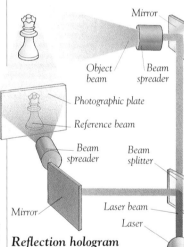

Mirror

Object beam — Beam spreader

Photographic plate

Reference beam

Beam spreader — Beam splitter

Laser beam

Mirror — Laser

### Reflection hologram
*The beams reach the plate from different directions. This gives a three-dimensional image when the hologram is viewed in ordinary light.*

### See also
Atom 34 • Electromagnetic radiation 74
Electron 34 • Infrared rays 75
Interference 79 • Microwaves 74
Nucleus 35 • Phase 73
Wavelength 72

# Lighting

Long ago, people had only the Sun, Moon, and stars to provide them with light. Later, the flames of candles and oil lamps were used. Today, electricity keeps homes and streets brightly lit.

***Flying dove***
*This photograph was taken as a stroboscope flashed on and off. It has "frozen" the movement of the bird's wings, which would otherwise be blurred.*

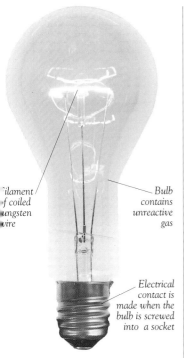

*Filament of coiled tungsten wire*

*Bulb contains unreactive gas*

*Electrical contact is made when the bulb is screwed into a socket*

## Light bulb

A hollow glass bulb containing a wire that glows when it is heated

A light bulb is a form of incandescent ▪ lighting. The bulb contains a piece of thin, coiled tungsten wire called a **filament**. The filament is heated by an electric current until it gets so hot that it glows white and gives off light. The bulb is filled with an unreactive gas, such as nitrogen or argon, to prevent the filament from burning out, as it would in air. In a **halogen bulb**, the gas contains a halogen ▪, such as iodine. This gives a brighter light, because the filament can be heated to a higher temperature.

## Discharge tube

A gas-filled tube that glows when electricity flows though it

A **neon lamp** consists of a discharge tube filled with neon gas and containing two electrodes. When an electric current passes between the electrodes, the gas glows bright red. In a **fluorescent lamp**, the discharge tube is filled with mercury vapor. When electricity flows through the vapor, the vapor emits invisible ultraviolet rays. The rays strike a phosphor coating on the inside of the tube, and the coating gives out white light by fluorescence ▪. A white street light that works in this way is a **mercury vapor lamp**. Fluorescent lamps use less electricity than normal light bulbs.

***Neon cowboy***
*City centers are full of colorful lights. Most of these lights contain discharge tubes. The color of the light from the tube depends on the gas or gases inside it.*

## Stroboscope

A bright lamp that continuously flashes on and off

A stroboscope is used to examine objects that rapidly rotate or move to and fro, such as moving parts in a machine. The stroboscope can be timed so that it flashes each time a moving part reaches a certain position, making the part appear stationary. With a flashing stroboscope, a camera can take a set of photographs of a fast-moving object. The pictures show exactly how it moves.

## Sodium vapor lamp

A lamp that glows with a bright yellow light

A sodium vapor lamp consists of two electrodes in a discharge tube of sodium vapor. When an electric current flows between the electrodes, the vapor glows yellow. Sodium vapor lamps are often used as street lights, because yellow light passes through fog better than white light.

*Electrode*

*Tube of sodium vapor*

*Electrode*

**Sodium vapor bulb**

### See also

Energy level 82 • Fluorescence 78
Halogens 137 • Incandescence 78

# Optics

The world appears before us because of the way light behaves. We can see because each eye has a lens that produces an image of our surroundings. Optics, the study of light, enables us to improve poor eyesight, to look at ourselves in mirrors, and even to see inside our own bodies.

## Optics

The study of light

Optics is mainly concerned with the ways in which light rays form images. These images occur when light rays coming from an object are reflected by mirrors and bent, or refracted, as they pass through lenses.

## Focal length

The distance from a lens or a curved mirror to the image of a distant object

The light rays that come from a distant object are parallel. A lens or mirror bends or reflects parallel rays so that they meet at the focal length. A camera lens has a focal length measured in millimeters. This indicates the size of the image produced by the lens. A longer focal length gives a larger image.

## Virtual image

An image seen in a shiny surface, such as a mirror, or through a lens

When you look at an object in a mirror, light rays from the object are reflected into your eyes. To your eyes, the light rays appear to be traveling in a straight line from a point behind the mirror. The eyes see an image of the object at this position. When you look at an object through a lens, light rays from the object are bent by the lens before they reach your eyes. The eye sees a virtual image which, because the rays have been bent, looks larger or smaller than the object. A virtual image appears in a position through which the light rays have not actually passed.

*Virtual image*
*When you see a reflection of an object in a mirror, it looks as if the object is positioned behind the mirror. This is because the light rays from the object are reflected from the mirror to the eye.*

*Object*

*Two sets of light rays from the tree*

*Virtual image of the tree*

## Mirror

A shiny surface that forms an image by reflecting light rays

A **plane mirror** is a flat mirror. It reflects light from an object to give a virtual image that is the same size as the object. A **convex mirror**, such as some rear-view mirrors, bulges outward and gives a smaller virtual image. This is because it is a **diverging mirror**, which means that light rays spread apart, or diverge, when they are reflected. A **concave mirror** curves inward, and can form a real image. This is because it is a **converging mirror**, which means that light rays converge, or move closer, when they are reflected. A concave mirror, such as a shaving mirror, can also form a large virtual image.

*Eye*

*Reflected rays*

*Plane mirror*

*To the eye, it looks as if the rays travel in a straight line*

*Flashlight*

*Mirrors and lenses*
*When you shine a flashlight through this stencil of a tree, the lens on the other side focuses the light rays and forms a real image. The mirror forms a virtual image.*

*The stencil of the tree is covered with colored plastic*

*Virtual image seen in the mirror*

# Lens

A curved piece of glass or plastic that forms an image by bending light rays

A **convex lens** bulges outward. It is a **converging lens**, which means that light rays come together, or converge, as they pass through the lens. This causes a convex lens to form a real image on a surface – the way the lens of a slide projector forms an image on a screen. A convex lens can also produce a large virtual image, as in a magnifying glass. A **concave lens** curves inward. It is a **diverging lens**, which means that light rays spread apart, or diverge, as they pass through the lens. A concave lens forms a small virtual image.

*The convex lens makes the light rays converge*

*Two sets of light rays from the tree*

*Light rays*

*Real image*

*Object*

*Convex lens*

### Real image
*Rays spread out from all points on the tree and pass through the convex lens. The lens bends the rays so that they converge to form a real image on the screen.*

# Focus

The position at which an image is sharp

An image that is sharp is said to be "in focus." A real image is sharp when the surface on which the image forms is at the focus of lens. In fact, the image is sharp over a range of distance called the **depth of field**. The verb focus can also mean to "make an image sharp," such as when you focus a pair of binoculars.

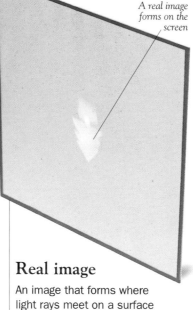

*A real image forms on the screen*

# Real image

An image that forms where light rays meet on a surface

Both a convex lens and a concave mirror can form a real image of an object. Light rays spread out from each point on an object. When some of these rays strike a lens, refraction causes the rays to bend as they pass through it. Rays from each point then come together and meet at a point on a surface, forming an upside-down image of the object. This is called a real image. A concave mirror reflects light rays so that they meet and form a real image. If no surface is present, the light rays actually pass through the point at which a real image forms.

## Fiber bundle
*Tiny beams of light can be seen emerging from this bundle of optical fibers.*

# Fiberoptics

The use of glass fibers to carry light rays

Light rays are able to pass along a thin glass thread or fiber, called an **optical fiber**. An outer coating of a different kind of glass reflects the light back into the center of the fiber, so that it cannot leave the fiber. Optical fibers are used to carry signals of laser light in telephone cables. An **endoscope** is used in medicine to produce images of the interior of the body. It is a flexible tube of optical fibers that is inserted into the body. It carries an image to an eyepiece at the other end.

# Spectacles

Lenses that correct poor vision

The eyes of most people with poor vision have a lens that does not form a sharp image on the retina at the back of the eye. They wear glasses with lenses that bend the light rays reaching their eyes from objects. A **contact lens** rests on the eye itself. Both types of lens help the lens in the eye to focus the light rays on the retina.

# Aberration

A distortion of an image produced by a lens or mirror

A lens or mirror of poor quality gives an image that is slightly blurred, because the light rays do not all meet at a single point.

## See also

Concave 173 • Convex 173 • Ray 76
Reflection 77 • Refraction 77

# Optical instruments

A world that we could not otherwise see is brought to us by optical instruments. Cameras and projectors provide photographs and movie films to entertain us. Microscopes and telescopes bring us magnified views of tiny creatures and distant objects.

*Exposure counter* *Shutter release button* *Shutter speed dial* *Film rewind/back cover release knob*

*Lens* *Lens housing*

**Single-lens reflex (SLR) camera**
*Adjusting the shutter speed alters the time for which the film is exposed to light. The rings around the lens housing adjust the aperture and the focus.*

## Camera

A machine that records images

A camera has a lens that forms a real image ■ of a scene on a light-sensitive material which stores the image. In a photographic camera, this material is a photographic film ■. A **movie camera** contains a moving strip of film that records many images, one after the other. In a television camera ■ or video camera ■, the image forms on a light-sensitive device that converts the image into electrical signals.

## Aperture

An opening that varies the amount of light entering a camera

Behind the lens of a camera is an **iris** or **diaphragm**, which contains a hole whose diameter can be varied. This hole is the aperture, and adjusting its size changes the brightness of the image. If the scene is dim, the aperture must be widened to take a good photograph. If the scene is too bright, the aperture must be narrowed. The size of the aperture is called a **stop**. An **f-number** tells the photographer the size of the stop. For example, *f*22 is a small aperture while *f*2 is large. The *f*-number is the focal length ■ of the lens divided by the diameter of the aperture.

## Shutter

The mechanism that lets light into a camera

When you press the shutter release button to take a photograph, the shutter opens to allow light from the lens to form an image on the film. The shutter usually opens for only a fraction of a second, so that moving objects appear still.

*Prism*

*Viewfinder*

*Hinged mirror*

*Shutter*

*Lenses for autofocusing and exposure*

**Cutaway camera**
*In this SLR camera, the mirror reflects the scene upward and through the prism to the viewfinder. Pressing the shutter release lifts the mirror to allow light through the shutter.*

## Flash

A bright light that flashes to take photographs at night or indoors

The flash provides either all the light or extra light needed to take a photograph in a dark or dim place. Most cameras have a built-in electronic flash. This contains a small tube of gas through which a strong pulse of electric current flows. The current makes the gas glow with bright light for an instant.

## Light meter

A device that measures the amount of light available to take a photograph

Many cameras have a built-in light meter, which is also called an **exposure meter**. It measures the brightness of the light reaching the camera from a scene. The meter contains a photocell ■ that changes the light into an electrical signal. This signal goes to a display, which shows whether the aperture at which the lens is set will give an over- or under-exposed photograph. The photographer can then adjust the aperture accordingly. In an automatic camera, the signal controls the aperture and the shutter, so that the correct amount of light reaches the film and produces a good photograph.

### See also

Film, photographic 125 • Focal length 84
Infrared rays 75 • Photocell 109
Real image 85 • Television camera 130
Video camera 131

# Wide-angle lens

A lens that produces images which give a wide view of a scene

A wide-angle lens has a short focal length. This gives it a wide field of view, so that a large part of a scene forms an image on the film.

**Picture with a wide-angle lens**

# Zoom lens

A lens that changes its field of view

A zoom lens can change from being a wide-angle lens to a telephoto lens. Its field of view varies over a certain range. It is called a zoom lens because it can "zoom in" on a scene.

**Picture with a normal lens**

# Telephoto lens

A lens that produces images in which distant objects appear close

A telephoto lens has a long focal length. This means it has a narrow field of view, so that only a small part of a scene forms an image on the film.

**Picture with a telephoto lens**

# Autofocus

A device that automatically enables a camera to take sharp pictures

You move a camera's lens in or out to focus rays of light coming from objects at different distances. An autofocus mechanism may contain a computer that checks the focus of the image and moves the lens until the image is sharp. Or the camera may move the lens as it sends out a scanning beam of infrared rays ■. The rays reflect from the object and return to a detector, which stops the lens in the right position for a sharp image.

# Viewfinder

The part of a camera that shows the photographer what will appear in the picture

The viewfinder may contain a separate lens that forms an image like that produced by the main lens. A **single-lens reflex (SLR)** camera uses the main lens as a viewfinder. A hinged mirror in front of the film sends the image to the eye instead of to the film. Pressing the shutter release button moves the mirror up so that the film is exposed to light coming through the lens.

# Movie projector

A machine that projects moving images onto a screen

Inside a movie projector, light from a lamp is condensed into a strong beam. The beam shines through a rotating shutter onto a moving strip of film. The shutter lets light through only when each picture on the film is in the right position. A lens projects and focuses the series of still, real images onto a screen, each for a fraction of a second.

# Projector

A machine that projects an image onto a screen

A **slide projector** projects color slides or transparencies. Light is shone through the slide, and a lens forms a real image on a screen.

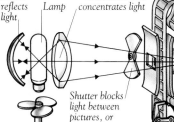

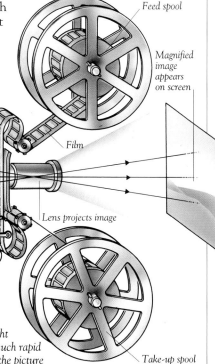

Mirror reflects light

Lamp

Condenser lens concentrates light

Feed spool

Magnified image appears on screen

Film

Shutter blocks light between pictures, or "frames"

Fan cools lamp

Lens projects image

Claw moves film

Take-up spool

**Projecting moving images**
*In a movie projector, a strip of separate photographs moves past a shutter. As the shutter rotates, the light flashes the images onto the screen in such rapid succession that no gaps are seen and the picture appears to be moving smoothly.*

Continued on next page ➤

# Microscope

An instrument that forms a magnified image of a small object

The simplest form of microscope is a **magnifying glass**, which is a powerful convex lens 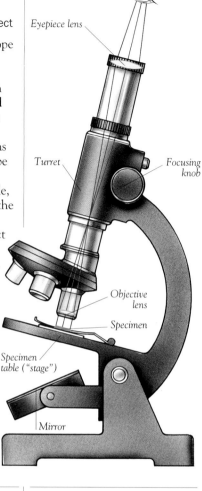. A microscope with more than one lens is called a **compound microscope**. It is a closed tube with an objective lens at the lower end, and an eyepiece lens at the top end. The object to be viewed, or the "specimen," is usually mounted on a glass slide, and then placed very close to the objective lens. This forms a large real image of the object inside the microscope. This image is then viewed through the eyepiece, which further magnifies the image to produce a very large virtual image of the object. Optical microscopes can magnify as much as 2,500 times.

*Compound microscope*
*This microscope has a turret containing different objective lenses that produce different levels of magnification. The mirror beneath the specimen table reflects light to illuminate the specimen.*

Labels on diagram: Eye, Eyepiece lens, Turret, Focusing knob, Objective lens, Specimen, Specimen table ("stage"), Mirror

# Scanning tunneling microscope

A very powerful microscope that uses electrons to view atoms

A scanning tunneling microscope has a very fine electrified needle that closely scans across a surface. Electrons flow, or "tunnel," between the tip of the needle and the atoms in the surface. The tip moves up and down to keep the number of tunneling electrons constant, and so follows the contours of the atoms in the surface. A computer then forms an image of the atoms.

# Electron microscope

A powerful kind of microscope that magnifies an object using electrons instead of light rays

A **transmission electron microscope** fires a beam of electrons through a thin specimen. Magnetic or electric fields then focus the beam onto a fluorescent screen, forming a picture. In a **scanning electron microscope**, an electron beam sweeps over a specimen. The reflected electrons are focused to form a picture.

*Microscopic creatures*
*Electron microscopes can magnify objects up to about a million times. This picture from an electron microscope shows a tiny dust mite.*

# Magnification

The ratio of the size of the image to the apparent size of the object

Magnification is usually written as a number with the symbol x, meaning "times." So a telescope with a magnification of 50x forms an image that is 50 times larger than the object itself.

# Objective

The lens in a telescope or microscope that is closest to the object being viewed

The objective gathers the light and gives a magnified real image of an object.

# Eyepiece

The lens through which you look to use a telescope or microscope

The simplest microscope, such as a magnifying glass, is really just an eyepiece lens. The eyepiece bends the light rays coming from an object, so that the rays strike the eye at a greater angle than they would if the rays had come directly from the object. This makes the image look much bigger than the object. In a telescope or microscope, the eyepiece lens bends light from the real image formed by the objective lens. This enlarges the image.

◄ Continued from previous page

# Condenser

A device used to give a bright light

A projector 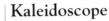 and a microscope may contain a condenser, which concentrates light onto the slide, film, or object being viewed. Light, usually from a bulb, passes through the condenser, which contains a pair of convex lenses. These bend the rays so that they converge on the slide, film, or object, and illuminate it brightly.

# Telescope

An instrument that forms a magnified image of a distant object

There are two kinds of telescope. A **refracting telescope** is a closed tube with an objective lens at one end and an eyepiece lens at the other end. A **reflecting telescope** is an open tube with a concave mirror  inside and an eyepiece outside. In both kinds of telescope, light rays from a distant object enter the tube. The rays are either bent by the objective or reflected by the mirror to form a real image of the object. The image is viewed through the eyepiece, which gives a magnified virtual image of the object. A refracting telescope may also have a third lens, to give an upright image. A reflecting telescope usually has a second mirror to send the light rays to the eyepiece.

# Kaleidoscope

A device that uses mirrors to form images in patterns

A kaleidoscope creates a colorful symmetrical pattern of triangular images arranged in a circle. At one end of the tube are small colored objects. Two mirrors run down the length of the tube, placed at an angle to each other to form a V shape. Each mirror forms a virtual image of the objects, as well as an image of the image in the other mirror. This gives a circle of images when you look through a peephole at the other end.

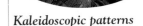

*Kaleidoscopic patterns*
*Angled mirrors inside the kaleidoscope create multiple reflected images of the colored objects – such as pieces of paper, plastic, or glass – at the bottom of the tube. Turning or shaking the kaleidoscope moves the objects and changes the pattern.*

# Binoculars

A pair of small refracting telescopes

Each telescope in a pair of binoculars contains two prisms 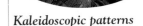. The prisms reflect light rays from an object to give an image that is upright and the right way around. They enable binoculars to be more compact, and so they are easier to handle, than normal telescopes.

*Binoculars*
*Inside binoculars, light is reflected four times by two prisms as it passes between the objective and the eyepiece. The prisms lengthen the distance traveled by the light rays, increasing the magnification possible in a short tube.*

# Periscope

A device that enables you to see objects that are out of view

You can use a periscope to see over the heads of a crowd, or around corners. A simple periscope is a tube with angled mirrors at each end. Light rays from a scene enter the top of the periscope. The top mirror reflects the rays down the periscope to the bottom mirror, which sends the rays to the eye. You see a virtual image of the scene as it appears at the level of the top mirror. A submarine periscope uses prisms instead of mirrors, with lenses between the prisms to magnify the image or to give a wide field of view.

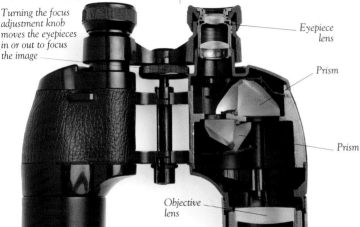

Turning the focus adjustment knob moves the eyepieces in or out to focus the image

Eyepiece lens

Prism

Prism

Objective lens

## See also

Atom 34 • Concave mirror 84
Convex lens 85 • Electron 34
Prism 76 • Projector 87 • Ray 76
Real image 85 • Virtual image 84

# Fire

Even though we may not always see the flames, we make much use of fire. Cars, aircraft, many heating systems, and most power stations burn fuel in engines, boilers, and furnaces.

**Fighting the flames**
*There are different fire extinguishers for putting out different kinds of fire. Use chemicals or foam, not water, on electrical fires.*

## Combustion

Burning

A substance or material that can catch fire or ignite is said to be **flammable**. It has to be heated to a temperature called the **ignition temperature**. A chemical reaction starts between the substance and oxygen in the air. This oxidation gives out heat, which keeps the material hot enough for combustion to continue, until all the material has burned.

**Fuelled by oxygen**
*When a candle burns in an enclosed space, such as this glass jar, the oxygen in the air around it is gradually used up.*

## Spontaneous combustion

Burning that starts without heat from external source

Some materials, like wet hay, can get hot enough internally to catch fire, even if not lit by a flame.

Glass jar

At first, the flame burns brightly

## Fire extinguisher

A device used to put out a fire

All fire extinguishers work by smothering a fire so that oxygen in the air cannot get to the burning material and so support the combustion. They use water or other liquids, foam, powder, or carbon dioxide gas.

As the flame uses up all the oxygen inside the glass jar, the water level rises and candle goes out

Dish of colored water

## Flame

A glowing gas produced in burning

The flame above a fire consists of gas produced by combustion. The gas burns where it meets the air, and becomes so hot that it glows, emitting light. The bright yellow flame of a candle or burning wood or coal contains glowing particles of carbon. A flash of flame occurs above a liquid fuel when it is heated to a temperature called its **flash point**. A mixture of air and hot vapor from the liquid fuel suddenly catches fire and burns fiercely.

## Explosion

A sudden blast

In an explosion, intense heat is released and the air rapidly blasts outward. A mixture of fuel vapor and air, for example, will explode because it burns very quickly and the heat generated causes the air to expand suddenly. Explosives contain chemical compounds that react instantly to give heat and large amounts of expanding gas, so oxygen from the air is not required. The reason atomic and hydrogen bombs are so powerful is that they release immense amounts of heat.

## Fuel

A substance used to provide heat

Fuels include wood, coal, natural gas, and gasoline. They are burned to provide heat for warmth and cooking, or to produce heat that is converted into movement and electricity.

### See also

Air 30 • Chemical reaction 144
Coal 164 • Explosive 161 • Heat 91
Light 76 • Natural gas 164
Oxidation 147 • Gasoline 165
Temperature 92 • Vapor 26

# Heat

Everything has heat, which is a form of energy. You are alive because your body makes heat to keep the parts of your body working properly. Heat is also used in a range of machines from cookers to rockets.

**Heating up**
*This electric element is heating the water that surrounds it by conduction. Convection currents then carry the hot water upward, while cool water moves in to be heated. The water at the surface cools as it evaporates.*

## Heat

The kind of energy that makes things hot or cold

Hot objects possess more heat energy ■ than cold objects. Heat is the movement or kinetic energy ■ of the particles of matter, such as molecules ■. An object gains heat and gets hotter if its particles move faster. If the particles slow down, it loses heat and cools. Heat energy always passes from a hotter object to a cooler object. We can produce heat in many ways, including by friction ■, combustion ■, and from electricity.

## Heat radiation

The flow of heat in the form of infrared rays, which do not need a material medium to transfer heat

All objects lose and gain heat by radiation. As an object's particles move, they give out infrared rays ■. By doing this, they lose some of their heat energy and slow down. Another object may absorb the infrared rays and will gain heat energy. The rays can travel through air, some solids and liquids, and even through a vacuum ■. Infrared rays are also called **radiant heat**. The Sun heats the Earth by radiation. The **solar constant** is the amount of heat energy that strikes the Earth. It is equal to 1,400 joules ■ per second per square meter of the Earth's surface – about the same as the heat of a one-bar electric heater on every square meter.

## Conduction, thermal

The flow of heat through a solid

A source of heat speeds up the particles in one part of a solid. These particles strike others and speed them up, allowing the heat to spread through the material and out into a surrounding liquid or gas. A thermal **conductor** is a material that carries heat in this way. Its **conductivity** is a measure of the rate at which heat flows. Heat flows easily through materials with a high conductivity.

**Hot and cold**
*This thermographic picture of a man's head is taken by a camera that senses infrared rays. The red and orange colors show the hottest parts.*

## Convection

The flow of heat through a fluid (a liquid or gas)

As a liquid or gas is heated, the hot part expands and becomes less dense. The hot fluid rises and mixes with the cooler part of the liquid or gas, spreading heat.

## Expansion

An increase in size when something gets hotter

Expansion happens when solids, liquids, and gases are heated. The particles speed up and move apart, causing an increase in size.

## Contraction

A shrinking in size when something gets colder

As most solids, liquids, and gases lose heat, their particles slow down and move closer together. This causes them to contract in size.

## Insulator, thermal

A material that resists the flow of heat

Insulators are poor conductors of heat. They include plastics, wood, cork, fiberglass, and air.

### See also

Combustion 90 • Energy 68
Friction 54 • Infrared rays 75
Joule 69 • Kinetic energy 68
Molecule 138 • Vacuum 26

*Continued on next page* ➤

## MEASURING TEMPERATURE

### Degree Celsius or degree Centigrade (°C)

Outside the USA, the most widely used unit of temperature

There are 100 degrees Celsius between the normal freezing point ▪ of water (0°C) and the boiling point ▪ of water (100°C).

### Degree Fahrenheit (°F)

A unit of temperature

There are 180 degrees Fahrenheit between the freezing point (32°F) and the boiling point (212°F) of water. To convert °F to °C, subtract 32, multiply by 5, and divide by 9.

### Kelvin (K)

The SI unit of temperature

Absolute zero has a temperature of 0K (zero kelvin), and one kelvin is equivalent to a degree Celsius. The kelvin scale does not have negative values.

### Temperature

The measure of hot or cold

The temperature of an object rises as it gets hotter and falls as it becomes colder. It is measured on a **temperature scale** in kelvins, degrees Celsius or Centigrade, or degrees Fahrenheit. The **absolute temperature** is the temperature in kelvins. A temperature scale is obtained by choosing two exact temperatures called **fixed points**, such as freezing and boiling points, and dividing the interval between into a certain number of degrees.

### Absolute zero

The lowest possible temperature

Nothing can have a temperature lower than absolute zero, which is –459.67°F (–273.15°C) or 0K. The motion of particles in all substances would cease at absolute zero. This temperature can never be attained, but temperatures just above it can.

### Thermometer

An instrument used to measure temperature

A common thermometer is a thin sealed tube containing a column of colored alcohol or mercury and marked with a temperature scale. As the temperature changes, this liquid expands or contracts and the level of the column rises or falls to indicate the temperature. A **maximum-minimum thermometer** works in the same way, and contains markers that indicate the highest and lowest temperatures reached over a period of time. Electrical thermometers contain electrical parts that vary in electrical resistance ▪ or voltage ▪ with temperature. A digital thermometer is an electrical thermometer that displays the temperature directly as a number.

### Thermostat

A device that is used to regulate temperature levels

A thermostat is able to detect temperature and switch a machine on or off. Furnaces may have thermostats that automatically turn off the furnace when the required temperature is reached. The temperature then falls; but the thermostat switches the furnace on again when the temperature drops too low.

### Bimetallic strip

A strip of metal that bends as it gets hotter

A bimetallic strip is made of two different metals, such as brass and iron. When heated, one metal expands more than the other, thus bending the strip. It unbends on cooling. In some thermostats, a bimetallic strip opens and closes a switch as it changes shape.

**0K**
(–459.67°F;
–273.15°C)
*Absolute zero*

**73K**
(–328°F;
–200°C)
*Air liquefies*

**234K**
(–36.2°F; –39°C)
*Mercury freezes*

**273K**
(32°F; 0°C)
*Water freezes*

**373K**
(212°F; 100°C)
*Water boils*

**457K**
(363.2°F;
184°C)
*Paper burns*

**184K (–328°F; –89°C)**
*Lowest temperature on Earth*

**331K (136°F; 58°C)**
*Highest temperature on Earth*

◀ Continued from previous page

# Lord Kelvin

Scottish physicist (1824–1907)

Kelvin was born William Thomson. In 1892, he was made Baron Kelvin of Largs for his work on undersea telegraph cables, which enabled signals to be sent across the Atlantic Ocean. Kelvin realized that there is a lowest possible temperature, absolute zero, and invented the absolute or basic temperature scale based on absolute zero. The degree in this temperature scale is called the kelvin after him.

*Temperature scale*
*This scale graphically shows the tremendous range of temperature between absolute zero and the fiery 14 million °C at the center of the Sun.*

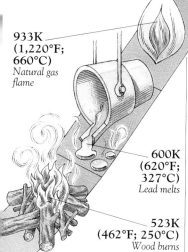

**933K**
**(1,220°F;**
**660°C)**
*Natural gas flame*

**600K**
**(620°F;**
**327°C)**
*Lead melts*

**523K**
**(462°F; 250°C)**
*Wood burns*

## See also

# Cryogenics

The study of matter at very low temperatures

Cryogenics includes the study of liquefied gases and effects, such as superconductivity ■, that occur when materials are very cold.

**5,800K**
**(9,980°F;**
**5,527°C)**
*Sun's surface*

**1,808K**
**(2,795°F;**
**1,535°C)**
*Iron melts*

**3,300K**
**(5,480°F;**
**3,027°C)**
*Metals can be welded*

## Pyrometer

An instrument for measuring high temperatures

A pyrometer measures the temperature of hot objects by detecting the heat or light they give off. A **thermopile** converts the heat rays into an electric current that goes to a meter to indicate temperature. An **optical pyrometer** measures brightness of light to obtain temperature.

## Thermal capacity

A measure of how much energy is needed to heat up a substance

A substance with a low thermal capacity needs a small amount of heat to change temperature, while a substance with a high thermal capacity needs a lot of heat. The **specific heat capacity** ($c$) of a substance is the amount of heat energy in joules ■ needed to raise the temperature of 1 kilogram of that substance by 1°C or 1 kelvin. It is measured in J/(kg °C) or J/(kg K).

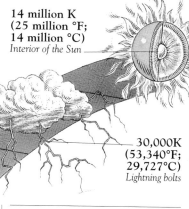

**14 million K**
**(25 million °F;**
**14 million °C)**
*Interior of the Sun*

**30,000K**
**(53,340°F;**
**29,727°C)**
*Lightning bolts*

# Vacuum flask

A flask that keeps substances hot or cold

Hot drinks stay hot for a long time in a vacuum flask, and cold drinks remain cold. Inside is a glass bottle with shiny double walls containing a vacuum ■. The shiny walls reflect heat radiation ■, and convection ■ and conduction ■ of heat cannot occur in the vacuum. In some countries it is also called a **Dewar flask**, after the Scottish scientist James Dewar (1842–1923), who invented it for use in his experiments.

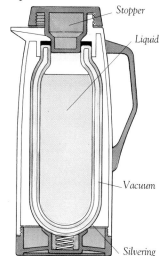

*Stopper*

*Liquid*

*Vacuum*

*Silvering*

*Vacuum flask*
*The flask works by preventing heat from escaping or entering. The stopper is made of an insulating material to reduce conduction through the neck of the flask.*

# Thermodynamics

Factories use heat energy to make materials such as plastics, and engines burn fuels to power machines. Thermodynamics is concerned with the forms heat energy can take, and how it can be made available for useful and efficient work.

## Thermodynamics

The study of heat energy and work

Thermodynamics looks at the amount of heat energy possessed by any system, such as the hot gas inside the cylinder of a gasoline engine ▪. Thermodynamics explains how such a system contains heat energy, and how the energy changes as the system does work ▪, such as moving the piston in the cylinder.

## Kinetic theory

The theory that explains the behavior of matter

The kinetic theory, or **kinetic model**, explains that particles of matter ▪ are always moving. The energy of an amount of matter is the total kinetic energy ▪ of its particles. Its temperature ▪ depends on this energy. Heating matter raises its temperature, because its particles move faster as their energy increases.

---

### See also

Absolute temperature 92
Boyle's law 22 • Charles' law 22
Kinetic energy 68 • Matter 23
Gasoline engine 67 • Pressure 52
Pressure law 22 • Temperature 92
Volume 174 • Work 70

---

*2 The water is poured away*

### Charles' law in action

*As the warm air in the bottle cools, it contracts, and the sides of the bottle cave in as the volume decreases. The volume can change because the sides are flexible. This keeps a constant pressure inside the bottle.*

*1 A plastic bottle is filled with hot water*

*3 The bottle top is quickly replaced, and the bottle collapses*

## Gas laws

Laws that explain how gases behave

The gas laws link the volume ▪, pressure ▪, and temperature of a quantity of any gas. They are Boyle's law, Charles' law, and the pressure law. A **perfect gas** or **ideal gas** is a theoretical gas that obeys the gas laws exactly. Real gases do not behave in this precise way. The kinetic theory explains the gas laws. Heating a gas causes its molecules to move faster. They strike the walls of a container with more force, increasing the pressure or the volume of the gas. Reducing the volume squeezes the molecules into a smaller space. They hit the walls more often and raise the pressure of the gas.

### Using Boyle's law

*Pushing the handle reduces the volume of the air inside the pump, raising its pressure. High-pressure air enters the balloon and stretches the rubber skin as it inflates.*

## Boyle's law

At a constant temperature, the volume of a quantity of a gas is inversely proportional to its pressure

If the pressure of a gas doubles, then its volume halves, and vice-versa. The temperature of the gas must not change.

## Charles' law

At a constant pressure, the volume of a quantity of gas is proportional to its absolute temperature

Absolute temperature ▪ is measured in kelvin (K). If this temperature rises by a tenth, for example from 300K to 330K, the volume of the gas increases by a tenth. The pressure of the gas must not change.

## Pressure law

At a constant volume, the pressure of a quantity of gas is proportional to its absolute temperature

Raising the absolute temperature of a gas by a tenth increases its pressure by a tenth. The volume must not change.

## Entropy

A measure of the disorder or randomness of a system

The particles in an apple or an iron nail are ordered. But if the apple rots away, or the nail rusts, the particles become less ordered, and the entropy of each amount of matter increases.

# Heating & cooling systems

Most buildings have machines that produce heat to warm rooms in cold weather and to heat water. Other machines may remove heat to cool the air in hot weather or to keep food cold and fresh.

## Refrigerator

A machine that makes things colder

A substance called a **refrigerant** circulates through a refrigerator. The refrigerant is a cool vapor ▦ at low pressure when it enters a compressor pump. The pump sends it on as a warm gas at high pressure to a tube outside the refrigerator called a condenser ▦, where it loses heat ▦ to the air and changes to a liquid. The liquid squirts through a hole into a tube called an evaporator. It is now at low pressure. It evaporates to become a cold vapor, taking heat from the air in the refrigerator. The vapor then returns to the pump. **Air conditioning** cools a room by transferring heat from the room to the air outside. A **heat pump** brings heat from the outside to warm a building. Both work in the same basic way as a refrigerator.

## Heat exchanger

A device that transfers heat from a hot object to a cooler object

A heat exchanger has two parts. A hot gas or liquid called a **coolant** flows through one part, transferring its heat to a cooler gas or liquid flowing through the second part. A car radiator ▦ is a type of heat exchanger. Hot water circulating from the engine loses heat to the air around the radiator.

### How a refrigerator works

The pump pushes refrigerant through a low-pressure pipe into a high-pressure pipe, from which it squirts through a tiny hole back into the low-pressure pipe.

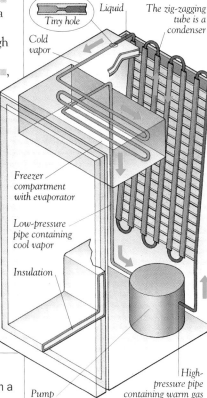

Tiny hole

Liquid

Cold vapor

The zig-zagging tube is a condenser

Freezer compartment with evaporator

Low-pressure pipe containing cool vapor

Insulation

Pump

High-pressure pipe containing warm gas

## Freezing mixture

A mixture that produces a low temperature

Crushed ice and salt make a freezing mixture. The salt dissolves as the ice melts. Each process takes in heat, cooling the surroundings to as low as $-20°C$ ($-4°F$).

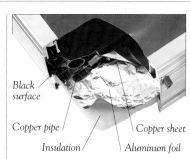

Black surface

Copper pipe

Insulation

Copper sheet

Aluminum foil

### Inside a solar panel

The black surface of the copper sheet gets hot when the Sun's rays pass through the transparent cover. This heats the water in the pipes. The shiny copper and aluminum stop heat loss by reflecting it onto the water pipes. The hot water is used to heat water in a tank.

## Solar heating

A heating system that uses the Sun's energy directly

Solar heating can help to heat a house or to provide hot water. Solar panels on the roof contain channels through which a fluid, such as water, flows. The Sun's rays heat the fluid, which in turn flows through a pipe inside the hot water tank, heating the water in the tank.

## Central heating

A heating system that produces heat from a central source

Many buildings have central heating to warm them. Water is heated by a boiler that burns gas or oil, or that is powered by electricity ▦. The heated water flows through pipes to radiators in the rooms. Alternatively, a heater may warm air that flows through pipes under the floors or into the rooms.

# Heat engines

We put heat to work in heat engines. These machines drive almost all our forms of transport both on land and at sea, in the air and in space. Heat engines also drive generators in power stations, supplying much of our electricity.

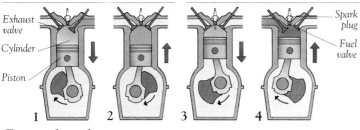

*Exhaust valve*
*Cylinder*
*Piston*
*Spark plug*
*Fuel valve*

1    2    3    4

**Four-stroke cycle**
*On the intake stroke (1), fuel enters the cylinder, where it is squeezed on the compression stroke (2). It ignites on the power stroke (3), pushing down the piston. The waste gases are forced out on the exhaust stroke (4).*

## Four-stroke engine

An engine that works on a cycle of four movements of a piston

Most cars have four-stroke gasoline engines ■. A stroke is a movement of the piston in each cylinder of the engine. The four-stroke cycle starts with the **intake stroke** (1). A fuel valve opens as the piston moves down, sucking fuel (gas vapor and air) into the cylinder. The **compression stroke** (2) follows. The valve closes and the piston moves up, compressing the fuel. The spark plug ignites the fuel, which burns rapidly. The heat causes the gases in the cylinder to expand, and the piston moves down on the **power stroke** (3) and does work, such as driving the car wheels. The cycle ends with the **exhaust stroke** (4). The exhaust valve opens as the piston rises, expelling waste gases.

### See also

Electric generator 110 • Kinetic energy 68
Gasoline engine 67 • Turbine 59

## Two-stroke engine

An engine that works on a cycle of two movements of a piston

Many motorcycles have two-stroke engines. A piston opens and closes holes, or **ports**, in a cylinder. As the piston rises on the first stroke (1), the fuel above the piston is compressed and is then ignited by the spark plug. Fresh fuel enters the area below the rising piston. On the second stroke (2), the piston is forced down, allowing waste gases to escape and pushing fuel up into the area above the piston.

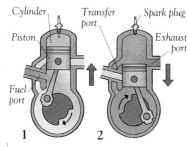

*Cylinder*
*Transfer port*
*Spark plug*
*Piston*
*Exhaust port*
*Fuel port*

1    2

**Two-stroke cycle**
*As the piston moves up, it compresses the fuel, which is then ignited. As the piston falls, new fuel is pushed through the transfer port to the area above the piston.*

## Heat engine

A machine that converts heat into work

A heat engine burns fuel to produce power and drive a machine. It does this by heating a gas, which expands as it gets hotter. The pressure of the expanding gas moves parts inside the engine, changing the heat energy into kinetic energy ■. An **internal combustion engine** is a heat engine that burns fuel inside the engine. Car engines, jet engines, and rocket engines are all internal combustion engines. An **external combustion engine** is a heat engine that burns fuel outside the engine. The steam turbine, used in large ships and power stations, is a type of external combustion engine. A separate boiler burns fuel to produce the hot steam that turns the turbine.

## Rotary engine

A gasoline engine that contains a rotating piston

The rotary engine is also called the **Wankel engine**, after its German inventor, Felix Wankel (1902–1988). The engine's triangular piston rotates in an oval chamber, enclosing three spaces that vary in volume. Ports in the chamber open and close to admit fuel and expel waste gases. In each space, the piston compresses a mixture of fuel and air, which is then ignited by a spark plug. The hot gases expand to drive the piston around and produce power.

## Safety valve

A valve that prevents a boiler from exploding

The pressure of steam builds up in a device that boils water, such as a boiler or pressure cooker. A safety valve lets steam escape before enough pressure builds to burst its container.

Vent — Steam inlet pipe

Boiler

*The first steam engine*
*The ancient Greek physicist Hero devised this engine. Steam from water heated in the boiler escaped through vents in the sphere, forcing the sphere to rotate.*

## Steam engine

An engine driven by hot steam

Old locomotive trains are powered by steam engines. In a steam engine, a piston moves up and down (or to and fro) in a cylinder, like the movement of a piston in a car engine. Hot steam at high pressure flows from a boiler to the cylinder. The steam expands in the cylinder, pushing the piston and providing power. In a **steam turbine**, rotating blades are driven by expanding steam. The turbine has separate sets of blades that work at high, medium, and low steam pressures. This allows the turbine to get more power from the steam.

## Gas turbine

An engine in which hot gas drives a turbine

Gas turbines can power machines such as electric generators. The engine contains a **combustion chamber**, in which a fuel burns continuously to heat air entering the gas turbine. The hot air expands and rotates the blades of a turbine, which is connected to a machine. The turbine also drives the blades of a compressor, which sucks air into the combustion chamber.

## Jet engine

An engine that produces a high-speed jet of air

Most aircraft are powered by jet engines. A jet engine is a gas turbine that burns jet fuel and drives only a compressor. As the engine burns fuel, a jet of hot air and other gases is forced from the exhaust of the engine and pushes it forward. A **turbofan** is a jet engine with a large fan at the front. The fan blows air around the gas turbine to join the jet at the rear, increasing the engine's thrust.

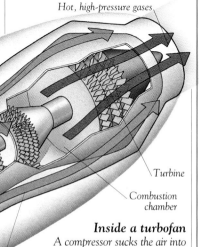

Hot, high-pressure gases

Cold air intake

Turbine

Combustion chamber

Turbofan blades

Compressor

Cold air flows around the engine

*Inside a turbofan*
*A compressor sucks the air into the combustion chamber, where it is mixed with fuel and burned. The large turbofan at the front blows some air around the engine and to the back, giving more power and reducing noise.*

## ENGINE BUILDERS

### Hero of Alexandria
Greek physicist (1st century AD)

Hero, or Heron, built the first steam engine, called the aeolipile. It consisted of a boiler beneath a hollow sphere which had two vents. Steam piped into the sphere emerged from the vents and made the sphere whirl around. The aeolipile had no practical use.

### James Watt
Scottish engineer (1736–1819)

The steam engine was developed in Britain from 1700 onward. James Watt built the first efficient steam engine in 1768. It soon led to improved steam engines that could drive machines of all kinds. The SI unit of power, the watt, is named after him.

### Frank Whittle
English engineer (born 1907)

Frank Whittle conceived the idea of the jet engine in 1929, and set about building one. However, the first jet-powered aircraft flew in Germany in 1939. Whittle's own engine was first used in an aircraft in 1941, and was the forerunner of the modern jet engine.

### Gottlieb Daimler
German engineer (1834–1900)

The earliest internal combustion engines used coal gas as a fuel. Daimler produced the first practical gasoline engine in 1883 and used it to power the first motorcycle in 1885.

# Sound

Scientific knowledge of sound brings us high-quality musical instruments, good concert halls and theaters, and machines that record sounds and play them back. We can also use sound to detect and see things that are hidden from view.

## Sound wave

The vibrations that occur in a material as a sound passes through it

You can hear people talking or singing because sound waves travel through the air from their mouths to your ears. A source of sound vibrates to and fro, and sets the air around it vibrating. The vibrations spread through the air as a series of regular changes in pressure. They travel at a speed of about 1,115 feet per second (340 meters per second). A sound wave consists of **compressions**, which are regions of high pressure. Each compression is followed by a **rarefaction**, a region of low pressure. You hear sound when the pressure changes reach your ears. Sound waves can also travel through liquids and solids.

High-pressure regions

## Volume

The loudness or softness of a sound

The volume of a sound depends on the pressure in the sound wave. Large pressure changes give a loud sound, and weak pressure changes a soft sound. Volume often depends on resonance ▪, especially in musical instruments. Vibrations produced by playing the instrument cause the body of the instrument or the air inside it to vibrate too. The amplitude ▪ of these vibrations builds up, so that the sound has more volume.

## Tone

The quality of a sound

Voices and musical instruments sound different because they have different tones, or **timbres**. A flute has a gentle tone and a drum a harsh tone, for example. The tone depends on the waveform ▪ of the sound wave. The waveform is the pattern of the pressure changes in the sound wave. Smooth pressure changes give a gentle tone, and sudden pressure changes give a harsh tone.

*In tune*
*When a tuning fork vibrates, it creates regions of high pressure, called compressions, and low-pressure regions, called rarefactions. These travel as sound waves to your ear.*

## Pitch

The sensation of how high or how deep a sound is

The pitch of a sound wave depends on its frequency ▪. The pitch is higher if the frequency is greater and the wavelength ▪ shorter. Women's and children's voices often have a high frequency, and a high pitch, while men speak and sing at a low pitch.

## Harmonic

An extra, higher sound wave

When you hear a sound that has a particular pitch, it is often not a pure note. This is because it is accompanied by sounds of a higher frequency, called harmonics or **overtones**. They are softer than the main sound wave, and they have twice, three times, four times the main frequency, and so on. The volume of each harmonic affects the tone of the sound.

Main note or / Second / Third
first harmonic    harmonic    harmonic

*Extra vibrations*
*The tone of a musical note depends on the loudness of the harmonics compared to each other and to the main note, or first harmonic. The second harmonic is produced by a string vibrating in two parts. The third harmonic consists of a vibration in three parts, and so on.*

## Acoustics

The scientific study of sound

The word acoustics refers not only to the study of sound, but also to the quality of sound produced in a public building, such as a concert hall. Here, good acoustics can make the sound of an orchestra, singer, or speaker clear and pleasant. The way in which the sound waves reflect from the walls and other surfaces is carefully controlled.

# Doppler effect

A change in pitch produced by the motion of a source of sound

As a police car or ambulance passes, you hear a sudden drop in the pitch of its siren. This is the Doppler effect. As the source of sound approaches, the pressure changes in the sound waves reach your ears more quickly. The frequency of the sound increases and its pitch is raised. As the source moves away, the pressure changes are spaced out more and the pitch drops. The Doppler effect also occurs with light waves. The frequency of light waves increases and decreases as a source of light moves toward or away from an observer.

# Echo

The repetition of a sound by the reflection of its sound wave

An echo occurs when a sound wave hits a barrier such as a large building or a cliff. The sound wave bounces off the surface, reaching your ears later than the rest of the sound wave, which reaches you directly.

# Beats

A regular variation in volume produced by two sounds

If two sounds are very close in pitch, you no longer hear both sounds but only one sound in which the volume regularly increases and decreases. Beats are caused by interference ▦ between the two sound waves.

# Echo location

A method of detecting objects using sound waves

A bat flying in the dark uses echo location. It makes squeaks that bounce off objects in its path. The bat hears the echoes, enabling it to detect the objects. **Sonar** ("sound navigation ranging") is a form of echo location. Sonar equipment on a vessel sends out pulses of sound and detects the echoes that come from a submerged object, such as a submarine or wreck. The sonar system converts the echoes into a picture of the object and its position on a screen. Geologists use sonar to find oil deposits beneath the Earth's surface.

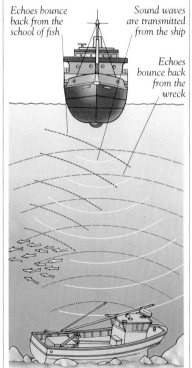

*Echoes bounce back from the school of fish*

*Sound waves are transmitted from the ship*

*Echoes bounce back from the wreck*

*Sounding out*
*The ship's sonar sends out pulses of sound (yellow) and detects the echoes coming from a wreck (red) and a shoal of fish (purple). The delay between the sound pulse and the echo depends on the an object's distance. The sonar measures the delays to find the depths of the objects.*

*Sound picture*
*An ultrasound scan of a baby in the womb.*

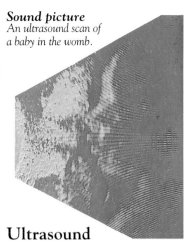

# Ultrasound

Sound that is too high in frequency to be heard by human ears

The blast of a dog whistle is an example of ultrasound. Ultrasound has a frequency of more than 20 kilohertz and has many uses in industry and medicine. Ultrasound scanners use pulses of ultrasound to view unborn babies inside their mothers. **Ultrasonics** is the study of ultrasound. **Infrasound** has a frequency of less than 20 hertz ▦, below the range of human hearing.

## MEASURING SOUND

### Speed of sound

About 1,115 feet per second (fps) at 68°F, 777 miles per hour (340 meters per second (m/s)

The speed of sound is less when the air is colder. At 32°F, for example, the velocity is 1,087 fps. Sound moves more than four times faster in water.

### Decibel (dB)

An approximate measure of the loudness of a sound

A sound of zero decibels (0 dB) can only just be heard, whereas the roar of a jet aircraft may reach 130 dB. Normal speech has a level of about 40 dB.

# Magnetism

Magnets and electric currents exert an invisible force on iron objects and other magnets. This force is magnetism. The Earth itself is a giant magnet with two magnetic poles. Electromagnets are formed by electric currents. They are used in machines such as cars, computers, and television sets.

## Magnet

An object that is magnetic

A magnet attracts iron and some other materials and attracts or repels other magnets within its magnetic field. If it is free to move, a magnet turns to line up with the Earth's magnetic field. Only certain materials are magnetic. These include some metals, such as iron, nickel, and cobalt, some alloys ▪, and some ceramics ▪. **Lodestone** is a magnetic mineral made of iron oxide. A **permanent magnet** is always magnetic, but a **temporary magnet** can gain and lose its magnetic force. A **keeper** is a bar of iron that you place on a permanent magnet to help keep its magnetism when you are not using it.

## Magnetic field

The area around a magnet in which it exerts force

A magnet only attracts objects when they are within its magnetic field. Two magnets push or pull on each other if their magnetic fields come together. At each point in the field, the magnet exerts a force in a certain direction. These directions follow **lines of force**, or **flux**, which loop around the magnet from one pole to the other. A wire carrying an electric current ▪ is also surrounded by a magnetic field while the current is flowing.

## Magnetic pole

One of two points in a magnet where its magnetism is strongest

A magnet has two poles called the north pole and south pole. The magnetic force is strongest at each pole. Opposite poles attract, so a north pole attracts a south pole. But like poles repel, and two magnets placed north pole to north pole will push each other away.

*Iron filings show lines of force*

## Compass

A device that points north–south

A magnetic compass contains a magnetized needle that swings on a pivot. The Earth's magnetic field attracts the needle so that one end is pulled toward the Earth's north magnetic pole, and the other end toward the south magnetic pole. But the direction of the true North Pole and South Pole lies at an angle to the direction shown by the needle. This angle varies from place to place.

## Domain

A small area of magnetism in a magnetic material

A magnetic material, such as iron or steel, is made up of many tiny regions of magnetism called domains. These are magnetic because the atoms ▪ inside them behave like miniature magnets. The moving electric charges of spinning electrons ▪ in the atoms produce magnetic fields. In a domain, the atoms line up in the same direction to form two magnetic poles. Normally, the poles of different domains point in different directions, so there is no overall magnetism. An outside magnetic field makes the poles of the domains line up in the same direction. This magnetizes the material, and it becomes a magnet.

*Opposite poles attract*

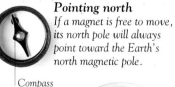

***Pointing north***
*If a magnet is free to move, its north pole will always point toward the Earth's north magnetic pole.*

*Compass points north*

*Magnet's north pole points north*

*Bar magnet floats on cork in water*

# Earth's magnetic field

The weak magnetic field that is present all over the Earth

The Earth is a huge magnet with north and south magnetic poles. These are located near the true North and South Poles, moving slightly from year to year. Compasses point to the north magnetic pole, and the angle between this direction and the true North Pole is the **magnetic declination**, or **magnetic variation**. In most places, the Earth's magnetic field is not horizontal but points down into the ground or up into the air. This is **magnetic dip**, and the angle between the magnetic field and a horizontal direction is called the **inclination**. The study of the Earth's magnetic field is called **geomagnetism**.

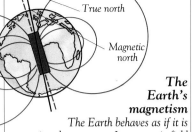

*True north*

*Magnetic north*

***The Earth's magnetism***
*The Earth behaves as if it is a giant bar magnet. Its magnetic field extends out into space. Scientists believe it is caused by electric currents in the Earth's metallic core.*

# Magnetic levitation

Suspending an object in a magnetic field

A **"maglev"** train works by magnetic levitation. The train floats above the track, supported by a strong magnetic field. A second magnetic field is used to propel the train along the track.

# Demagnetization

The removal of magnetism

You can remove an object's magnetism by dropping it, hammering it, or heating it. An electric coil with a rapidly changing magnetic field also demagnetizes objects. This method is called **degaussing**.

# Electromagnet

A form of magnet that works by electricity

An electromagnet consists of a coil of wire wound around a piece of iron. When an electric current flows through the coil, the iron becomes a magnet. The electromagnet loses its magnetism when the current is turned off. A **solenoid** is an electromagnet with a long cylindrical coil.

*Like poles repel*

# Magnetometer

An instrument that detects and measures magnetism

You use a magnetometer to measure the strengths of magnetic fields in machines and to detect sunken or buried metal objects. Satellites and space probes carry magnetometers to measure the magnetic fields in space and around planets.

# Magnetic induction

The production of magnetism in another object by a magnet

Placing an object made of a magnetic material in a magnetic field turns it into a magnet. This is called magnetic induction. The magnetic field makes the domains in the object line up to point in one direction. This forms two magnetic poles, turning the object into a magnet.

***Magnetism from electricity***
*In an electromagnet (shown above), electric current flows through the wire, producing a magnetic field. The wire is coiled many times to increase the field.*

## See also

Alloy 166 • Atom 34
Ceramics 159
Electric current 104
Electron 34
Superconductivity 113

# Static electricity

The crackles you may hear as you pull off a sweater are caused by tiny sparks of electricity traveling through the air. The sweater gains a static electric charge when it rubs against your hair or clothes. Lightning is a huge spark caused by static electricity in the clouds.

*Gold-leaf electroscope*
*This plastic comb becomes charged when you rub it against wool. You can measure the charge by bringing the comb to a gold-leaf electroscope and seeing how far the gold leaf moves out from the rod.*

*Charged plastic comb*

*Cap*

*Gold leaf*

*Scale*

## Electricity

A form of energy produced by the movement of electrons

Electrons ▪ are tiny, moving particles inside atoms ▪. In some substances, electrons can be made to leave their atoms and move to other atoms in the same substanc, or to atoms in another substance. This movement of electrons produces electrical energy ▪, or electricity. There are two kinds of electricity – static electricity and current electricity.

## Electroscope

An instrument that detects an electric charge

A **gold-leaf electroscope** contains a metal rod with a thin leaf of gold at the base and a cap at the top. When you bring an electrically charged object to the cap, it makes the leaf move out from the rod. The charge makes electrons move up or down the rod. The leaf and rod each gain the same kind of charge, so the rod repels the leaf.

## Static electricity

A form of electricity in which electric charge remains static

Rather than flowing in a current, static electricity stays in one place. Rubbing a plastic pen with a handkerchief creates a static electric charge because electrons move from the handkerchief to the pen. The plastic pen is an electrical insulator ▪, so when it gains electrons, they stay where they are instead of flowing away. The pen becomes charged and will attract small pieces of paper. Unless the plastic pen is rubbed on the handerkerchief again, its extra electrons will gradually disperse, and the pen will lose its charge. The study of static electricity is called **electrostatics**.

## Electric charge

A quantity of electricity

When the atoms in an object gain electrons, the object gets a **negative charge**. This is because each electron carries a tiny negative charge. When the atoms in an object lose electrons, the object gets a **positive charge**. The amount of charge an object has depends on how many electrons are gained or lost by its atoms. Objects with opposite charges attract each other, while objects with the same charges repel each other. An object with no overall electric charge is **neutral**.

## Electric field

The area around a charged object in which it exerts a force

An electrically charged object is surrounded by an electric field. This is the area within which the object exerts a force on other charged objects. It is also called an **electrostatic field**.

# Electrostatic induction

The way in which a charged object produces an electric charge in another object

The electric field around a charged object affects a nearby object. A negative field repels electrons in the second object. These move away from the surface of the object, giving it a positive charge. A positive charge on the first object attracts electrons, giving the surface of the second object a negative charge. This is electrostatic induction. The two oppositely charged objects attract each other.

# Electrophorus

A device that makes and carries an electric charge

An electrophorus consists of a plastic disk and a metal disk with an insulated handle. Rubbing the plastic disk makes it gain an electric charge. Placing the metal disk on the plastic one causes it to become charged by induction. You carry the charged electrophorus by its insulated handle, which stops the charge from flowing away.

*Van de Graaff generator*
*This large Van de Graaff generator produces enough static electricity to make the girl's hair stand on end when she touches it.*

# Lightning conductor

A metal rod that attracts lightning

A lightning conductor, or lightning rod, is fixed to the top of a building. A metal cable connects the rod to the ground. Lightning tends to strike the rod rather than the building. The cable carries the strong electric current ▓ down to the ground, where it is discharged harmlessly into the earth.

# Electrostatic generator

A machine that continuously generates electric charge

An electrostatic generator builds up a powerful charge in an object. It is used in scientific research and in industry. A **Wimshurst machine** is a small generator that contains two rotating disks in which electric charge builds up. This is collected by metal combs. A **Van de Graaff generator** contains a moving belt that becomes charged as it passes over a row of metal points. The belt carries the charge to a hollow metal dome at the top of the generator. If you place another metal dome next to the generator, you can make large sparks of static electricity leap between the two domes.

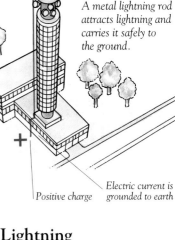

*Bolt of lightning*

*Lightning conductor*

*Negative charge*

**Lightning**
*If lightning strikes a building, it can cause serious damage. A metal lightning rod attracts lightning and carries it safely to the ground.*

*Positive charge*

*Electric current is grounded to earth*

# Lightning

A huge spark of electricity that occurs during a thunderstorm

A thundercloud becomes highly charged as positive and negative charges separate between the top and bottom of the cloud. The negative charge at the bottom of the cloud causes a positive charge to build up in the ground by electrostatic induction. Lightning occurs when a strong pulse of electric current suddenly flows between the two opposite charges. Heat from the current makes the air glow, which you see as a bright flash, or spark. It also causes the air to expand suddenly, producing a loud thunder clap.

## See also

# Current electricity

Electricity that flows in a current is a clean and efficient source of energy that is easy to transport. Wires carry the electricity generated by power stations to homes and industries, where it provides heat and light and powers motor-driven machines. Portable batteries supply electricity for smaller electric machines.

## Electric current

The flow of electric charge through a substance

Electric charge can only flow through a substance that conducts electricity, such as copper wire. Charge flows through the wire when an electromotive force drives electrons ▪ into the conductor. The electrons are negatively charged ▪, so they repel electrons ahead, causing them to jump from one atom to the next. As electrons in the conductor move from atom to atom, the charge is carried along the wire in a flow that is called electric current.

## Direct current (DC)

Electric current which flows in one direction only

A battery ▪ produces direct current. An electromotive force from the battery makes electrons move along a wire in a particular direction. The electrons cannot reverse the direction of their flow.

## Alternating current (AC)

Electric current in which electrons change direction many times per second

The type of electricity that comes from power stations ▪ to most homes and factories is alternating current. This is because it is easier to send alternating current over long distances than direct current. In the alternating current of the electricity supply, the electrons move back and forth along a wire 50 or 60 times a second. This rate is the **frequency** of the supply.

*Bulbs in series*
*Both bulbs are dim because they each get only half the voltage produced by the batteries.*

## Series circuit

A circuit that connects a source and components one after the other

The components in a series circuit share the voltage of the source, so each component gets less voltage. A break in any part of the circuit stops the current flowing.

## Circuit, electrical

The path along which an electric current flows

An electrical circuit consists of a source of energy (such as a battery), connecting wires, and electrical components such as lamps, switches, resistors ▪, or capacitors ▪. The current flows out from the power source and around the circuit, unless the circuit is broken.

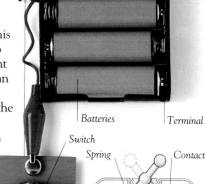

*A double circuit*
*Direct current from this set of batteries flows through two circuits – a series circuit to the left and a parallel circuit to the right.*

Batteries    Terminal

Switch
Spring    Contact

*Operating the switch makes the metal spring touch the contact, and current flows through the switch*

## Switch

A device that completes or breaks an electrical circuit

When you turn on a light, the switch closes a gap in a circuit. This allows the current to flow through the light bulb. When you turn off the light, the switch opens the gap and breaks the circuit, stopping the flow of current.

## Conductor, electrical

A substance through which electricity can flow

Most metals are good electrical conductors. Their atoms have free electrons that move easily. The passage of electricity through a substance is called electrical **conduction**. Electrical **conductivity** is the ease with which current flows.

## Electromotive force (emf)

The force that makes electrons move in an electric current

Electrons cannot produce a current without being pushed by an electromotive force. This is produced by a source of electrical energy, such as a battery. The electromotive force acts upon the electrons inside the battery. It pushes them out into the circuit, where they start other electrons moving. The difference in the electromotive force between any two points in a circuit is called the **potential difference (PD)**. This causes the current to flow because electrons always move from a point of high potential to a point of low potential. The electromotive force of a source is also called its **voltage**. Both emf and PD are measured in volts.

## Terminal

The point at which an electric current leaves or enters an electrical device

Wires connect to the terminals of batteries and electrical components. Electrons leave through the negative terminal of a battery.

## Insulator, electrical

A substance that blocks the flow of electricity

An insulator does not conduct electricity because its atoms have no free electrons. Plastics and ceramics are good insulators. **Insulation** is the use of insulators to make electrical devices safe to handle. The coverings on wires and electrical components are made from insulators.

*This wire is insulated with a plastic coating*

### Parallel circuit

A circuit that splits into branches

Current flows to all branches of the circuit, so that each branch gets the full voltage of the source. A break in one branch of the circuit stops the current only in that branch.

*Bulbs in parallel*
*The bulbs in the two branches of the parallel circuit glow brightly because they each get the full voltage produced by the batteries.*

### Resistance

The degree to which a substance resists electric current

All electrical conductors, except superconductors ■, have a certain amount of electrical resistance. This means that they convert some of the electrical energy passing through them into heat. Resistance is low in good conductors.

### MEASURING ELECTRIC CURRENT

## Ampere or amp (A)

The SI unit of electric current

1 ampere is equal to the current that produces a force of 2 ten-millionths of a newton ■ between two infinitely long parallel wires 1 meter (3.3 ft) apart. It is named after André Ampère ■.

## Volt (V)

The SI unit of potential difference

1 volt makes a current of 1 ampere produce 1 joule of energy every second. It is named after the physicist Alessandro Volta ■.

## Ohm ($\Omega$)

The SI unit of electrical resistance

1 ohm of resistance makes a potential difference of 1 volt produce a current of 1 ampere. It is named after Georg Ohm ■.

## Coulomb (C)

The SI unit of electric charge

1 coulomb is the charge that is delivered by a current of 1 ampere flowing for 1 second. It equals the charge of 6 million million million electrons. It is named after Charles Coulomb ■.

## Farad (F)

The SI unit of capacitance

A capacitor with a capacitance of 1 farad stores a charge of 1 coulomb when you apply a PD of 1 volt. A microfarad ($\mu$F) is one-millionth of a farad. It is named after Michael Faraday ■.

*Continued on next page* ➤

Battery

## Resistor

An electrical component that has a particular resistance

A resistor determines the amount of electric current ▪ that flows through an electrical circuit ▪. A fixed resistor has a set electrical resistance ▪.

*Variable resistor*

You can vary the resistance of a **variable resistor**, or **rheostat**. The resistance of a thermistor ▪ falls as its temperature rises.

### Electrical resistance
*This variable resistor (above) controls the amount of current flowing through the light bulb, making it glow brighter or dimmer.*

## Ohm's law

The resistance of a conductor equals the potential difference across it divided by the current flowing through it

The amount of current that flows through an electrical conductor ▪ depends on the resistance of the conductor and on the potential difference ▪, or voltage, across it. The current decreases as the resistance increases, but it increases as the voltage increases. To find the resistance in ohms, you divide the potential difference in volts by the current in amperes. This law was discovered by Georg Ohm ▪.

### Measuring voltage
*By attaching a multimeter to the terminals of this light bulb, you can measure the voltage, or potential difference, across them. Here, the potential difference equals*

## Capacitor

An electrical component that stores electric charge

A capacitor contains two metal conducting plates separated by an electrical insulator ▪ called a **dielectric**. Connecting the plates to a source of electricity builds up an electric charge in the capacitor. A capacitor is also called a **condenser**, and **capacitance** is the degree to which it can store electricity.

## Voltmeter

An instrument that measures potential difference

A voltmeter measures the voltage, or potential difference, between two points in a circuit.

Light bulb

## CIRCUIT SYMBOLS

| | |
|---|---|
|  | Simple switch |
|  | Single cell |
|  | Battery of cells |
|  | Power supply |
|  | Ammeter |
|  | Galvanometer |
|  | Voltmeter |
|  | Motor |
|  | Bulb |
|  | Fuse |
|  | Resistor |
| | Variable resistor |
| | Capacitor |

## Potentiometer

An electrical component that produces a variable voltage

A potentiometer, or **pot**, contains a resistor. You apply a fixed voltage to the resistor and move a contact along it to tap the current. The contact's position affects the potential difference between it and the end of the resistor. This is the variable voltage.

## Ammeter

An instrument that measures current

An ammeter measures the amount of current flowing through a circuit. A **galvanometer** detects and measures a small electric current.

*Multimeter*
A multimeter (below) measures current voltage, or resistance

*Multimeter*

### See also

◄ *Continued from previous page*

# Pioneers of electricity

Scientists have known about the power of static electricity for more than 2,000 years. But it is only in the last 200 years that scientists have discovered how to generate current electricity, one of our most useful forms of energy.

**Faraday's ring**
*Michael Faraday investigated electromagnetic induction using this induction ring. It was the first transformer.*

## Thales

Greek scientist and philosopher (c.640–c.550 BC)

Thales found that rubbing amber caused it to attract light objects. This was because of static electricity ■. Our word electricity comes from *elektron*, the Greek word for amber.

## Benjamin Franklin

American scientist and statesman (1706–90)

Franklin put forward the idea that electricity consists of electrical "fluid" made up of positive and negative electric charges ■. In 1752, Franklin flew a kite in a thunderstorm to prove that lightning is electrical. Electricity from the thunderclouds flowed down the wet kite string and charged a capacitor. After this, lightning rods became widely used to ground lightning.

*A dangerous experiment*
*Franklin risked his life by flying a kite in a storm. Others were killed trying the same experiment.*

## Luigi Galvani

Italian anatomist (1737–98)

In 1791, Galvani noticed that the legs of a dead frog twitched when they were touched by two different metals. The legs moved because the metals reacted with chemicals in the frog's muscles to produce an electric current ■. **Alessandro Volta** (1745–1827), an Italian physicist, invented the first battery in 1800. It used different metals to produce electric current.

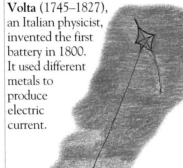

## Hans Oersted

Danish physicist (1777–1851)

In 1820, Oersted placed a compass needle beside a wire carrying an electric current. The needle moved, showing that an electric current produces a magnetic field ■. Oersted had discovered electromagnetism, which is used in most modern electrical machines.

## Michael Faraday

English physicist (1791–1867)

Faraday was inspired by Oersted's discovery of electromagnetism. In 1821, he used it to make the first electric motor. In 1831, he discovered electromagnetic induction ■ and invented the transformer ■. An American physicist, **Joseph Henry** (1797–1878), also made this discovery at the same time. Later in 1831, Faraday invented the electric generator ■.

## Nikola Tesla

Croatian–American physicist (1856–1943)

Tesla discovered that electrical machines work better using alternating current rather than direct current. In 1888, he invented the induction motor ■. He also made the Tesla coil, which produces the high-frequency signals used in radio and television. An American engineer, **George Westinghouse** (1846–1914), developed Tesla's machines to build power stations.

### See also

# Electricity production

We produce electricity to power machines in two main ways. Batteries are a portable source of low power, while electricity with much greater energy comes to us through wires from power stations. Other sources of electricity include solar cells.

## Battery

**A device that produces and stores electric current**

A battery can consist of one electrical cell, or a set of cells connected together. Many batteries contain primary cells, which lose their store of electricity after a certain amount of use. A **storage battery**, or **accumulator**, can be recharged with electricity and used again. It contains one or more secondary cells.

## Electrical cell

**A device in which a chemical reaction produces an electric current**

A simple cell contains two rods or plates, called **electrodes**, that are made of different metals. These are placed in a substance called an **electrolyte**. Connecting the electrodes causes the metals in the electrodes to react with the chemical compound in the electrolyte. Electrons ▪ flow from one electrode to the other as the reaction proceeds. Current then flows out from the cell, around the wires in an electrical circuit ▪, and back to the cell.

### Simple primary cell
*An electric current flows when zinc and copper electrodes are placed in a dilute solution of sulfuric acid $(H_2SO_4)$.*

Copper electrode

*Hydrogen gas $(H_2)$ is released as hydrogen ions $(H^+)$ in the acid gain electrons*

*Flow of electrons lights the bulb*

Zinc electrode

*As the zinc dissolves in the acid, the zinc atoms lose electrons, which flow to the copper electrode*

*Electrons flow out of the cell, through the wire, and back into the cell*

## Dry cell

**A sealed electrical cell that is dry in use**

Most batteries are dry cells. The most common type of dry cell is the **Leclanché cell**, which uses zinc and manganese as electrodes and produces 1.5 volts. An alkaline manganese cell or "long-life battery" contains powdered zinc, a mixture of manganese(IV) oxide and carbon, and potassium hydroxide as an electrolyte. These are sealed in a steel case.

## Primary cell

**An electrical cell that cannot be recharged**

Most batteries used in flashlights and cassette recorders are primary cells. They go "dead" after a while and have to be replaced. This is because the electrodes and the electrolyte change as they react together and produce electricity. When the change is complete, the reaction cannot continue and the cell stops working.

## Fuel cell

**A device that uses up fuel to produce electricity**

The Space Shuttle carries fuel cells that consume hydrogen gas and oxygen gas as fuel. Each cell contains an electrolyte between a pair of porous plates. Hydrogen and oxygen are fed into the plates. As they flow out of the holes in the plates, they react with the electrolyte. As the fuel and electrolyte react, the plates become charged with electricity and produce an electric current.

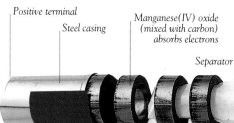

Positive terminal

Steel casing

Manganese(IV) oxide (mixed with carbon) absorbs electrons

Separator

Zinc in electrolyte paste produces electrons

Metal rod collects electrons

Negative terminal

### Long-life battery
*The steel casing of this alkaline manganese cell does not take part in the reaction. It prevents the potassium hydroxide electrolyte from leaking out.*

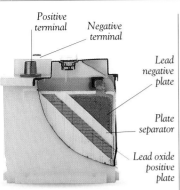

Positive terminal  Negative terminal

Lead negative plate

Plate separator

Lead oxide positive plate

**Car battery**
*A car has a battery to produce current for starting the car. The battery contains secondary cells that are recharged with electricity by the car's alternator (a type of generator) when the engine is running.*

## Secondary cell

An electrical cell that can be recharged with electricity

Feeding an electric current to the electrodes of a secondary cell reverses the chemical changes inside the cell. It restores the metals in the electrodes and the chemical compound in the electrolyte. A car battery is a **lead-acid accumulator**. It contains electrode plates of lead and lead(IV) oxide immersed in an electrolyte of sulfuric acid.

## Thermoelectricity

Electricity produced directly from heat

A **thermocouple** produces an electric current when it is heated. It contains a pair of wires made of different metals and joined together at each end. When one joint is kept cold and the other heated, the difference in temperature causes electrons inside the wire to move around, producing an electric current. The amount of current produced depends on the temperature difference between the two joints. By measuring the current, a thermocouple can be used as a type of thermometer.

## Photoelectric effect

Changing light into electricity

The photoelectric effect is a release of electrons caused by light or other radiation falling on certain materials. It can produce an electric current. A **photocell** is a sensing device that generates an electrical signal when struck by light, infrared rays, or ultraviolet rays. Photocells are used in the light meters ▦ of cameras, in automatic doors, burglar alarms, and many other automatic machines. Some kinds of photocell require a source of electric current to make them work. **Photovoltaic cells** require no electric current. **Solar cells**, which power calculators, small motors, or other electrical equipment by turning sunlight into electricity, are photovoltaic.

*Electricity from the Sun*
*By connecting the solar cell inside a calculator to a multimeter, you can measure the electricity generated when sunlight falls on the cell. This cell gives a potential difference of 1.8 volts.*

Printed circuit under keys

Solar cell

Calculator display

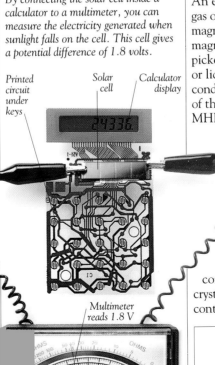

Multimeter reads 1.8 V

**Boat with a silent engine**
*This Japanese boat uses MHD to suck water into the tubes at the front of its hull, and force it out again at the rear, driving the boat forward.*

## Magnetohydrodynamics (MHD)

Producing electricity from a moving liquid or gas

An electric current ▦ forms in a gas or liquid that passes through a magnetic field generated by strong magnets. The current can be picked up by electrodes in the gas or liquid, which must be able to conduct electricity. Power stations of the future may be able to use MHD to produce electricity.

## Piezoelectricity

Electricity produced from crystals

Certain crystals produce an electric current when they are squeezed or made to vibrate. Many watches contain a vibrating quartz crystal that gives out an accurate control signal to keep good time.

## See also

Electric current 104
Circuit, electrical 104 • Electron 34
Light meter 86 • Photodiode 115

## Fleming's rules

Rules that relate the current in a wire to its movement and a surrounding magnetic field

When a current flows through a wire in a magnetic field ■, a force acts on the wire. This happens in an electric motor ■. If the directions of the current and the field are known, Fleming's left-hand rule can be used to work out the direction of the force moving the wire. When a wire moves through a magnetic field, a current is generated in the wire. This happens in a generator. Fleming's right-hand rule can be used to work out the direction of the current if the directions of the field and the wire's motion are known.

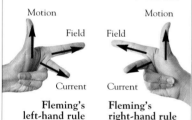

| Motion | Motion |
| --- | --- |
| Field | Field |
| Current | Current |
| **Fleming's left-hand rule** | **Fleming's right-hand rule** |

## Electromagnetic induction

The use of magnetism to produce electricity

When you move a copper wire through the magnetic field around a magnet, an electric current flows in the wire. This is electromagnetic induction. It also occurs if the magnet moves past the wire or if both are still and the magnetic field changes in strength.

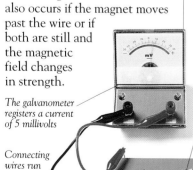

*The galvanometer registers a current of 5 millivolts*

*Connecting wires run under the board*

## Transformer

A device that changes the voltage and current of an electricity supply

Computers and other machines have parts that can work only if they receive less voltage than that of the normal household supply. A transformer changes the voltage. It contains two coils of wire wound around an iron core. Alternating current at a particular voltage goes to the first coil, and produces a changing magnetic field. This field causes the second coil to produce current with a different voltage. The difference in voltage depends on the number of turns of wire in each coil.

## Electric generator

A machine that converts movement into electricity

Power stations contain electric generators, which are driven by a turbine and generate an electric current. Inside a generator, a coil of wire rotates in the magnetic field between the poles of a magnet or electromagnet ■. Alternatively, the magnet may rotate while the coil remains still. In both cases, an electric current flows in the coil. An **alternator** is a generator that produces an alternating current ■. An electric generator is also called a **dynamo**.

### Mini generator

*As this coil of wire spins within the magnetic field produced by the bar magnets, a tiny electric current flows through the coil. The current can be measured on a galvanometer.*

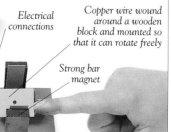

*Electrical connections*

*Copper wire wound around a wooden block and mounted so that it can rotate freely*

*Strong bar magnet*

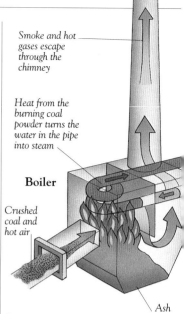

*Smoke and hot gases escape through the chimney*

*Heat from the burning coal powder turns the water in the pipe into steam*

**Boiler**

*Crushed coal and hot air*

*Ash*

## Power station

A building that produces a region's electricity supply

Power stations produce the supply of electricity that comes to your home. A **thermal power station** burns a fuel, such as coal, to boil water into steam. In a **nuclear power station**, a nuclear reactor ■ produces heat to make steam. In both types of power station, the steam goes to a steam turbine, which drives an electric generator. A **hydroelectric power station** contains a turbine driven by falling water from a dam. This turbine drives the generator.

## Converter

A device that changes alternating current to direct current, or vice versa

Electronic machines work by direct current (DC) ■, but the normal supply is alternating current (AC). A converter that changes only AC to DC is a **rectifier**. It has a diode ■ that passes current flowing in one direction, but not in the reverse direction. This gives direct current but an uneven voltage. **Smoothing** means connecting a capacitor ■ to a rectifier to give an even voltage.

◄ Continued from previous page

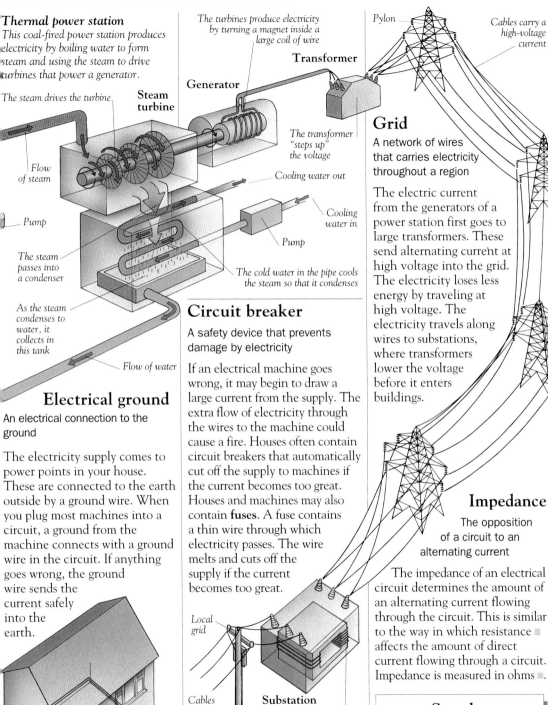

### Thermal power station
*This coal-fired power station produces electricity by boiling water to form steam and using the steam to drive turbines that power a generator.*

The turbines produce electricity by turning a magnet inside a large coil of wire

**Transformer**

Pylon

Cables carry a high-voltage current

**Generator**

**Steam turbine**

The steam drives the turbine

Flow of steam

Pump

The steam passes into a condenser

As the steam condenses to water, it collects in this tank

Flow of water

The transformer "steps up" the voltage

Cooling water out

Cooling water in

Pump

The cold water in the pipe cools the steam so that it condenses

## Grid
A network of wires that carries electricity throughout a region

The electric current from the generators of a power station first goes to large transformers. These send alternating current at high voltage into the grid. The electricity loses less energy by traveling at high voltage. The electricity travels along wires to substations, where transformers lower the voltage before it enters buildings.

## Electrical ground
An electrical connection to the ground

The electricity supply comes to power points in your house. These are connected to the earth outside by a ground wire. When you plug most machines into a circuit, a ground from the machine connects with a ground wire in the circuit. If anything goes wrong, the ground wire sends the current safely into the earth.

## Circuit breaker
A safety device that prevents damage by electricity

If an electrical machine goes wrong, it may begin to draw a large current from the supply. The extra flow of electricity through the wires to the machine could cause a fire. Houses often contain circuit breakers that automatically cut off the supply to machines if the current becomes too great. Houses and machines may also contain **fuses**. A fuse contains a thin wire through which electricity passes. The wire melts and cuts off the supply if the current becomes too great.

## Impedance
The opposition of a circuit to an alternating current

The impedance of an electrical circuit determines the amount of an alternating current flowing through the circuit. This is similar to the way in which resistance affects the amount of direct current flowing through a circuit. Impedance is measured in ohms.

Local grid

Cables below ground

Substation

Transformer "steps down" the voltage

### Electricity to your home
*The grid takes electricity from the power station to a substation, where a transformer reduces the voltage so that it is suitable for use in the home.*

Power point

Fuse box or circuit breaker

Ground

### See also
Alternating current 104 • Capacitor 106
Diode 114 • Direct current 104
Electric motor 112 • Electromagnet 101
Magnetic field 100 • Nuclear reactor 40
Ohm 105 • Resistance 105

# Electrical machines

Many of our machines spring into action at the flick of a switch. But electricity, either from batteries or the household supply, not only gets machines moving – it can also enable machines to perform very precise sets of actions.

Terminal

Battery

The coil of wire is a rotor

The coil of copper wire rotates in the magnetic field of the bar magnets

Circuit wires run beneath the board and emerge at brushes

## Electric motor

**A machine that uses electricity to produce movement**

An electric motor basically contains a coil of wire suspended in the magnetic field ▦ of a magnet or electromagnet ▦. When an electric current flows through the coil, it produces its own magnetic field. The two fields push or pull on each other so that the coil rotates and drives the shaft of the motor. The rotating coil is called a **rotor**, or **armature**, and the stationary magnet or electromagnet is called a **stator**. Many motors contain **brushes**, which feed current to the rotating coil. A device called a **commutator** connects the coil and brushes. It changes the direction of the current every half-turn, which is necessary to keep the coil turning continuously. Changing the current's direction reverses the forces acting on each side of the coil, so that the coil is pushed upward on one side and then pulled down on the other side.

Strong bar magnet

The ends of the wire coil run along the shaft to the electrical contacts, or brushes

Mounting allows coil to rotate freely

## Induction motor

**An electric motor that works by electromagnetic induction**

Inside an induction motor is a rotating cylinder containing metal bars. This cylinder is surrounded by electromagnets. An alternating current goes to the electromagnets, which produce a changing magnetic field. Electromagnetic induction ▦ occurs, and the magnetic field generates a current in the metal bars of the cylinder. This current produces its own magnetic field. The two fields interact, pushing or pulling on each other so that the cylinder rotates. If the cylinder is connected to a shaft or flywheel, it can be used to power a machine.

The strong bar magnet is a stator

Electrical contacts form brushes

### Basic electric motor
*Current flows when the free ends of the wire coil touch the brushes. The curved brushes act as a simple commutator. They do not form a complete circle, so the circuit is broken each time the coil is vertical. The coil's momentum carries it on just far enough for each end of the wire to touch the other brush, completing the circuit and reversing current. The repeated making and breaking of the circuit keeps the coil turning.*

## Stepper motor

**An electric motor that rotates by exact amounts**

Cameras and computer disk drives contain parts that need to move with very precise actions. Such parts are moved by stepper motors, which are controlled by electrical signals. A signal goes to a coil around a cylindrical magnet. The coil generates a magnetic field that makes the magnet rotate a certain distance, but no farther.

# Linear motor

An electric motor that moves in a line instead of rotating

A linear motor is a form of induction motor that moves along a metal track. The motor contains electromagnets that generate a magnetic field. This induces a current in the track, which produces its own magnetic field. The two magnetic fields interact to move the motor along the track. Linear motors drive magnetic levitation ▪ trains.

# Relay

An electrical device that switches a current on and off

A machine driven by a powerful electric motor requires a large current. A relay enables a person to turn the machine on and off in safety, using a simple switch that uses a small current. The simple switch sends the small current to a relay. The relay contains an electromagnet or an electronic part that closes a heavy-duty switch, completing the circuit and sending a powerful current to operate the machine.

*Floating train*
*Electromagnets enable this magnetic levitation train in Sydney, Australia, to travel a few millimeters above the track. Linear motors propel the train forward.*

# Electric bell

A bell that rings continuously when its button is pressed

The button of an electric doorbell is a switch. When you press the button, it sends an electric current to the bell, making it ring. The current causes an electromagnet inside the bell to generate a magnetic field. This field pulls a hammer forward, so that it strikes the bell. As it moves, the hammer breaks the circuit. This cuts off the current, so that the magnetic pull ceases. A spring pulls the hammer back to its original position, allowing the current to flow again. The bell keeps ringing because this series of actions is repeated over and over again, for as long as you keep pressing the button.

# Superconductivity

The ability to conduct electricity without resistance

When a metal is cooled almost to absolute zero ▪, it loses its electrical resistance ▪ and becomes a **superconductor**. A very strong electric current can flow in a superconductor, enabling electromagnets made of superconductors to generate very powerful magnetic fields. Superconductors are used in magnetic levitation trains as well as in scientific equipment. Some new ceramic materials become superconducting at temperatures of about −238°F (−150°C), well above absolute zero. These new materials may make superconductivity more practical, leading to powerful machines that use less energy.

*Electromagnets*

*Make-and-break circuit contact*

*Hammer*

*Bell*

**Electric bell**
*Electromagnets pull the hammer forward to strike the bell, breaking the circuit. It then springs back, completing the circuit.*

# Metal detector

A device that locates buried metal

A metal detector contains a coil of wire called a **search coil**. An electric current flows through the search coil to produce a magnetic field. When this field enters a metal object hidden underground, electromagnetic induction causes electric currents called **eddy currents** to flow in the metal. The eddy currents produce another magnetic field, which induces an electric signal in the detector's search coil. The signal flashes a light, gives a reading on a meter, or produces a sound in earphones to indicate a find.

## See also

Absolute zero 92 • Electromagnet 101
Electromagnetic induction 110
Magnetic field 100
Magnetic levitation 101
Resistance 105

# Electronics

Machines such as computers, automatic cameras, and television sets perform amazing feats of calculation, control, and communication. Electronics enables these machines to work. It is the only technology capable of the fast and complex operations that are needed.

## Electronics

The branch of science that deals with electrical signals

The numbers on a calculator, the sounds coming from a tape player or a radio, and the pictures on a television set are all formed by electrical signals. The signals represent the numbers, sounds, and pictures. They consist of groups of electrons ■ traveling at very high speed through circuits that contain electronic components such as transistors. The components are made of semiconductors or vacuum tubes ■, which vary the flow of electrons through them to produce and process the signals.

## Doping

Adding another substance to a semiconductor

Very small amounts of other substances can be added to semiconductors in order to give them particular electrical properties. For example, an **n-type semiconductor** contains a substance called a **donor**, which provides extra electrons. And a **p-type semiconductor** contains a substance called an **acceptor**, which takes up electrons, leaving spaces for electrons called **holes**. The extra electrons and holes are called **carriers** or **charge carriers**, because they can move through the semiconductor, transferring an electric charge as they move.

## Semiconductor

A material that varies in electrical conductivity

Most electronic components, such as diodes and transistors, are made of a semiconductor, such as silicon. The semiconductor can change its ability to conduct electricity. It may pass a large or small electric current, or it may block the current. This allows semiconductors to produce and process electrical signals.

## Diode

An electronic component that can either pass or block a current

A diode contains small pieces of p-type and n-type semiconductors joined together. Electrons move easily across the junction from the electron-rich n-type region to holes in the p-type region, but not in the reverse direction. The diode therefore passes a current flowing in one direction and blocks a current flowing the other way. A diode can be used as a type of converter ■ called a rectifier.

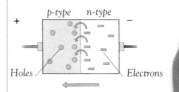

*How a diode works*
*A steady stream of electrons flows across the junction from the n-type region to the p-type region. But if the current is reversed, the electrons stop.*

## Thermistor

An electronic component that detects heat

A thermistor contains a semiconductor that releases electrons when it gets hotter. This decreases its resistance, so that the current flowing through the semiconductor increases. Most temperature gauges use thermistors to measure heat.

## Flip-flop

An electronic component that stores an electrical signal

A flip-flop is also called a **bistable circuit**. In a computer, electrical signals in binary code go to a set of flip-flops. Logic gates in the flip-flops change so that the signals are stored until they are needed.

## Light-emitting diode (LED)

An electronic component that emits light

An LED is a diode that gives out light or infrared rays ■ when electrons enter holes as a current flows through the diode. LEDs consume less current and last longer than light bulbs, so they are often used as warning or safety lights. Remote control units contain LEDs that convert electrical signals into invisible infrared control signals.

*Light-emitting diode (LED)*

**A diode and an LED in series**
*The LED lights up only if the current flows in the right direction. When the current is reversed, the diode prevents the current from passing and the LED does not light up.*

*Diode*

*Battery pack*

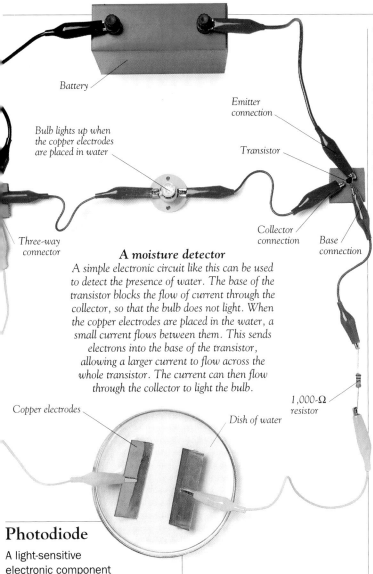

Battery

Emitter
connection

Bulb lights up when
the copper electrodes
are placed in water

Transistor

Three-way
connector

Collector
connection

Base
connection

## A moisture detector

*A simple electronic circuit like this can be used to detect the presence of water. The base of the transistor blocks the flow of current through the collector, so that the bulb does not light. When the copper electrodes are placed in the water, a small current flows between them. This sends electrons into the base of the transistor, allowing a larger current to flow across the whole transistor. The current can then flow through the collector to light the bulb.*

Copper electrodes

Dish of water

$1,000\text{-}\Omega$
resistor

## Transistor

**An electronic component that switches or amplifies a current**

Collector

Base

Emitter

Transistors are important components in computers and amplifiers. A transistor contains three pieces of semiconductor in a p-n-p or n-p-n arrangement. The central piece is called the **base**, and the outer pieces are the **emitter** and **collector**. A main current flows through the whole transistor, while a small control signal goes to the base. The control signal either sends electrons into the base or attracts them away from it. This movement of electrons affects the passage of current through the whole transistor. The base is able to pass or block the current, switching the transistor on or off. It may also vary the current so that the transistor amplifies the control signal.

## Photodiode

**A light-sensitive electronic component**

Photodiodes detect light and infrared signals and convert them into electrical signals. When a ray of light or an infrared ray strikes the diode, it frees some electrons in the semiconductor. These move across the junction between the n-type material and the p-type material, allowing a current to flow through it. A photodiode is used as a light detector in a compact disc player ■. A **charge-coupled device (CCD)** is an array of photodiodes. It is used in a video camera to convert an image into an electrical picture signal.

## Silicon-controlled rectifier (SCR)

**An electronic component that controls an electric current**

An SCR or **thyristor** contains four pieces of p-type and n-type semiconductors in a p-n-p-n arrangement. A small signal fed to the inner pieces of the SCR controls the flow of a large current through it. SCRs are used in dimmer switches for electric lights, in speed regulators for electrical appliances, and in relays ■.

## Logic gate

**An electronic component that processes electrical signals**

The microprocessor ■ of a computer contains logic gates, which are made of various arrangements of transistors. A logic gate receives electrical signals in binary code ■. The transistors switch on or off to produce another binary signal as a result. Sets of logic gates add up numbers in calculators and computers.

### See also

Binary code 123

Compact disc player 126

Converter 110 • Electron 34

Infrared rays 75 • Microprocessor 122

Relay 113 • Vacuum tubes 116

*Continued on next page ➤*

## ELECTRONICS SYMBOLS

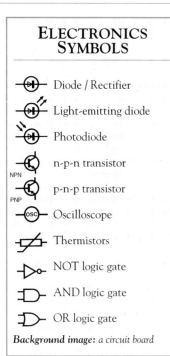

— Diode / Rectifier

— Light-emitting diode

— Photodiode

— n-p-n transistor
NPN

— p-n-p transistor
PNP

—(OSC)— Oscilloscope

— Thermistors

—|>o— NOT logic gate

—|D— AND logic gate

—|D>— OR logic gate

*Background image: a circuit board*

# Printed circuit

**A board on which electronic components are mounted**

Electronic machines contain microchips and other components connected in complex circuits. The components plug into a printed circuit board. The board is printed with metal lines that conduct electricity and connect the components.

# Oscillator

**A device that converts direct current (DC) into alternating current (AC)**

Electronic components in an oscillator produce a current that alternates ■ at a particular frequency ■. Oscillators generate high-frequency electrical signals in radios, radar, and computers.

# Integrated circuit

**A complete set of electronic components in one unit**

An integrated circuit is also called a **microchip**, **silicon chip**, or **chip**. It consists of a single piece of semiconductor ■, usually silicon, that contains thousands of linked components, such as transistors ■ and diodes ■. A microchip is made by doping ■ tiny regions of **wafer**, a thin slice of semiconductor, to form all the components. A tiny integrated circuit can carry out many complex actions – so many, in fact, that the circuit of a whole computer may be connected in one chip.

# Vacuum tube

**An electronic component in a sealed glass tube**

A vacuum tube is also called a **valve** or **tube**. Vacuum tubes were the first electronic components; they are still used. They perform the same actions as diodes and transistors. A vacuum tube contains metal electrodes sealed in a vacuum inside a glass tube. Electrons ■ flow across the vacuum between the electrodes to process electrical signals.

*Cathode ray oscilloscope*
*The electron beam can be deflected vertically by charging the Y-plates, or horizontally by charging the X-plates. The brightness of the spot on the screen is controlled by the grid.*

# John Fleming
English engineer
(1849–1945)

Fleming founded electronics in 1904, when he invented the vacuum tube. This tube was a kind of diode. A team led by the American engineer **William Shockley** (1910–89) invented the transistor in 1947. This led to the development of microchips and compact electronic machines.

*Fleming's vacuum tube*

# Cathode ray tube (CRT)

**A tube in which a beam of electrons lights up a screen**

Television sets, radar screens, and computer monitors contain a CRT. In a CRT, a filament is heated so that it gives off **cathode rays**, which are beams of electrons. The electrons move from one end of the tube and strike a screen at the other end, showing up as a spot of light. When an electrical signal is fed to metal plates or coils inside the tube, it produces electric or magnetic fields. The fields deflect the beam so that the spot of light moves over the screen to form a picture. An **oscilloscope** is a CRT that shows the changing voltage of an electrical signal as a curved line on a screen.

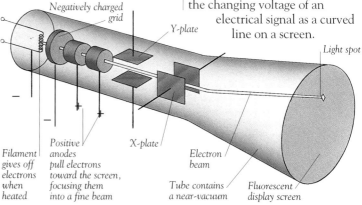

*Negatively charged grid*

*Y-plate*

*Light spot*

*Filament gives off electrons when heated*

*Positive anodes pull electrons toward the screen, focusing them into a fine beam*

*X-plate*

*Electron beam*

*Tube contains a near-vacuum*

*Fluorescent display screen*

◄ Continued from previous page

# Computers

Playing games, forecasting weather, guiding aircraft – these are just some of the many things a computer can be instructed to do. In each activity, the computer processes information according to strict rules.

**Computer design**
*This computer model shows the flow of air over the wings of an airplane. Computer modeling can effectively test new designs, making it unnecessary to build expensive prototypes.*

**Supercomputers**
*Supercomputers, such as this CRAY X-MP/48, can carry out millions of instructions each second.*

## Computer

An electronic machine that handles information or data

When a computer receives data, such as a collection of names, it can process the data and produce a result, such as a list of names in alphabetical order. A computer may also store the data and the result. **Hardware** is machinery, such as computers and printers ▪. The instructions, or programs ▪, that enable computers to perform tasks are called **software**. A **personal computer** (PC), or microcomputer ▪, is a computer that is used by only one person at a time, such as a home computer. A large computer used by many people at once is a **mainframe**. A **supercomputer** is a powerful computer used to perform complex tasks, such as weather forecasting or designing new cars.

## Information technology

The use of machines to handle, process, and transmit information

Many kinds of electronic and telecommunications ▪ equipment, including computers, are used to handle and transmit information. Collecting, handling, and storing information is called **data processing**. A business, for example, may use a data processing computer to work out its accounts.

## Real time

Getting instant results

Some computers take a few seconds, or even minutes, to react to a set of instructions. A computer that gives you instant results as you feed information into it works in real time. Real-time working is important in computers that must react immediately to a constant flow of information, such as computers that navigate aircraft.

**Computer trainer**
*A flight simulator helps pilots learn to fly without leaving the ground. It simulates most aspects of flying an airliner.*

## Parallel computer

A powerful new kind of computer

A computer splits a task up into many small operations. Most computers carry out the operations one after another. A parallel computer performs whole groups of operations at the same time, enabling it to work much faster. A **neural network** is an experimental computer designed to imitate the workings of a human brain. The parts of the computer that process information are linked together in a similar way to your brain's nerve cells, or neurons.

## Artificial intelligence (AI)

The ability of a computer to think and work like a human being

A computer that has some degree of artificial intelligence can assess its own performance and work out ways to improve it. A computer can be programmed to play a game of chess, for example, but an intelligent computer can learn from each game it plays, so that it is able to play better the next time. At present, no computer has full artificial intelligence. Artificial intelligence research has produced speech recognition ▪ and expert systems ▪.

### See also

# Computer software

Without software, a computer is just a useless box of electronic components. But with the huge variety of computer programs that are available, it becomes a machine that can do almost anything.

**See also**

Binary code 123 • Disk 120
Memory 121 • Microchip 116
Microcomputer 120 • Modem 121

## Program

A set of instructions used by a computer

The program contains all the instructions needed for a computer to carry out a particular task, such as word processing or playing a game. The instructions are in the form of electrical signals that control the computer. The signals that make up a program are stored on a disk ▦ or microchip ▦. A diagram called a **flowchart** shows how the instructions are arranged in a computer program.

## File

A piece of information used by a computer

A file may be a list, a document, a picture, some computer music, and so on. Each file has its own name.

*How this book was prepared*
*The author's text was sent to the publisher's office on floppy disks. The disks were then fed into a computer and the text was edited in a word processing program.*

## Computer language

A code used to write a program

The instructions that control a computer consist of long sets of code numbers called **machine language**. It is difficult to write a computer program in machine language, so programmers use easier codes called computer languages. An **assembly language** uses abbreviations for the actions that the computer carries out. A **high-level language** uses whole words to describe the actions, such as REPEAT and NEXT. These languages include **BASIC**, which stands for "beginners all-purpose symbolic instruction code," **Pascal**, **C**, and **COBOL**. A program called a **compiler** or an **interpreter** converts instructions written in high-level language into machine code instructions.

## Word processor

A computer program that helps you to write letters and documents

Once you have typed some text into a computer, a word processor can then line up the words to form columns and check the spelling. You can also change any words and insert or remove passages. When all is perfect, the document can be printed. A **desktop publishing (DTP)** program enables you to produce documents of high quality that include pictures. A microcomputer ▦ with a word processing program is also known as a word processor.

## Database

A program that assembles a collection of information

A database contains a particular set of information, such as details of all the books that you can buy. It is stored on disk or CD-ROM. The computer allows you to get information from a database in several ways. For example, it could give you a list of all the books on a particular subject, or all the books written by one author.

## Object-oriented programming (OOP)

A method of writing better computer programs

Many computer programs use very long sets of instructions. These are likely to contain some errors that could make the computer go wrong. OOP is a way of writing programs in which the programmer has to describe real objects and events. It helps to reduce errors, because the programmer is more likely to spot any mistakes in the program.

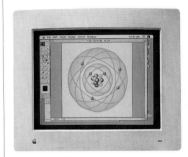

*Computer graphics*
*Some of the illustrations in this book were drawn with computer software. This picture shows the artwork of the atom from pages 34 and 35. Images drawn on computers are called computer graphics.*

## Expert system

A program that contains knowledge about a particular subject

Using an expert system is like consulting a human expert on a particular subject. It can use the information it contains to answer any questions you have on that subject. For example, a medical expert system can diagnose an illness from symptoms that occur.

## Speech recognition

A way of feeding information into a computer with the human voice

If a microphone is connected to a computer, a speech recognition program is able to recognize spoken words and obey their instructions.

## Virus

A program that destroys information stored in a computer

A virus can get into a computer from a floppy disk containing the virus program or via a modem █. It may enter the computer's memory █ and make it destroy all the information it holds, or it may copy itself again and again, so that it uses up all the memory. Other computers may be "infected" with the virus via networks or disks. Antivirus programs check computers and disks for viruses.

**Desktop publishing**
*When the text has been edited and the pictures chosen, the pages are designed with a desktop publishing program. The position of the text and pictures can be altered until the page looks just right.*

# CONCEIVING THE COMPUTER

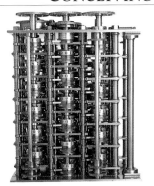

**Babbage's difference engine**
*It was while Babbage was building this calculating machine that he had the idea for his mechanical computer.*

## Charles Babbage

English mathematician (1791–1871)

In 1823, Babbage started building a mechanical calculator, called the difference engine, to calculate tables of figures. He also planned to build a machine that he could program to perform different kinds of calculations. Babbage never built this machine, called the analytical engine, but it would have been like a mechanical computer. The mathematician **Ada Lovelace** (1815–52) also worked on the analytical engine.

## Spreadsheet

A program that performs calculations on a table of numbers

A spreadsheet displays a grid of rows and columns. The computer does calculations with numbers placed in the rows and columns. If one number is changed, the computer recalculates to show how the change affects other numbers and to give new totals. Spreadsheets are mainly used in business to display and forecast sales and profits.

## John von Neumann

American mathematician (1903–57)

The first electronic computers were not easy to reprogram and give new tasks. Von Neumann, who was born in Hungary, was the first to suggest that the program to operate the computer should be stored in the computer's memory. The computer could then switch quickly from one task to another. All modern computers work in this way.

## Alan Turing

English mathematician (1912–54)

One of the first electronic computers, called Colossus, was built in Britain in 1943 to crack enemy codes. Turing was one of the team that developed it. He also made important advances in the theory of computers. The **Turing test** is a rule used to find out whether a computer can think. Turing believed that a computer can think if the way it performs a task cannot be told apart from the way a human being performs the same task.

**Counting the cost**
*The publisher uses a spreadsheet to calculate the cost of the book and how many copies to print.*

# Computer hardware

A computer has four basic parts, or units. You feed information into the computer with an input unit, such as a keyboard. The processing unit performs a task and then shows you the result on an output unit, such as a screen. The memory unit stores information and instructions.

## Monitor

A computer screen

A monitor receives signals from the computer and forms a picture. It works in the same way as a television receiver ▪. Some computers have liquid crystal display ▪ screens. A computer screen is also called a **visual display unit (VDU)** or **cathode ray tube (CRT)**.

## Microcomputer

A compact computer

A microcomputer basically consists of a keyboard, a monitor, and a box containing the memory and processing units. A **peripheral** is a further device, such as a printer, that can be connected to the microcomputer. A microcomputer is often called a **PC**, which stands for **personal computer**. A **laptop** or **notebook** is a portable microcomputer.

## Disk

A device that stores information and computer programs

A computer disk, or **disc**, is usually coated with a magnetic material. It records information and programs as magnetic signals in binary code ▪. The disk is placed in a **disk drive**. The drive has a **read-write head** that can move to different parts of the disk and store or "write" new information on the disk, or retrieve or "read" information already there. A **floppy disk** is a single flexible disk housed in a plastic or card case. A **hard disk** is a set of rigid disks housed in a sealed box. An **optical disk** is another kind of computer disk. Information is retrieved from it using a laser beam. Sometimes the laser also writes information on the disk. One form of optical disk is the **CD-ROM**, which is a compact disc ▪ used to store very large amounts of information, including pictures and sounds.

*Computer hardware*
*This picture shows a typical microcomputer –
with its monitor, keyboard, and mouse – linked to a laser printer. This book was designed and edited using such equipment.*

*Color monitor*

*Inside the computer are the processing unit and the hard and floppy disk drives that enable it to work*

*Box of floppy disks*

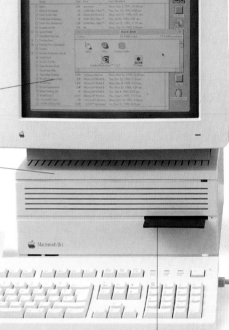

Macintosh IIci

*Keyboard*

*Disks are fed into the floppy disk drive*

*Sector boundary*

*Concentric tracks*

*Sector*

*Recording surface*

***Floppy disk***
*On a floppy disk, information is ordered into tracks and sectors, rather like a filing system. To retrieve information, the disk drive moves the read-write head to the correct sector and track, and rotates the disk. A hard disk works in a similar way.*

## Keyboard

A device that has a set of keys to feed information into a computer

Most keyboards are **alphanumeric keyboards**. The keys are marked with **characters**, which are letters, numbers from 0 to 9, and symbols such as ? and &. Pressing the keys operates switches that feed letters and numbers into the computer. **Function keys** make the computer perform set tasks. The tasks depend on the program ▪ used. A **concept keyboard** uses pictures instead of letters, numbers, and symbols.

# Interface

An electrical component that connects a computer to another piece of equipment, or peripheral

An interface sends signals from a computer to operate an external device such as a printer. A **serial interface** sends signals along a single wire one after the other. A **parallel interface** sends groups of signals along a set of wires at the same time. A **port** is the socket on the computer into which you plug a cable to a printer or other external device. When a computer starts to communicate with another piece of equipment, it is called **handshaking**.

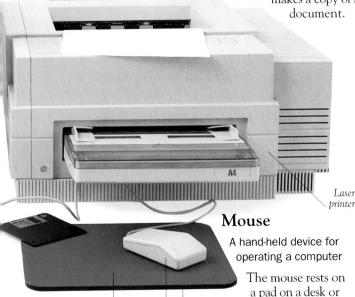

Mouse pad | Mouse

Laser printer

# Memory

The part of a computer that stores information and programs

If you type a list of names and addresses into a computer, you can store the list in the computer's memory. You can then retrieve the list from the memory and use it again at any time. The memory also holds the programs that you use to make the computer carry out its tasks. The memory consists of microchips ▪ and disks.

# Printer

A device that prints information produced by a computer

An **impact printer** works rather like a typewriter. Its print head has raised letters and numbers that print onto paper when the print head strikes an inked ribbon. A **dot-matrix printer** has a print head with a set of raised pins. As the pins strike the ribbon, they print letters or numbers in the form of patterns of dots. An **ink-jet printer** works by squirting a jet of ink through fine nozzles. A **laser printer** uses a laser to form an image, which is then printed in the same way that a photocopier ▪ makes a copy of a document.

# Mouse

A hand-held device for operating a computer

The mouse rests on a pad on a desk or table. As you move the mouse on the pad, it causes a pointer on the screen to move in the same direction. Inside the mouse is a ball that rotates as the mouse moves over the pad. The ball's movement sends signals to the computer to move the pointer in the same way. The screen displays a number of **icons**, which are small pictures that represent files ▪, programs, or other operations. Moving the pointer to an icon and clicking a button on the mouse opens a file or starts a program.

# Data capture

Feeding information into a computer

A keyboard is just one of several devices used for data capture. **Optical character recognition (OCR)** uses an optical scanner, which "reads" a document such as a page of a book or a magazine article and feeds it into a computer. A **digitizer** feeds in a picture such as a photograph or a drawing. All these devices convert the information into binary code.

# Computer network

A group of computers that are connected together

Several computers in a network can exchange information, or make use of a powerful central computer or a central database. A **terminal** is a keyboard and screen linked to a network.

# Electronic mail

Messages sent by computer

Messages typed into a computer can be sent through computer networks. The messages travel along telephone lines, and a central computer stores them until the user requests them.

# Modem

A device that connects a computer to the telephone system

A modem enables computers that are far apart to exchange information along a telephone line. Modems convert the computer signal into a telephone signal and back again. Modem means modulator-demodulator.

---

## See also

Continued on next page ➤

## Operating system

Instructions that a computer needs in order to work

An operating system is needed to start up a computer. It is a special program ▦ that enables a computer to perform basic tasks, such as accepting data from a keyboard ▦, storing it in the memory ▦, and displaying it on the screen. The computer is then able to run other programs. The operating system may be stored in a microchip ▦ in the computer, or on a disk ▦.

## Buffer

A microchip in a computer that stores data temporarily

A buffer holds data that is waiting to be used by a computer or a piece of computer equipment, and sends the data on as soon as it is needed. For example, the instructions you type into a microcomputer are usually held in a buffer until you press the "enter" or "return" key. Other devices, such as printers, also have buffers. When a document is to be printed, the instructions and information are passed from the computer to the printer, where they are stored in a buffer. This allows the computer to perform other tasks while the document is being printed.

## Microprocessor

A part of a computer that performs tasks and calculates results

All computers have a microchip called a **central processing unit**, or **CPU**. In a microcomputer ▦, the CPU is called a microprocessor. The CPU receives data from the computer's keyboard or memory. By following the instructions of a program, the CPU processes the data and displays the result on the screen. It may add up numbers, for example, and display the total.

## Read-only memory (ROM)

The part of a computer's memory whose contents cannot be changed

ROM is **permanent memory**, which retains information when the computer is switched off. It consists of microchips inside the computer. Once data has been recorded onto a ROM chip, it cannot normally be altered or removed, and can only be read. The content of the ROM chip is usually fixed at the time the computer is made. In a microcomputer, for example, the ROM may store important programs, such as the operating system. A **PROM** is a **programmable read-only memory**. Data is written onto a blank PROM by the user, after which it cannot be altered. An **EPROM** (**erasable programmable read-only memory**) consists of microchips whose contents can be changed by the user.

### A computer dissected
*Here is the computer on page 120 with its cover removed. Some parts, such as the clock and the buffers, are too small to be seen and occur in a number of places.*

## Clock

Part of a computer that sends out an electronic control signal

The microchips in a computer are operated by a control signal. The clock produces this signal, which consists of electric pulses that pass at a constant rate. The clock ensures that all the computer's components are working in step with each other. The signal is measured in megahertz or MHz (millions of pulses per second). A computer with a faster clock than another computer is more powerful and can perform tasks more quickly.

Screen socket

Mains supply socket

Fan

***Power supply unit***
*The power supply unit (PSU) enables the computer to be connected to the electricity supply. It also contains a fan to keep the PSU cool.*

Speaker

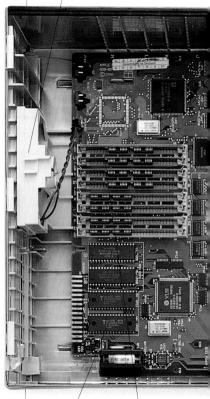

Read-only memory (ROM) microchips

Random-access memory (RAM) microchips

***Hard disk drive***
*This drive reads and writes information on a hard disk. Its storage capacity is 40 Mb.*

◄ *Continued from previous page*

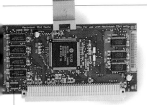

*This circuit board is called an accelerator, because it makes the computer work faster*

*The bus carries signals from one part of the computer to another*

*This circuit board, called a video card, controls the operation of the computer screen*

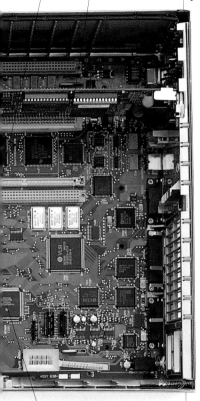

*The central processing unit (CPU) processes data according to instructions in the computer program*

**Floppy disk drive**
*This drive can read and write information on floppy disks. Its storage capacity is 1.44 Mb.*

## Random-access memory (RAM)

**The part of a computer's memory whose contents can be changed**

RAM consists of integrated circuits, or microchips, in the computer. These chips store data and programs that are fed into the computer on a disk, or typed in using the keyboard. The data can be altered and new data and programs can be added at any time. This type of memory is called random-access memory because data can be retrieved from any part of it, in any order. **Dynamic RAM**, or **DRAM**, is a microchip that needs a constant signal to hold data and programs. **Static RAM**, or **SRAM**, does not need a constant signal. RAM may be **volatile**, which means that the contents of the memory are lost when the computer is switched off.

## Binary code

**The code that computers use**

Many different kinds of data go into and come out of a computer. They include words, numbers, pictures, and music. The computer has to convert any data that is not already in the form of numerals – such as letters, the parts of a drawing, and musical notes – into code numbers. The letter A, for example, becomes 65. The computer then converts these code numbers into binary numbers ■, such as 01000001, which is the binary number for 65. The binary code consists of a signal made up of pulses of electricity that are on (1) or off (0). The number 13 becomes the binary code on-on-off-on, because its binary number is 1101. Microchips in the computer then process and store these electrical code signals.

## Bit

**A numeral in a binary number used by a computer**

A computer uses electrical signals that are groups of on-off pulses. A group of pulses represents a binary number made up of the numerals 1 and 0. Each numeral is called a bit, so 1101 is a four-bit number. A powerful microcomputer processes signals with 16-bit or 32-bit numbers. The word bit is actually short for the term "binary digit."

## Byte

**A binary code signal with eight bits**

When a computer stores data, it converts the data into a long sequence of binary numbers. These binary numbers are changed into signals in binary code. Each number has eight bits and is called a byte. The capacity of a memory unit, such as a RAM or a disk, is measured by the total number of bytes that it can store. This is given in **kilobytes** (K/Kb/KB), which each contain 1,024 bytes, and in **megabytes** (M/Mb/MB), which each contain 1,048,576 bytes. A computer may process bytes in groups called **words**. Each word contains two or more bytes.

## Bus

**A set of wires or metal strips that carries signals from one part of a computer to another**

A bus is a kind of communication route within a computer, enabling electrical signals in binary code to travel from place to place. In a microcomputer, buses connect all the components to the CPU.

### See also

# Printing & photography

Written words and pictures bring us much of our knowledge of the world, and especially of the past. Today, printing and photography let this knowledge reach millions of people.

## Printing

The process of making copies of text and pictures using ink

A **printing press** contains a printing plate, upon which are text or pictures. Ink is applied to the plate, and the letters or pictures take up the ink. Paper, or another material, is then pressed against the plate, and the ink transfers to the paper to produce a copy of the text or pictures. **Color printing** usually uses four plates that print a picture in black, yellow, cyan, and magenta inks. The four colors merge to give a full-color picture.

## Gravure

A method of printing using recessed letters and pictures

The letters and pictures are etched into the printing plate. The plate is inked and then wiped, so that ink collects only in the recessed parts.

## Letterpress

A method of printing using raised letters and pictures

A letterpress printing plate has raised letters and pictures, so that ink collects only on the raised parts of the plate.

## Photocopier

A machine that makes instant copies of documents

Inside a photocopier is a lens that projects an image of a document onto a metal drum. This causes a charge of static electricity ▪ to form on the parts of the drum where the image is dark. The drum rotates, and dark powder is applied to it. The powder sticks only to the charged parts of the drum. The powder then transfers to a piece of paper pressed against the drum, forming an image of the document on the paper.

## Photography

The process of recording an image with a camera

When you take a photograph with a camera ▪, the camera lens ▪ forms an image of a scene on light-sensitive photographic film inside the camera. The film is then developed in a solution of chemicals, and the image appears on the film. A **color slide** is developed color film that shows the scene as it was photographed. Most films are developed to form a **negative**, an image of the scene in which light and dark and the colors are reversed. Prints are made from a negative by projecting an image of the negative on to photographic printing paper. This light-sensitive paper is similar to the film in the camera. Developing the paper reverses the negative, revealing the original scene again.

*Light-sensitive film*

***Taking the picture***
*Light is briefly focused through the lens onto a section of the film inside the camera.*

*Container for spool and chemicals*

*Mixing jar*  *Chemicals*

*Timer*

*Spool*

***Developing the film***
*The exposed film is transferred onto a spool and developed in a chemical solution for a set amount of time.*

## Lithography

A method of printing using flat letters and pictures

In lithography, the printing plate is smooth and the letters and pictures are formed of lacquer. The plate is first wetted, and the lacquered parts reject the water. The plate is then inked. The lacquered parts take up the ink and the wet surface rejects the ink, leaving only the letters and pictures covered by ink.

*Spool*

*Negative film*

***The negative***
*The film is then placed in another chemical solution called a fixer. The resulting negative film is washed in water to remove all the chemicals and is then hung up to dry.*

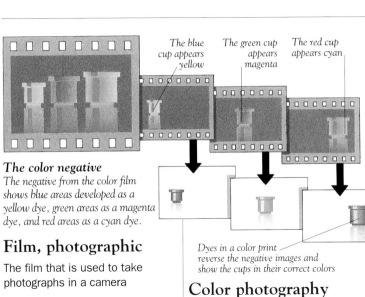

The blue cup appears yellow

The green cup appears magenta

The red cup appears cyan

### Color photography

This illustration shows what happens if you photograph blue, green, and red cups. A color film has three layers that react to blue, green, and red light. It gives a negative in which these colours show up as yellow, magenta, and cyan. Color photographic paper has the same three layers. Making a color print reverses the process and gives the correct colors again.

### The color negative
The negative from the color film shows blue areas developed as a yellow dye, green areas as a magenta dye, and red areas as a cyan dye.

# Film, photographic

The film that is used to take photographs in a camera

A black-and-white film contains a layer of silver compounds ▦. When you take a photograph, an image forms as the film is exposed to light. The compounds struck by light begin to change to silver. Placing the film in a **developer**, a solution of chemical compounds, completes this change. Another solution, a **fixer**, dissolves the unchanged compounds. This gives a negative, with dark silver in the parts of the image that were light. The same process is used to make a print from the negative on photographic paper, which also contains silver compounds.

### The enlarger
The small image on the negative must be enlarged to give a good-size print. A light shines through the negative, and a lens projects a larger image onto photographic paper.

Housing for light

Negative

Height control

The lens magnifies the image

Enlarger

Timer

Photographic printing paper

Dyes in a color print reverse the negative images and show the cups in their correct colors

# Color photography

The process of making color prints and color slides

A **color film** has three separate layers of silver compounds. These are sensitive to the blue, green, and red light in the image. Developing a **color slide film** first changes the dark parts of the image into dark silver. The layers of silver are then replaced by yellow, magenta, and cyan dyes ▦, so that the film contains three images in these colors. These combine to give a full-color picture when you view a slide. A **color print film** is the same, except that the light parts of the image are changed into dyes instead of the dark parts. This gives a **color negative**, from which color prints are made on color photographic paper.

Bath of developer

Print

### Developing a print
Once it has been exposed to light from the enlarger, the paper is developed and fixed with chemicals (in the same way as a film) to reveal the image.

### The color print
The yellow light from the negative exposes layers in the paper sensitive to red and green. These are dyed cyan and magenta, which combine to produce blue. In the same way, the other cups appear in their proper colors.

# Instant photography

A method of producing photographs immediately after taking them

Some cameras use special film that is like a color slide film fixed to a plastic base. The plastic sheet emerges from the camera after pressing the shutter ▦ to take the picture, and a color photograph appears on the film only a minute later. The film contains chemicals; these are released as the film emerges and develop the picture.

### The final picture
After developing and fixing, the image produced on the paper is light in areas that were dark on the negative, and vice versa. The print is washed and dried, and the scene that was originally photographed is ready for the album.

# Sound recording

All methods of sound recording store an electrical signal, which comes from either a microphone or an electric musical instrument. The signal is then reproduced to power loudspeakers or earphones which play back the recorded sounds.

## Digital recording

A method of recording that converts sound into numbers

Compact discs and some cassette tapes are digital recordings. To make the recording, a computer measures the electrical signal from a microphone thousands of times each second. It reproduces the measurements as a series of numbers in binary code ▦, which consists of on-off pulses of electric current. The pulses are recorded on a magnetic tape called a **digital audio tape (DAT)** or a **digital compact cassette (DCC)** or on a compact disc. Digital recording is of very high quality, because it is easier to record the pulses of current than the signal itself.

### Recording sound
*Digital audio recording equipment produces very high-quality sound.*

## Analog recording

A method of recording that copies sound in another form

Many tapes and records are analog recordings. A magnetic tape records the changing electrical signal that comes from a microphone as a changing pattern of magnetism along the tape. On the surface of a vinyl record (such as an LP), the changing signal is stored as a wiggly groove. These are copies of the signal in another form. The copies are not exact, and analog recordings always have some background noise.

## Microphone

A device that changes sound into electric current

A microphone picks up the sound waves ▦ of music, speech, or other sounds. The energy in the sound waves changes rapidly, depending on the frequencies ▦ of the waves. The microphone converts the waves into an electrical signal that varies at the same frequencies as the sound waves.

*A microphone converts the sound of the girl's voice into an electrical signal*

*The DAT recorder records the signal as pulses of electric current*

*The pulses are stored on a DAT cassette*

## Record

A plastic disc that records sound as a spiral groove

To play a record, you place it on a revolving turntable and lower a sharp **stylus** into its groove. The stylus vibrates as the groove moves past it. The vibrations are turned into electrical signals, which are amplified and fed into loudspeakers to create sounds.

## Compact disc

A plastic disc that records sound as a series of tiny notches

A compact disc contains a spiral track of millions of tiny notches pressed into an aluminum layer that covers the disc. A layer of smooth, clear plastic covers and protects the aluminum. Inside a **compact disc player**, a laser ▦ beam scans the disc as it spins at high speed. The tiny notches alter the way the beam reflects from the surface of the shiny aluminum. A detector converts the changing reflections into electrical pulses. These are changed into electrical signals, which are amplified and fed into loudspeakers to produce sounds.

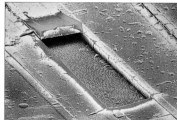

### Microscopic music
*This magnified picture of a compact disc shows the plastic coating peeled back to reveal the notched layer of aluminum.*

*The electric pulses are converted into notches on the surface of a compact disc*

# Amplifier

A machine that increases the strength of an electrical signal

The electrical signal from a microphone is very weak. An amplifier makes the signal much stronger so that it can power a loudspeaker and reproduce sound. The weak signal goes to the amplifier, which also gets a strong electric current from the household supply or from batteries. The amplifier changes the current into a strong copy of the weak signal, and this strong signal is sent to the loudspeaker. A **preamplifier** is a part of the amplifier containing volume and tone controls.

# Loudspeaker

A device that reproduces sound

Tape recorders and compact disc players, radios, television receivers, and stage sound systems have loudspeakers. Some machines have **earphones**, which are small loudspeakers that fit in the ears. A loudspeaker receives a strong electrical signal from an amplifier, and changes the signal into sound. In most loudspeakers, the signal goes to a coil of wire fixed to a large cone. The coil is suspended inside a magnet. The signal produces a changing magnetic field ■ in the coil, which moves to and fro and causes the cone to vibrate and produce sound waves.

*The compact disc player scans the disc with a laser beam, changing the pattern of notches into electrical signals*

# Stereophonic sound

Recorded sound that gives a sense of where the sound is coming from

Stereophonic sound, or **stereo**, requires two loudspeakers or earphones. The tape, record, or disc records a pair of electrical signals with different mixes of sounds. These go to the two loudspeakers. The sounds, such as different instruments, come from either loudspeaker or seem to come from a position in between.

# Magnetic tape

Metal-coated plastic tape on which sound is recorded as magnetism

The surface of magnetic tape can be magnetized and demagnetized. A **tape recorder** records either the electrical signal from a microphone in analog recording, or electric pulses in digital recording, as magnetic patterns along a reel of tape. On playback, the recorder changes these patterns back into electrical signals, which go to an amplifier and loudspeakers to reproduce the sound. A **cassette tape** is a small reel of tape in a container, and a **cassette recorder** records on and plays back cassette tapes.

*The loudspeaker changes the signal back into sound*

## See also

Binary code 123 • Frequency 71
Laser 82 • Magnetic field 100
Memory 121 • Sound wave 98
Telephone 128

# Thomas Alva Edison

American inventor (1847–1931)

Edison was the first to discover how to record sound. In 1877, he made a phonograph that recorded sound onto a drum covered in tinfoil. He also developed a microphone that improved the telephone ■ and a device that produced moving pictures. In 1879, both Edison and the English scientist **Joseph Swan** (1828–1914) invented the electric light bulb.

**Edison's phonograph, 1877**

# Synthesizer

An electronic musical instrument

A synthesizer makes sounds electronically. It can reproduce sounds of musical instruments or create new sounds. A **sampler** stores sounds as digital recordings in its memory ■. The sampler can then reproduce the sounds. It can also alter their pitch and duration.

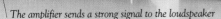

*The amplifier sends a strong signal to the loudspeaker* | *Cone*

# Telecommunications

Telecommunications play an important part in our lives. We can speak to people anywhere in the world on the telephone, while radio and television bring entertainment, sports, news, the arts, and education right into our homes.

## Telecommunications

**The methods used to send messages and information instantly over long distances**

Telephone, television, and radio are the main forms of telecommunications. They send, or **transmit**, sounds, written words, computer data, and pictures from place to place. The information is changed into electrical signals, light signals, or radio signals, which can all travel at high speed. Receivers turn the signals back into sounds, words, computer data, and pictures. When many transmitters and receivers of telecommunications are linked together, they form a **network**.

## Telephone

**A device that sends spoken messages between two people**

When you make a telephone call, you speak into the **mouthpiece** of the telephone. This contains a small microphone ▪, which changes the sound of your voice into an electrical signal. The signal travels via exchanges to the telephone of the person you are calling. When the person answers, a signal returns from the speaker's mouthpiece and goes to the **earpiece** of your telephone. This contains a small loudspeaker ▪, which changes the signal back into the sound of the speaker's voice.

## Cellular telephone

**A portable telephone**

A cellular telephone is a small radio transmitter and receiver. It sends and receives a call in the form of a radio signal. The signal goes to a nearby station in a network of stations that each serves an area called a **cell**. As a caller moves from one cell to the next, the telephone automatically connects to the next station.

Loudspeaker    Earpiece

Microphone    Mouthpiece

**Talking by telephone**
*The sound waves of your voice vibrate a thin metal disk in the microphone, altering the electrical signal sent by the telephone. A vibrating membrane in the loudspeaker of the receiving telephone converts the signal back into sound.*

## Exchange

**A center that connects many telephones together**

Telephone signals pass through a network of exchanges, which connect two telephones making a call. An electrical signal travels along wires to your telephone. But between exchanges the signal may be changed to a light signal, which travels along optical fibers ▪, or a radio signal, which may travel via a communications satellite ▪.

## Fax

**A machine that sends a copy of a document by telephone**

Fax is short for **facsimile**, which means a replica of something. A fax machine scans a document and changes the light and dark parts into an electrical signal. The signal travels by telephone lines to the receiving fax machine, which prints the light and dark parts on paper to give a copy of the document. A document can also be typed into a **telex** machine, which sends an electrical signal by telephone to another telex that prints out the document.

# Radio

A way of sending and receiving sounds without using wires

A person on the radio speaks into a microphone, which changes the sound into an electrical signal. The radio station changes this signal into radio waves ▪, which it sends out, or **broadcasts**, from a transmitter. An **antenna (aerial)** picks up the radio waves. It is connected to a radio receiver, which changes the waves back into sound so that you can hear the person speaking.

# Radio receiver

A machine that detects radio waves and produces sound

Many different carrier waves from different radio stations strike the antenna of a receiver. The waves change to weak electrical signals in the antenna. These signals go to the **tuner** in the receiver, which selects the signal coming from the particular station you wish to hear. **Demodulation** changes the signal to an electrical signal that is identical to that produced by the microphone at the radio station. This signal finally goes to an amplifier ▪ and then a loudspeaker, which reproduces the sound of the speaker's voice.

# Carrier wave

The radio wave sent out by a transmitter

Each radio station transmits a carrier wave with a particular wavelength ▪ or frequency ▪. The wave is made to carry a copy of the original sound waves by a process called modulation. There are four main groups of carrier waves. These are **long waves**, **medium waves**, and **short waves**, which have long, medium, and short wavelengths, and **VHF** (very-high-frequency) waves. Long and short waves have a long range, medium waves a medium range, and VHF waves a short range.

AM carrier wave

*High amplitude*

*Low amplitude*

FM carrier wave

*High frequency*

*Low frequency*

### Modulating carrier waves
*In AM carrier waves, the height of the crests and the depth of the troughs of the waves vary. In FM carrier waves, the frequency of the waves changes.*

# Guglielmo Marconi

Italian inventor (1874–1937)

Marconi invented radio communication. In 1895, just seven years after the discovery of radio waves by Heinrich Hertz ▪, Marconi succeeded in transmitting a radio message in Morse ▪ code. The first voice broadcast took place in 1906, after the invention of modulation by the Canadian engineer **Reginald Fessenden** (1866–1932).

Guglielmo Marconi, 1896

# Modulation

A way of making radio waves carry sounds

The electrical signal from a microphone at a radio station constantly changes in level. This signal varies, or modulates, the carrier wave broadcast by the station. It makes the carrier wave vary at the same rate as the sound level changes. In **amplitude modulation (AM)**, the strength, or amplitude ▪, of the radio wave varies. In **frequency modulation (FM)**, the frequency of the wave varies. In a receiver, the wave is demodulated, or changed back to the original electrical signal.

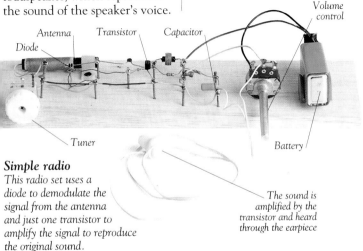

### Simple radio
*This radio set uses a diode to demodulate the signal from the antenna and just one transistor to amplify the signal to reproduce the original sound.*

Antenna

Diode

Transistor

Capacitor

Volume control

Tuner

Battery

*The sound is amplified by the transistor and heard through the earpiece*

## See also

*Continued on next page ➤*

## Vladimir Zworykin

American engineer (1889–1982)

Zworykin, who was born in Russia, developed the electronic system of television in the 1920s. He based his invention on the cathode ray tube ▨. In 1928, the American inventor **Philo T. Farnsworth** (1906–71) developed the image pick-up tube that made today's television camera possible.

## Television

A way of sending pictures using radio waves or cables

Television cameras and microphones change moving pictures and sound into electrical signals. These, in turn, are changed by the television station into radio waves by modulation ▨ (as in sound radio) and then transmitted to your home.

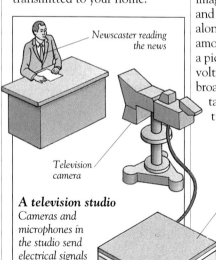

Newscaster reading the news

Television camera

**A television studio**
*Cameras and microphones in the studio send electrical signals to the television station, which then broadcasts the signals.*

## Television transmitter

A device that is used to send television pictures

When a television program is broadcast, signals are sent out to transmitters, which are often mounted on tall masts. The transmitters broadcast the signals as radio waves to homes, and antennas pick up the waves. Television receivers change the waves back into the pictures seen on the television screen. The sound works in exactly the same way as in radio ▨. In **cable television**, the electrical picture and sound signals travel along a cable from the television station or a satellite ground station to the receiver in the home.

## Television camera

A camera that takes pictures for television

The lens ▨ of a television camera forms a real image ▨ of a scene on a tube inside the camera. The tube converts the light in the picture into an electrical picture signal by **scanning**. It splits the image into 525 horizontal lines, and detects the amounts of light along each line. These varying amounts of light are changed into a picture signal that varies in voltage ▨. The signal is then broadcast. A television camera takes a whole picture 30 times every second.

Ground stations beam radio waves to satellites overhead

Television station

## Communications satellite

A satellite that relays telephone calls and television programs

Telephone calls and television programs may travel between continents via communications satellites. These orbit the Earth about 22,400 miles (about 36,000 kilometers) above the equator. They circle the Earth every 24 hours, the same time it takes for the Earth to revolve once. This means that they remain in the same position above a particular place on the Earth's surface. The satellites receive radio signals from ground stations below. They then send the signals back to ground stations on other continents and to **satellite dishes** on homes.

*Satellites travel in a special orbit, called a geostationary orbit, which makes them appear to be stationary in the sky*

*Transmitter masts broadcast radio waves from the television station to antennas on the roofs of houses*

# Television receiver

A set that shows television pictures

Choosing a program operates a tuner in the receiver and selects a **channel**, which is a carrier wave ▨ transmitted at a particular frequency ▨ by a television station. The carrier wave is demodulated to produce an electrical picture signal, which goes to the picture tube, or cathode ray tube. An **electron gun** at the back of the tube fires a beam of electrons ▨ at the screen in front. On the screen are **phosphors**, substances that light up when struck by the electron beam. The picture signal controls the beam so that it moves over the screen in the same way that the television camera scans the image. A picture forms 30 times a second and appears to move. A color television receiver contains three beams that strike red, green, and blue phosphors.

# Color television

A way of sending television pictures in full color

Television cannot send every color in a picture separately, so it sends just the three primary colors ▨ (red, green, and blue), which can be mixed to form all other colors. A color television camera contains three tubes that detect the amounts of red, green, and blue light in a picture. The tubes reproduce the three colors as three electrical picture signals. These signals are sent to a color receiver, which shows three overlapping pictures in red, green, and blue. The three colors merge to form a full-color picture. There are two main color television systems. These are **NTSC (National Television Systems Committee)**, which is used in North America and Japan, and **PAL (phase alteration line)**, used in Europe and Australia.

# Video

A method of recording television pictures on tape

A **video camera**, or **camcorder**, is a portable television camera. A **videotape** in the camera records an electrical picture signal in the same way that a magnetic tape ▨ records sound. A **video cassette recorder**, or **VCR**, records the signal onto videotape. When you replay the tape, it reproduces the electrical picture signal, which goes to a television receiver. A **video disc** records television pictures in the same way that a compact disc ▨ records sound.

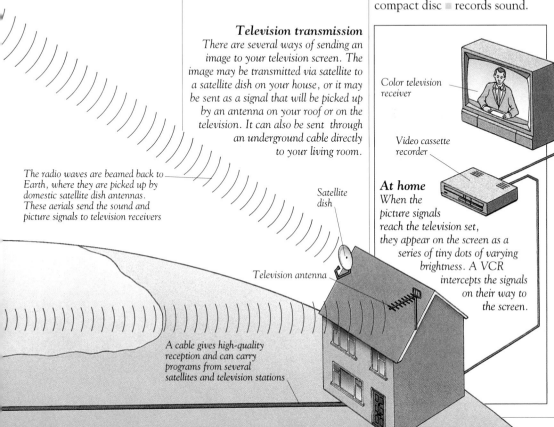

*Television transmission*
*There are several ways of sending an image to your television screen. The image may be transmitted via satellite to a satellite dish on your house, or it may be sent as a signal that will be picked up by an antenna on your roof or on the television. It can also be sent through an underground cable directly to your living room.*

Color television receiver

Video cassette recorder

*The radio waves are beamed back to Earth, where they are picked up by domestic satellite dish antennas. These aerials send the sound and picture signals to television receivers*

Satellite dish

**At home**
*When the picture signals reach the television set, they appear on the screen as a series of tiny dots of varying brightness. A VCR intercepts the signals on their way to the screen.*

Television antenna

*A cable gives high-quality reception and can carry programs from several satellites and television stations*

# Elements

An element is any substance that cannot be broken down into simpler substances. Water, for example, is made up of hydrogen and oxygen, so it is not an element. However, oxygen gas and hydrogen gas cannot be split into anything simpler, so they are elements.

## Element

**A substance that contains only one kind of atom**

All substances are made of particles called atoms . There are just over a hundred different types of atom. Each has its own atomic number . In most substances, two or more types of atom are mixed together or combined as a compound . Only a few of the millions of substances that exist are made of just one kind of atom. These are the elements, or **chemical elements**. One example is oxygen, which contains only oxygen atoms. Ninety of the elements occur naturally, but a few have been made by scientists.

**Potassium in water**
*Potassium, an element, bursts into flame on contact with water because it is highly reactive. Its reactivity causes it to occur naturally only as potassium compounds.*

**Pure gold**
*This picture shows yellow veins of pure gold in quartz rock. Pure gold can be found naturally because it does not react easily with other elements.*

## Metal

**An element that is shiny and usually hard and strong**

Most elements are metals. Metals include iron, gold, silver, and lead. All metals, except mercury, are solid at room temperature (68°F, 20°C). Most metals have a high density , and conduct heat and electricity well. Many are useful for making things because they are strong and can be formed into different shapes. Metals are often mixed with other metals to form alloys .

## Allotrope

**A different physical form of an element**

A few elements have more than one physical form, because their atoms can link up in different ways. Diamond and graphite are hard and soft allotropes of carbon. They contain only carbon atoms, but have very different physical properties.

## Chemical symbol

**A letter code that represents an element**

Scientists throughout the world use the same chemical symbols as a kind of shorthand. Several symbols are just a single letter, such as "C" for carbon and "S" for sulfur. Other symbols have two letters, such as "Co" for cobalt and "Cl" for chlorine. Most symbols come from the element's English name, but a few come from other languages, such as Greek, Latin, and Arabic. Iron has the symbol "Fe," which comes from *ferrum*, the Latin word for iron.

## Metalloid

**An element that is partly a metal and partly a nonmetal**

It is not easy to classify every element as either a metal or a nonmetal. Although some elements look like metals, they break easily and are poor conductors of electricity. These elements are metalloids. They include silicon and germanium.

## Nonmetal

**An element that is not a metal**

Nonmetals include elements that are gases at room temperature (20°C, 68°F), such as hydrogen and oxygen. Solid nonmetals, such as sulfur and iodine, usually break easily, have a low density, do not shine, and are poor conductors  of heat and electricity.

### See also

Alloy 166 • Atom 34
Atomic number 34
Compound 138
Conductor, electrical 105
Conductor, thermal 91 • Density 23
Reactive 146

# SOME COMMON ELEMENTS

| Name | Details |
|------|---------|
| Aluminum | Light metal extracted from bauxite. Used to make kitchen foil and light, strong alloys for aircraft. Easy to recycle. Discovered 1825. |
| Argon | Colorless gas present in air. Used to fill light bulbs. Discovered 1894. |
| Calcium | Metal extracted from lime. Used in alloys. Compounds used in plaster and cement. Discovered 1808. |
| Carbon | Nonmetal that occurs in several forms. **Diamond** is a hard crystal used in jewelry and drills. **Graphite** is a soft, black solid used as a lubricant and in pencils. **Carbon black** is a fine powder used in making rubber. **Coke** is a form of carbon used to make steel. **Carbon fibers** are used to make strong materials. Known since ancient times. (**Buckminsterfullerene** is a newly discovered form of carbon, with molecules of 60 atoms linked in a sphere). |
| Chlorine | Green-yellow gas extracted from salt. Used as a disinfectant and bleach. Discovered 1774. |
| Copper | Reddish metal found naturally as an element Extracted from chalcopyrite. Used to make pipes, coins, and electric wire, and the alloys brass and bronze. Known since ancient times. |
| Fluorine | Pale yellow gas extracted from fluorine compounds. Most reactive of all the elements. Compounds used in toothpaste and drinking water to fight tooth decay. Discovered 1886. |
| Gold | Yellow metal found as an element. Used in jewelry. Known since ancient times. |
| Helium | Colorless, unreactive gas found in natural gas deposits. Tiny traces found in air. Used to fill balloons and airships. Discovered 1868. |
| Hydrogen | Colorless gas obtained from water or methane. Used as fuel and to make important materials such as ammonia. Discovered 1766. |
| Iodine | Violet, solid nonmetal extracted from Chile saltpeter. Used in medicine. Discovered 1811. |
| Iron | Metal extracted from hematite, siderite, and other iron ores. Used to make cast iron and steel. Known since ancient times. |
| Lead | Metal extracted from galena. Used in roofing and to make car batteries and alloys. Protects against radiation. Known since ancient times. |
| Magnesium | Silvery-white metal extracted from dolomite. Burns with a bright light. Used to make light alloys, flares, and fireworks. Isolated 1808. |

| Name | Details |
|------|---------|
| Mercury | Liquid metal extracted from cinnabar. Once used in thermometers, dentistry, and mercury vapor lamps, now used mainly in industrial processes. Known since ancient times. |
| Nickel | Metal extracted from pentlandite. Used in corrosion-resistant alloys for cutlery and coins. Nickel plating used to protect metals from corrosion. Discovered 1751. |
| Nitrogen | Colorless gas that makes up 78% of air. Used in light bulbs and in the manufacture of fertilizers. Discovered 1772. |
| Oxygen | Colorless gas present in air. **Ozone** is an allotrope of oxygen that forms a layer in the upper atmosphere. Oxygen is the most abundant element on Earth, its compounds forming water and rocks. Essential for life, and widely used in industry. Discovered 1774. |
| Plutonium | Radioactive metal made in nuclear reactors from waste uranium fuel. Used in reactors and nuclear weapons. Discovered 1940. |
| Potassium | Highly reactive, soft metal extracted from potassium compounds. Compounds used as fertilizer. Discovered 1807. |
| Silicon | Metalloid extracted from silica. Used to make transistors and microchips. Discovered 1823. |
| Silver | Metal found as an element and extracted from silver ores. Used in jewelry and tableware. Known since ancient times. |
| Sodium | Soft, reactive metal extracted from salt. Compounds used in chemical industry. Discovered 1807. |
| Sulfur | Yellow, solid nonmetal found naturally as an element. Used in chemical industry and to treat rubber. Known since ancient times. |
| Tin | Soft metal extracted from cassiterite. Used in alloys. Known since ancient times. |
| Titanium | Hard metal extracted from rutile and ilmenite. Used in light, corrosion-resistant alloys and white paints. Discovered 1791. |
| Uranium | Radioactive metal extracted from pitchblende and carnotite. Used in nuclear reactors. Discovered 1789. |
| Zinc | Metal extracted from zinc blende. Used to make batteries, and brass and other alloys. Iron is galvanized with zinc to prevent rusting. Discovered 1746. |

*Background picture: sulfur crystals*

*Continued on next page* ➤

# THE ELEMENTS

| Name | Symbol | Atomic number | Atomic mass | Type |
|------|--------|---------------|-------------|------|
| Actinium | Ac | 89 | 227.02 | metal |
| Aluminum | Al | 13 | 26.98 | metal |
| Americium | Am | 95 | 243 | metal |
| Antimony | Sb | 51 | 121.75 | metalloid |
| Argon | Ar | 18 | 39.95 | gas |
| Arsenic | As | 33 | 74.92 | metalloid |
| Astatine | At | 85 | 210 | solid nonmetal |
| Barium | Ba | 56 | 137.34 | metal |
| Berkelium | Bk | 97 | 247 | metal |
| Beryllium | Be | 4 | 9.01 | metal |
| Bismuth | Bi | 83 | 208.98 | metal |
| Boron | B | 5 | 10.81 | metalloid |
| Bromine | Br | 35 | 79.91 | liquid nonmetal |
| Cadmium | Cd | 48 | 112.40 | metal |
| Calcium | Ca | 20 | 40.08 | metal |
| Californium | Cf | 98 | 251 | metal |
| Carbon | C | 6 | 12.01 | solid nonmetal |
| Cerium | Ce | 58 | 140.12 | metal |
| Cesium | Cs | 55 | 132.91 | metal |
| Chlorine | Cl | 17 | 35.45 | gas |
| Chromium | Cr | 24 | 51.99 | metal |
| Cobalt | Co | 27 | 58.93 | metal |
| Copper | Cu | 29 | 63.55 | metal |
| Curium | Cm | 96 | 247 | metal |
| Dysprosium | Dy | 66 | 162.50 | metal |
| Einsteinium | Es | 99 | 254 | metal |
| Erbium | Er | 68 | 167.26 | metal |
| Europium | Eu | 63 | 151.96 | metal |
| Fermium | Fm | 100 | 257 | metal |
| Fluorine | F | 9 | 18.99 | gas |
| Francium | Fr | 87 | 223 | metal |
| Gadolinium | Gd | 64 | 157.25 | metal |
| Gallium | Ga | 31 | 69.72 | metal |
| Germanium | Ge | 32 | 72.59 | metalloid |
| Gold | Au | 79 | 196.97 | metal |
| Hafnium | Hf | 72 | 178.49 | metal |
| Hahnium | Ha | 105 | 262 | metal |
| Helium | He | 2 | 4.00 | gas |
| Holmium | Ho | 67 | 164.93 | metal |
| Hydrogen | H | 1 | 1.01 | gas |
| Indium | In | 49 | 114.82 | metal |
| Iodine | I | 53 | 126.90 | solid nonmetal |
| Iridium | Ir | 77 | 192.20 | metal |
| Iron | Fe | 26 | 55.85 | metal |
| Krypton | Kr | 36 | 83.80 | gas |
| Lanthanum | La | 57 | 138.91 | metal |
| Lawrencium | Lr | 103 | 257 | metal |
| Lead | Pb | 82 | 207.19 | metal |
| Lithium | Li | 3 | 6.94 | metal |
| Lutetium | Lu | 71 | 174.97 | metal |
| Magnesium | Mg | 12 | 24.31 | metal |
| Manganese | Mn | 25 | 54.94 | metal |
| Mendelevium | Md | 101 | 256 | metal |

| Name | Symbol | Atomic number | Atomic mass | Type |
|------|--------|---------------|-------------|------|
| Mercury | Hg | 80 | 200.59 | liquid metal |
| Molybdenum | Mo | 42 | 95.94 | metal |
| Neodymium | Nd | 60 | 144.24 | metal |
| Neon | Ne | 10 | 20.18 | gas |
| Neptunium | Np | 93 | 237 | metal |
| Nickel | Ni | 28 | 58.71 | metal |
| Niobium | Nb | 41 | 92.91 | metal |
| Nitrogen | N | 7 | 14.01 | gas |
| Nobelium | No | 102 | 254 | metal |
| Osmium | Os | 76 | 190.2 | metal |
| Oxygen | O | 8 | 15.99 | gas |
| Palladium | Pd | 46 | 106.4 | metal |
| Phosphorus | P | 15 | 30.97 | solid nonmetal |
| Platinum | Pt | 78 | 195.09 | metal |
| Plutonium | Pu | 94 | 242 | metal |
| Polonium | Po | 84 | 210 | metalloid |
| Potassium | K | 19 | 39.10 | metal |
| Praseodymium | Pr | 59 | 140.91 | metal |
| Promethium | Pm | 61 | 145 | metal |
| Protactinium | Pa | 91 | 231 | metal |
| Radium | Ra | 88 | 226 | metal |
| Radon | Rn | 86 | 222 | gas |
| Rhenium | Re | 75 | 186.20 | metal |
| Rhodium | Rh | 45 | 102.91 | metal |
| Rubidium | Rb | 37 | 85.47 | metal |
| Ruthenium | Ru | 44 | 101.07 | metal |
| Rutherfordium | Rf | 104 | 261 | metal |
| Samarium | Sm | 62 | 150.35 | metal |
| Scandium | Sc | 21 | 44.96 | metal |
| Selenium | Se | 34 | 78.96 | solid nonmetal |
| Silicon | Si | 14 | 28.09 | metalloid |
| Silver | Ag | 47 | 107.87 | metal |
| Sodium | Na | 11 | 22.99 | metal |
| Strontium | Sr | 38 | 87.62 | metal |
| Sulfur | S | 16 | 32.06 | solid nonmetal |
| Tantalum | Ta | 73 | 180.95 | metal |
| Technetium | Tc | 43 | 99 | metal |
| Tellurium | Te | 52 | 127.60 | metalloid |
| Terbium | Tb | 65 | 158.93 | metal |
| Thallium | Tl | 81 | 204.39 | metal |
| Thorium | Th | 90 | 232.04 | metal |
| Thulium | Tm | 69 | 168.93 | metal |
| Tin | Sn | 50 | 118.69 | metal |
| Titanium | Ti | 22 | 47.90 | metal |
| Tungsten | W | 74 | 183.85 | metal |
| Uranium | U | 92 | 238.03 | metal |
| Vanadium | V | 23 | 50.94 | metal |
| Xenon | Xe | 54 | 131.30 | gas |
| Ytterbium | Yb | 70 | 173.04 | metal |
| Yttrium | Y | 39 | 88.91 | metal |
| Zinc | Zn | 30 | 65.38 | metal |
| Zirconium | Zr | 40 | 91.22 | metal |

**Background picture:** *a cross section of a meteorite containing iron*

◄ *Continued from previous page*

# Discovery of elements

More than 2,000 years ago, Aristotle, a Greek philosopher, believed that all substances were made up of just four elements – earth, fire, air, and water. It was only in the 17th century that people began to realize what elements are really like. Scientists today continue to search for new elements by making them artificially in tiny amounts.

## Robert Boyle

Irish scientist (1627–91)

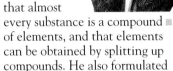

Boyle realized the true nature of elements ▪. He understood that almost every substance is a compound ▪ of elements, and that elements can be obtained by splitting up compounds. He also formulated Boyle's law ▪.

## Henry Cavendish

English scientist (1731–1810)

Cavendish discovered hydrogen in 1766. He formed water by exploding a mixture of hydrogen and air with an electric spark. This disproved the old idea that water itself was an element. Cavendish also measured the gravitational constant, which defines the strength of the force of gravity ▪.

## Karl Scheele

Swedish chemist (1742–86)

Scheele searched for unknown elements and discovered many new chemical compounds. He was the first to produce oxygen and chlorine, but it was only in later years that scientists realized they are elements. Scheele may also have discovered other elements without knowing it.

## Antoine Lavoisier

French chemist (1743–94)

Lavoisier showed that air is not an element, but a mixture of gases. He also showed that water is a compound of hydrogen and oxygen. He founded the system of naming compounds and gave several elements their names. Lavoisier also explained that burning is a reaction with oxygen in the air.

## Humphry Davy

English chemist (1778–1829)

Davy discovered that if he passed an electric current through a compound, he could split it into its elements. In this way, he discovered potassium and sodium in 1807, and magnesium, barium, calcium, and strontium in 1808.

*Humphry Davy's apparatus*
*Davy obtained sodium by passing electricity through salt in this apparatus.*

Terminal     Terminal

## Jöns Berzelius

Swedish chemist (1779–1848)

Berzelius discovered selenium in 1818, silicon in 1823, and thorium in 1829. He prepared the first accurate table of the atomic masses ▪ of elements and invented the system of using chemical symbols ▪ for elements.

## Dmitri Mendeleyev

Russian chemist (1834–1907)

In 1869, Mendeleyev classified the 63 elements then known into groups and invented the periodic table ▪. He used the table to predict the existence of three new elements, all of which were discovered a few years later. Every element found since then has fitted into his table. The element mendelevium was named after him in 1955.

## Marie Curie

Polish–French chemist (1867–1934)

Polish-born Marie Curie discovered polonium and radium in 1898 while researching in Paris. She detected these elements by their intense radioactivity ▪. Together with her husband, the French physicist **Pierre Curie** (1859–1906), she processed about four tons of ore for less than a gram of radium. Pierre Curie discovered piezoelectricity ▪ in 1880.

### See also

Atomic mass 34 • Boyle's law 94
Chemical symbol 132 • Compound 138
Element 132 • Gravity 49
Periodic table 136 • Piezoelectricity 109
Radioactivity 36

# Periodic table

There are similarities between certain elements. Sodium and potassium are both very reactive metals, while argon and helium are both unreactive gases. The elements can be arranged into different groups according to their properties.

## Periodic table

An arrangement of the elements according to the similarities and differences between them

In the periodic table, the elements ▦ are placed in vertical columns called **groups**, and horizontal rows called **periods**. They appear in order of atomic number ▦, starting with the lowest first. Hydrogen has its own place at the top of the table. The position and properties of each element are determined by the arrangement of electrons ▦ in the shells of its atoms ▦.

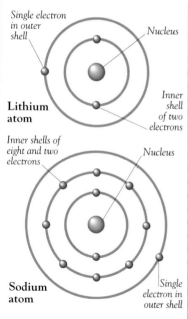

*Single electron in outer shell*

*Nucleus*

**Lithium atom**

*Inner shell of two electrons*

*Inner shells of eight and two electrons*

*Nucleus*

**Sodium atom**

*Single electron in outer shell*

### Electron shells
*The elements lithium and sodium are placed in group I of the periodic table. This is because their atoms have just one electron in their outer shell.*

## Alkaline earth metals

The elements beryllium, magnesium, calcium, strontium, barium, and radium

The alkaline earth metals ▦ form group II of the periodic table. They have two electrons in the outer shell of their atoms, making them less reactive than the alkali metals. The oxides of these metals react with water to form alkalis.

*Each box gives basic details about an element*

| | Group I | Group II |
|---|---|---|
| | **1**<br>**H**<br>Hydrogen | |
| | **3**<br>**Li**<br>Lithium | **4**<br>**Be**<br>Beryllium |
| | **11**<br>**Na**<br>Sodium | **12**<br>**Mg**<br>Magnesium |

| **19**<br>**K**<br>Potassium | **20**<br>**Ca**<br>Calcium | **21**<br>**Sc**<br>Scandium | **22**<br>**Ti**<br>Titanium | **23**<br>**V**<br>Vanadium | **24**<br>**Cr**<br>Chromium | **25**<br>**Mn**<br>Manganese |
|---|---|---|---|---|---|---|
| **37**<br>**Rb**<br>Rubidium | **38**<br>**Sr**<br>Strontium | **39**<br>**Y**<br>Yttrium | **40**<br>**Zr**<br>Zirconium | **41**<br>**Nb**<br>Niobium | **42**<br>**Mo**<br>Molybdenum | **43**<br>**Tc**<br>Technetium |
| **55**<br>**Cs**<br>Cesium | **56**<br>**Ba**<br>Barium | ▶ **57**<br>**La**<br>Lanthanum | **72**<br>**Hf**<br>Hafnium | **73**<br>**Ta**<br>Tantalum | **74**<br>**W**<br>Tungsten | **75**<br>**Re**<br>Rhenium |
| **87**<br>**Fr**<br>Francium | **88**<br>**Ra**<br>Radium | ▶▶ **89**<br>**Ac**<br>Actinium | **104**<br>**Rf**<br>Rutherfordium | **105**<br>**Ha**<br>Hahnium | | |

**Group I   Group II**

*Atomic number*

**79**<br>**Au**<br>Gold

*Name of element*   *Chemical symbol*

| Alkali metals | Alkaline earth metals |
|---|---|
| Transition metals | Actinide series |

▶ **Lanthanide series**

| **58**<br>**Ce**<br>Cerium | **59**<br>**Pr**<br>Praseodymium | **60**<br>**Nd**<br>Neodymium |
|---|---|---|

▶▶ **Actinide series**

| **90**<br>**Th**<br>Thorium | **91**<br>**Pa**<br>Protactinium | **92**<br>**U**<br>Uranium |
|---|---|---|

## Alkali metals

The elements lithium, sodium, potassium, rubidium, cesium, and francium

The alkali metals form group I of the periodic table. They are called alkali metals because when they react with water they form alkalis. They all have one electron in the outer shell of their atoms, making them very reactive. They react vigorously or even explosively with water and acids ▦, for example.

### Natural salt deposits
*Crystals of salt beside the Dead Sea in Israel. Salt (sodium chloride) is a compound of sodium and chlorine, reactive elements from groups I and VII.*

## Lighter than air

*Helium, a light noble gas, is often used to fill children's balloons. Helium is in group 0 and is so unreactive that it cannot catch fire, making it safe to use in balloons and airships.*

## Noble gases

The elements helium, neon, argon, krypton, xenon, and radon

The noble gases form group 0 of the periodic table. They are also called the **inert gases**, or the **rare gases**, though they are not totally inert (unable to be changed by chemical reactions) nor are they all rare. The noble gases are unreactive, forming very few compounds with other elements. This is because their atoms have a very stable outer shell, containing a maximum number of electrons (two for helium, eight for the other gases).

## Transition elements

Elements that lie between groups II and III in the periodic table

The properties of the transition elements are midway between the metals of group II and group III. The transition elements are either reactive or unreactive metals. They include iron, zinc, nickel, copper, silver, gold, chromium, platinum, and mercury. Transition elements are used in many alloys ▥, and often form colored compounds ▥. An inner shell in the atoms of transition elements is incomplete or only partly filled with electrons.

## See also

Acid 149 • Alloy 166 • Atom 34
Atomic number 34 • Compound 138
Electron 34 • Element 132
Metal 132 • Nonmetal 132

## Halogens

The elements fluorine, chlorine, bromine, iodine, and astatine

The halogens are the gases and solid nonmetals ▥ of group VII. All are poisonous. Halogens have seven electrons in the outer shell of their atoms, making them very reactive. They can form covalent and ionic compounds with other elements. A **halide** is a compound of a halogen and another element. Salt (sodium chloride) is a halide.

| | | | | | 2 **He** Helium |
|---|---|---|---|---|---|
| 5 **\*B** Boron | 6 **C** Carbon | 7 **N** Nitrogen | 8 **O** Oxygen | 9 **F** Fluorine | 10 **Ne** Neon |
| 13 **Al** Aluminum | 14 **\*Si** Silicon | 15 **P** Phosphorus | 16 **S** Sulfur | 17 **Cl** Chlorine | 18 **Ar** Argon |

| 26 **Fe** Iron | 27 **Co** Cobalt | 28 **Ni** Nickel | 29 **Cu** Copper | 30 **Zn** Zinc | 31 **Ga** Gallium | 32 **\*Ge** Germanium | 33 **\*As** Arsenic | 34 **Se** Selenium | 35 **Br** Bromine | 36 **Kr** Krypton |
|---|---|---|---|---|---|---|---|---|---|---|
| 44 **Ru** Ruthenium | 45 **Rh** Rhodium | 46 **Pd** Palladium | 47 **Ag** Silver | 48 **Cd** Cadmium | 49 **In** Indium | 50 **Sn** Tin | 51 **\*Sb** Antimony | 52 **\*Te** Tellurium | 53 **I** Iodine | 54 **Xe** Xenon |
| 76 **Os** Osmium | 77 **Ir** Iridium | 78 **Pt** Platinum | 79 **Au** Gold | 80 **Hg** Mercury | 81 **Tl** Thallium | 82 **Pb** Lead | 83 **Bi** Bismuth | 84 **\*Po** Polonium | 85 **At** Astatine | 86 **Rn** Radon |
| | | | | | Group III | Group IV | Group V | Group VI | Group VII | Group 0 |

| Nonmetals | Noble gases |
|---|---|
| Lanthanide series | Other metals |

### Note

An alternative numbering system that lists the vertical columns as Groups 1–18 is also used. Hydrogen does not belong to any one group.

*\* These elements are often called metalloids*

| 61 **Pm** Promethium | 62 **Sm** Samarium | 63 **Eu** Europium | 64 **Gd** Gadolinium | 65 **Tb** Terbium | 66 **Dy** Dysprosium | 67 **Ho** Holmium | 68 **Er** Erbium | 69 **Tm** Thulium | 70 **Yb** Ytterbium | 71 **Lu** Lutetium |
|---|---|---|---|---|---|---|---|---|---|---|
| 93 **Np** Neptunium | 94 **Pu** Plutonium | 95 **Am** Americium | 96 **Cm** Curium | 97 **Bk** Berkelium | 98 **Cf** Californium | 99 **Es** Einsteinium | 100 **Fm** Fermium | 101 **Md** Mendelevium | 102 **No** Nobelium | 103 **Lr** Lawrencium |

# Molecules

Most pure substances are made up of tiny particles called molecules. These are identical groups of atoms of one or more elements. Each substance has its own kind of molecule. Glucose, a type of sugar, contains glucose molecules, and water is made of water molecules. They are so small that a drop of water contains more molecules than there are grains of sand on a large beach.

## Molecule

A group of atoms that are linked together

A molecule contains atoms ▪ of elements ▪ linked together in fixed proportions. Many chemical compounds and some elements contain molecules. Water contains the elements oxygen and hydrogen combined together, so each water molecule contains two hydrogen atoms linked to one oxygen atom. Nitrogen gas has molecules made of two nitrogen atoms. Molecules may have a few or very many atoms. The atoms are held or linked together by bonds ▪.

### Water molecule
A water molecule is made up of two atoms of hydrogen linked to a single atom of oxygen.

O

H    H

**Water (H₂O)**

## Substance

A particular type of material

A substance is a material that has a definite identity, such as water, air, salt, sugar, alcohol, wax, or talcum powder. A pure substance contains only one compound or element.

## Avogadro's hypothesis

Equal volumes of all gases, under the same conditions of temperature and pressure, contain the same number of molecules

This hypothesis, suggested by the physicist Amedeo Avogadro ▪ in 1811, was the first explanation of molecules. It means that the volume of a gas depends on the number of particles it contains. A liter of any gas at normal temperature and pressure contains about 25,000 million million million molecules.

*1 A burette with a fine nozzle is filled with a solution of 1 cm³ of olive oil in 1,000 cm³ of alcohol*

*2 The surface of the water is lightly dusted with talcum powder*

*3 The tap is opened to let drops fall into a dish. By counting the number of drops in 1 cm³ of oil solution, the volume of one drop can be calculated*

*Shallow dish of water*

## Compound

A substance in which the atoms of two or more elements are combined together

A compound is also called a **chemical compound**. It contains fixed proportions of elements linked in molecules or in a giant structure ▪. The **chemical name** of a compound shows the elements within it. Salt's chemical name is sodium chloride, showing that it is a compound of sodium and chlorine. A compound's properties may be very different from those of the elements it contains. Sodium is a soft metal, and chlorine is a poisonous gas. It is not safe to eat either sodium or chlorine, yet salt is an important food.

### How large is a molecule?
*Molecules are so small that their size cannot be measured using a ruler. One way to find out what size they are is to create a layer of olive oil just one molecule thick on the surface of water. The area of the oil layer is then measured. If the volume of the oil is known, the depth of the layer can be calculated from the area of the oil layer. As the layer is only one molecule thick, the depth of the layer gives the size of an oil molecule. The answer will be in the region of one ten-millionth of a centimeter.*

*4 One drop of the oil solution is allowed to fall gently into the dish*

*5 When a drop of the solution falls into the dish, the alcohol dissolves and the oil pushes the powder aside, spreading out until it is just one molecule thick*

*6 The diameter of the oil patch is measured and its area calculated*

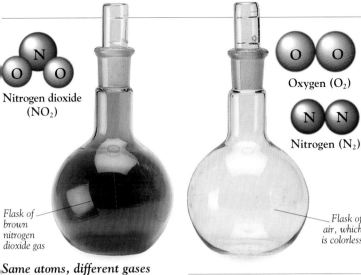

Nitrogen dioxide (NO₂)

Oxygen (O₂)

Nitrogen (N₂)

*Flask of brown nitrogen dioxide gas*

*Flask of air, which is colorless*

## Same atoms, different gases

*Nitrogen dioxide gas contains oxygen and nitrogen atoms linked as nitrogen dioxide molecules. Air is mostly made up of the same atoms but linked in pairs as molecules of oxygen and nitrogen.*

## Chemical formula

A group of letters and numbers that show how elements are combined in a compound

A chemical formula, or **molecular formula**, uses chemical symbols ▣ to show the elements present in a compound. Numbers show the proportions in which the elements are combined. A water molecule contains two atoms of hydrogen (H) and one atom of oxygen (O), so the chemical formula of water is $H_2O$. Salt (sodium chloride) contains equal numbers of sodium ions ▣ (Na) and chloride ions (Cl), so its formula is NaCl. Elements have formulas, too. For example, nitrogen (N) has the formula $N_2$, because each nitrogen molecule has two atoms. Ethanoic acid, which is in vinegar, has a formula of $C_2H_4O_2$. It also has a **structural formula** of $CH_3COOH$. This shows how the atoms of hydrogen, oxygen, and carbon (C) are arranged in a molecule. It can also be written as:

*The lines between the atoms are the bonds that hold them together*

$$
\begin{array}{ccc}
& H & O \\
& | & \| \\
H - & C - & C \\
& | & \backslash \\
& H & O - H
\end{array}
$$

## Brownian motion

The movement of tiny solid particles in a liquid or gas

Tiny solid particles in a liquid or gas can be seen zigzagging at random when observed through a microscope. Their sudden changes of direction are caused by collisions with the fast-moving molecules of the liquid or gas. The molecules themselves are too small to be seen. This effect was first seen in 1827 by the British botanist Robert Brown while studying pollen grains in water.

*Nitrogen molecule in the air*

*Smoke particle*

*Oxygen molecule in the air*

### Brownian motion

*Brownian motion demonstrates the existence of molecules. It can be seen by observing the movement of smoke particles in air through a microscope. The air molecules collide with the smoke particles, making them move at random. It is possible to see the motion of the smoke particles, but not the molecules that cause the motion.*

## Stereochemistry

The branch of chemistry that studies the shape of molecules

The shape of molecules is very important, because the molecules of two different compounds may contain the same atoms linked together in different ways. The shape of a compound's molecules is shown by its structural formula.

## Relative molecular mass (RMM)

The mass of a molecule relative to the mass of an atom of carbon–12

Relative molecular mass is also called **molecular weight**. It is found by adding up the atomic masses ▣ of the atoms in the chemical formula of a compound or element. Water has a chemical formula of $H_2O$. Hydrogen has an atomic mass of 1 and oxygen 16, so the relative molecular mass of water is 18. One mole ▣ of a compound or element has a mass in grams equal to its relative molecular mass.

*Movement of smoke particle*

*Molecules in the air hit the smoke particle from all directions*

### See also

Atom 34 • Atomic mass 34

Avogadro 178 • Bond 140

Chemical symbol 132 • Element 132

Giant structure 140 • Ion 144

Mole 146

*Continued on next page ➤*

# Bond

## A force that holds atoms, ions, or molecules together

All substances contain atoms 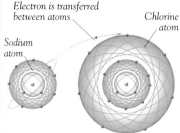 or ions 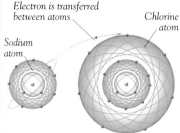 held together by **chemical bonds**. For example, bonds join two hydrogen atoms to an atom of oxygen to form a water molecule 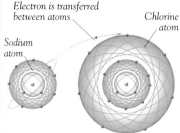. A molecule is linked to other molecules by bonds called intermolecular forces. Bonds are caused by electrical attraction between atoms, ions, or molecules.

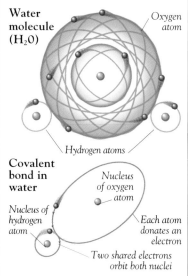

**Water molecule ($H_2O$)**

Oxygen atom

Hydrogen atoms

**Covalent bond in water**

Nucleus of oxygen atom

Nucleus of hydrogen atom

Each atom donates an electron

Two shared electrons orbit both nuclei

**Covalent bonds in water**
*A water molecule contains hydrogen and oxygen atoms linked by covalent bonds.*

# Covalent bond

## A bond between atoms, in which the atoms share electrons

Covalent bonds occur in compounds formed by nonmetals 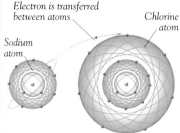, such as hydrogen and oxygen in water. Two atoms each donate an electron 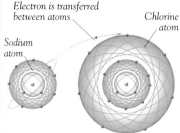 to form a pair of electrons that are shared by both atoms. This pulls the two atoms together. A **dative bond** or **coordinate bond** is a covalent bond in which one atom donates both electrons. A **double bond** is a pair of covalent bonds between two atoms, with each atom donating two electrons.

*As the gas burns, the lamp's mantle heats up and glows brightly, giving a strong light*

# Ionic bond

## A bond between atoms, in which electrons transfer from one atom to another

An ionic bond is also called an **electrovalent bond**, or a **polar bond**. It occurs in a compound 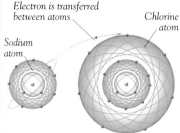 of a metal 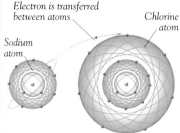 with a nonmetal, such as salt (sodium chloride). Each metal atom loses one or more electrons, which are taken up by the nonmetal atom. The atoms then become ions with positive and negative electric charges. The opposite charges on the ions attract each other, holding the ions together in an ionic bond. Ionic bonds also form between groups of atoms, as well as pairs of atoms.

Electron is transferred between atoms

Chlorine atom

Sodium atom

**Ionic bonds in salt**
*Above, you can see how electrons transfer from sodium atoms to chlorine atoms, giving positive sodium ions and negative chloride ions that attract each other.*

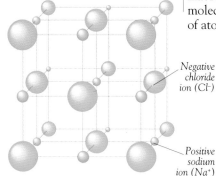

Negative chloride ion ($Cl^-$)

Positive sodium ion ($Na^+$)

# Giant structure

## A substance composed of a network of atoms

Many crystals 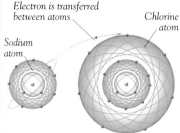 are giant structures. Salt (sodium chloride) is made of sodium and chloride ions all connected together in a huge network that extends throughout a salt crystal. This is a **giant ionic structure**. Diamond contains carbon atoms joined to each other by covalent bonds. This is a **giant covalent structure**. Plastics 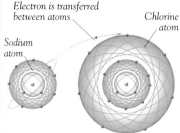 are made of **macromolecules** – very large molecules that contain thousands of atoms linked together.

**The structure of salt**
*The picture on the left shows how sodium and chloride ions are arranged in a crystal of salt (sodium chloride). Salt has a giant ionic structure. Each negatively charged chloride ion is surrounded by positively charged sodium ions. The ions are held in place by ionic bonds.*

◄ Continued from previous page

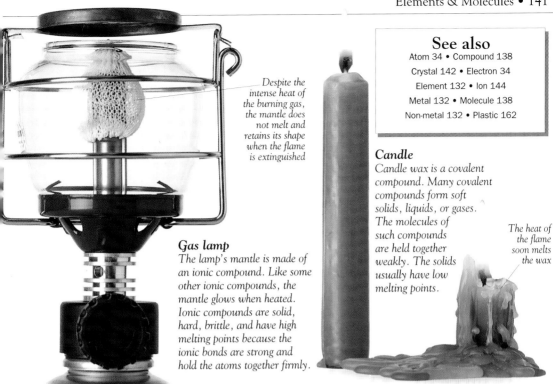

*Despite the intense heat of the burning gas, the mantle does not melt and retains its shape when the flame is extinguished*

## See also

Atom 34 • Compound 138
Crystal 142 • Electron 34
Element 132 • Ion 144
Metal 132 • Molecule 138
Non-metal 132 • Plastic 162

## Candle

Candle wax is a covalent compound. Many covalent compounds form soft solids, liquids, or gases. The molecules of such compounds are held together weakly. The solids usually have low melting points.

*The heat of the flame soon melts the wax*

## Gas lamp

The lamp's mantle is made of an ionic compound. Like some other ionic compounds, the mantle glows when heated. Ionic compounds are solid, hard, brittle, and have high melting points because the ionic bonds are strong and hold the atoms together firmly.

# Intermolecular force

A bond between two molecules

There are weak forces of electrical attraction between individual molecules. These are called **van der Waal's forces**. They are much weaker than the covalent bonds that hold atoms together strongly in molecules, or the ionic bonds that hold ions together in ionic compounds.

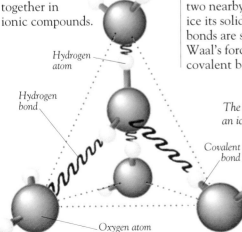

*Hydrogen atom*

*Hydrogen bond*

*Covalent bond*

*Oxygen atom*

# Hydrogen bonds

Bonds that hold together molecules containing hydrogen

Hydrogen bonds are a type of intermolecular force. They hold together hydrogen-containing molecules, such as water molecules in ice. The hydrogen atoms in a water molecule are attracted to the oxygen atoms in two nearby molecules. This gives ice its solid structure. Hydrogen bonds are stronger than van der Waal's forces, but weaker than covalent bonds and ionic bonds.

### The structure of ice

*The picture at left shows part of an ice crystal. As water freezes, hydrogen bonds form and join the water molecules together in a solid structure. The bonds form between the hydrogen atoms and oxygen atoms in nearby molecules.*

# Combining power

The proportion in which an element combines with other elements

Each element ▪ has a certain combining power, which is also called its **valency** or **valence**. For example, hydrogen has a combining power of 1, oxygen 2, and carbon 4. When elements combine to form compounds, they do so in fixed proportions, determined by their combining power. This means that two proportions of hydrogen must combine with one of oxygen to give water ($H_2O$), but four proportions of hydrogen must combine with one of carbon to give methane ($CH_4$). Carbon and oxygen combine in proportions of 1 to 2, to give carbon dioxide ($CO_2$). Some elements have more than one combining power. Iron has combining powers of 2 and 3. The combining power is given in Roman numerals in the compound's name, such as iron(II) chloride ($FeCl_2$) and iron(III) oxide ($Fe_2O_3$).

# Crystals

Many crystals have such beautiful shapes and colors that we use them as ornaments and gems. Their regular internal structure also makes crystals important in industry. Quartz crystals, for example, are used in clocks to keep good time, while silicon crystals are used in electronic circuits, and diamonds in drilling tools.

### Quartz crystal
*In a quartz crystal, silicon and oxygen atoms link together to give a rhombohedral structure.*

## Crystallography
The study of crystals

Crystallographers find out the arrangement of the particles inside crystals. **X-ray crystallography** uses X-rays ▪ to determine the structure of a crystal. A beam of X-rays passes through the crystal and strikes an X-ray film. The X-rays bend, or diffract ▪, as they pass between the particles, and form a pattern of spots on the film. The crystallographer works out the arrangement of the particles from the pattern of spots. X-ray crystallography is used to examine minerals and alloys and to work out the structure of DNA, which is important in understanding genetics.

*1 Copper(II) sulfate solution after one hour*

*2 Tiny copper(II) sulfate crystals begin to form after two hours*

## Crystal

A solid containing a regular arrangement of particles

If you leave some salty water exposed to the air, it forms tiny white crystals of salt as the water evaporates. Many compounds ▪ form crystals when they leave solutions ▪. Most molten compounds also form crystals as they solidify. Most elements ▪, such as iodine, form crystals too. The process of forming crystals is called **crystallization**. As a crystal forms, atoms ▪, ions ▪, or molecules ▪ link together in a regular network called a **lattice**. The crystal grows as more atoms, ions, or molecules join the lattice. The shape of the lattice gives the crystal its particular shape. Salt crystals are tiny cubes, for example.

## Crystal system

The basic structure of a crystal

A crystal belongs to one of seven crystal systems (shown in the box on page 143). These are the seven basic ways in which atoms or other particles may link up inside a crystal. The crystals of a substance in a particular crystal system all have the same basic shape. All substances that crystallize in the cubic system form cube-shaped crystals, for example. However, corners may be missing and crystals often lump together, so that the crystals look different. The seven systems are called **cubic, tetragonal, orthorhombic, monoclinic, hexagonal, trigonal** or **rhombohedral**, and **triclinic**.

*3 In four hours, the crystals are have grown so that their triclinic structure is visible*

### Growing crystals
*Crystals form as water evaporates from a strong copper(II) sulfate solution.*

# William Henry Bragg

English physicist
(1862–1942)

In 1915, Bragg
discovered X-ray
crystallography
with his son
**William Lawrence Bragg**
(1890–1971). Using this
method, the English biochemist
**Dorothy Hodgkin** (born 1910)
later discovered the structures
of vitamin B12 and penicillin.
X-ray investigations of DNA
by the English crystallographer
**Rosalind Franklin** (1920–58)
led to the discovery of its
structure in 1953.

# Polymorphous

Having crystals that form more
than one definite shape

Polymorphous compounds form
crystals with different crystal
systems and different shapes.
Calcium carbonate, for example,
forms the mineral calcite, which
is rhombohedral and may
occur as crystals shaped like
tilted blocks. It also forms
the mineral aragonite,
which is orthorhombic
and often occurs as long,
needle-shaped crystals.
The ability of a
compound's crystals to
have different shapes is
called **polymorphism**.

## Amorphous

Having no definite shape

Amorphous substances do not
form crystals and do not have
any particular shape or regular
internal structure. They include
substances such as glass, which
can be molded into any shape,
and which shatters into
fragments of many shapes and
sizes when it breaks.

# Liquid crystals

Liquids that have similar
properties to crystals

The molecules in a liquid crystal
line up in a regular pattern, similar
to the arrangement of particles in
solid crystals. The molecules affect
the light rays passing through the
liquid crystals. Heating the liquid
changes the alignment of the
molecules and causes the light to
change color at different
temperatures. This enables liquid
crystals to be used as simple
thermometers.

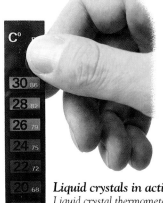

***Liquid crystals in action***
*Liquid crystal thermometers
change color as temperature
changes. Here, you can see
how the heat from a person's thumb
changes the color along the scale.*

# Liquid crystal display (LCD)

A screen on which dark letters and
numbers appear

Calculators and some computers
use a liquid-crystal display. The
screen has layers of liquid crystal
and materials that polarize
light. When you press a key, a
letter or number appears because
the calculator sends an electrical
signal to the liquid crystal. This
changes the pattern of molecules
in the liquid crystal. The new
pattern of molecules causes the
polarized light to be blocked by
the polarizing materials, forming
a dark image of a letter or
number on the screen.

# CRYSTAL SYSTEMS

Each crystal system has a basic
block of particles (red) with a
particular shape. These are
defined by imaginary **axes of
symmetry**, which give the
lengths of any three edges
(black) that meet at a corner
and the angles at which they
meet. As a crystal grows,
particles join onto this basic
shape so that it gets larger and
larger. The maximum number
of identical faces varies from
six (cubic) to two (triclinic).

## Cubic system

All the edges are at
right angles, and all
are equal in length

## Tetragonal system

All the edges are at
right angles, and two
edges are equal length

## Orthorhombic system

All the edges are at
right angles, and all
are different in length

## Monoclinic system

Two edges are at right
angles, and all edges
are different in length

## Hexagonal system

Two edges are at 120
degrees and equal in
length, while the third
edge is at a right angle
to the others

## Rhombohedral or Trigonal system

All edges are equal and
not at right angles

## Triclinic system

None of the edges is
equal and none is at
right angles

# Chemical reactions

If you leave a bicycle out in the open air for a long time, elements in the air, the rain, and the bicycle will combine to form a new substance – rust! This process is called a chemical reaction. Chemical reactions enable elements to combine and produce all the different substances in the world.

## Chemical reaction

A process that changes one substance into another

When you make toast, you cause a chemical reaction to take place. Bread contains carbohydrate ■, a compound ■ of the elements carbon, hydrogen, and oxygen. Heating the bread changes the carbohydrate into black carbon, which forms on the surface of the bread. Water (hydrogen oxide) also forms and escapes into the air as a vapor ■. In a chemical reaction, the atoms ■ of elements in substances rearrange to form new substances, which contain the same atoms but in different combinations. Substances that take part in chemical reactions are called **reactants** or **reagents**. A reaction may stop at a point where the reactants and the products of the reaction exist together. This is called **chemical equilibrium**.

*Chemical equations*
*The equation below represents the reaction pictured on the right. The hydrogen ions from the acid (H+) are replaced by magnesium ions (Mg2+), releasing the hydrogen as a gas.*

## Reversible reaction

A chemical reaction that can go forward or backward

Making toast is not a reversible process; you cannot treat the toast to get untoasted bread back. But in some chemical reactions, the products can react together to give the original substances. Heating blue copper sulfate crystals turns them into white powder and water vapor, which escapes. Adding water then reverses this reaction to give the blue crystals again.

## Chemical equation

A way of showing what happens in a chemical reaction

To write a chemical equation, you take the chemical formulas ■ of the reactants and link them with an arrow to those of the products. The reaction of hydrogen ($H_2$) and oxygen ($O_2$) forms water ($H_2O$). The chemical equation is: $2H_2 + O_2 \rightarrow 2H_2O$. There must be the same total number of atoms of each element on each side of the equation. The equation shows that two molecules ■ of hydrogen react with one molecule of oxygen to give two molecules of water.

## Ion

An atom or group of atoms that carries an electric charge

When atoms or radicals gain electrons ■, they form ions with a negative electric charge ■. Such ions are called **anions**. When atoms or radicals lose electrons, they form ions with a positive charge. These ions are called **cations**. Many compounds contain ions joined together by ionic bonds ■. The formation of ions is called **ionization** or **dissociation**. It occurs when compounds dissolve or melt. A chemical reaction may take place as the ions join up again in new combinations. The combining power ■ of ions depends on the number of electric charges that they have.

*A chemical reaction*
*Both sides of this balance hold the same equipment and amounts of reactants. When the magnesium ribbon is dropped into the flask, it reacts with the sulfuric acid and releases hydrogen gas. This is the reaction described by the chemical equation in the bottom left-hand corner.*

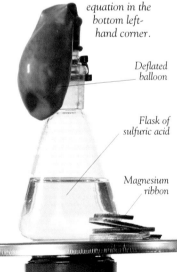

Deflated balloon

Flask of sulfuric acid

Magnesium ribbon

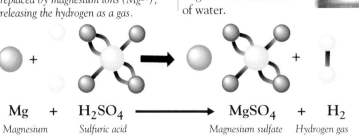

| Mg | + | $H_2SO_4$ | $\longrightarrow$ | $MgSO_4$ | + | $H_2$ |
|---|---|---|---|---|---|---|
| *Magnesium* | | *Sulfuric acid* | | *Magnesium sulfate* | *Hydrogen gas* | |

## Effervescence

The formation of gas bubbles in a liquid by chemical reaction

Adding water to Epsom salts gives a fizzy solution. As the powder dissolves, a chemical reaction occurs that produces a gas. The gas forms bubbles as it escapes from the solution.

The balloon stops the hydrogen gas from escaping and inflates as the gas rises from the flask

The pointer shows that the masses are equal

The magnesium and sulfuric acid react, releasing bubbles of hydrogen gas by effervescence

## Conservation of mass

No change in mass occurs during a chemical reaction

The products of a chemical reaction always have the same total mass ▪ as that of the reactants (provided that none escape). The same atoms are present, though rearranged, at the end of a reaction as at the start, so their total mass cannot change.

## Catalyst

A substance that speeds up a chemical reaction but that does not change itself

The exhaust ▪ system of a car may contain a catalyst. It speeds up a chemical reaction that changes polluting gases in the exhaust fumes into harmless or less harmful gases. **Catalysis** is the process of speeding up reactions by using a catalyst. A **promoter** is a substance that improves a catalyst. A catalyst is also called an **accelerator**.

### Conservation of mass
The gas produced by this reaction causes a small lifting or "buoyant" force on the balloon (see page 51). If the balance is adjusted to allow for this before the reaction takes place, it will be level when the reaction is complete, proving that the masses on both sides are equal.

The flask gets hotter as heat is produced in the reaction

## Fermentation

A chemical reaction that changes starch or sugars into ethanol and carbon dioxide

Bread and alcoholic drinks are made by fermentation. This process uses yeasts, which are biological catalysts that break down starch or sugar in the ingredients of the bread or drink to form carbon dioxide gas ($CO_2$) and alcohol (ethanol). The release of carbon dioxide is used in bread making; gas bubbles make dough rise when it is "proofing" before baking. Ethanol is the alcohol in drinks such as wine or beer.

As the dough ferments, or proofs, carbon dioxide forms and makes the dough rise

Fresh dough mixture

### Bread
The flour in the dough contains starch. Yeast makes the starch change first to sugar, and then to carbon dioxide.

## Radical

A group of atoms that does not change during a chemical reaction

Silver nitrate ($2AgNO_3$) reacts with copper (Cu) to give copper nitrate ($Cu(NO_3)_2$) and silver ($2Ag$). The group of atoms that forms the nitrate ($NO_3$) part of the molecules does not change, so it is a radical. It contains one atom of nitrogen and three of oxygen.

Continued on next page ➤

# Mole (mol)

The SI unit of amount of substance

The mole is a measure of the number of atoms ▪, molecules ▪, or ions ▪ in a substance. It equals the number of carbon–12 atoms that together have a mass of 12 grams (about 602,000 million million million). This number is known as **Avogadro's** ▪ **number**, or **Avogadro's constant**. One mole of any substance has a mass in grams equal to its atomic mass ▪ or its molecular mass ▪. Oxygen has an atomic mass of 16. Oxygen gas has molecules of two atoms each, so 1 mole of oxygen gas has a mass of 32 grams. Similarly, one mole of hydrogen gas ($H_2$) has a mass of 2 grams. One mole of oxygen always reacts with two moles of hydrogen to give two moles of water.

1 mole of copper

1 mole of iodine

*Moles and molecules*
*A mole of copper has a mass of 64 grams and a mole of iodine 127 grams, yet each has the same number of atoms.*

# Reactivity series

A list of elements that shows how easily they react

Elements that form ions easily are said to be very **reactive**. The reactivity series orders elements according to how reactive they are. Sodium, a very reactive metal, is higher up in the series than gold, a very unreactive metal. The series is also called the **electrochemical series** or the **electromotive series**. **Electropositive** elements are those which form positive ions. They include hydrogen and all metals. Nonmetallic elements are **electronegative** elements, because they form negative ions.

## *Precipitation reaction*
*When solutions of potassium iodide and lead nitrate are mixed together, a yellow precipitate called lead iodide forms. Potassium nitrate also forms, but it is soluble, so it stays in solution.*

# Precipitation

The formation of an insoluble solid in a solution

When two soluble compounds ▪ dissolve in a solvent, such as water, they may react together to produce an insoluble compound called a **precipitate**. This appears as a powder in the solution and may sink to the bottom. Soap reacts with dissolved minerals in hard water to give a precipitate of a white scum.

# Reduction

A chemical reaction in which a substance loses oxygen

Iron ore is a compound of iron and oxygen. Heating the ore with carbon removes the oxygen to give iron. This process is reduction. The carbon is a **reducing agent**, a substance that removes oxygen. The carbon is oxidized and carbon dioxide is formed. Reduction and oxidation always occur together in a pair of reactions called a **redox reaction**. Reduction also has a more general meaning: it is a reaction in which atoms of an element gain electrons ▪. A reducing agent provides the electrons, so it is also known as an **electron donor**.

# Hydrogenation

A process in which hydrogen combines with another substance

Hydrogenation is used to make margarine. Combining natural liquid oils with hydrogen turns them into solid margarine.

*The solutions of lead nitrate and potassium iodide are colorless*

# Decomposition

The splitting up of a compound

A chemical reaction ▪ may cause a single compound to split up into its elements, or into simpler compounds. Heating bread to make toast is decomposition, because a carbohydrate ▪ in the bread splits up into carbon and water. **Double decomposition** is a reaction in which two compounds first split up and then reform into two new compounds.

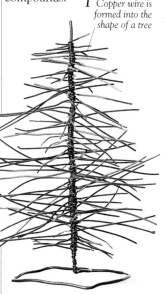

*1 Copper wire is formed into the shape of a tree*

# Polymer

A compound with large molecules that contain many small molecules linked together

Plastics are polymers, and so too are some natural substances, such as rubber, starch, and cellulose. They are made from **monomers**, which are compounds with small molecules. In a chemical reaction called **polymerization**, molecules of these monomers link together, often in long chains, to form the large molecules of a polymer.

◄ *Continued from previous page*

# Synthesis

The formation of a compound from simpler compounds or elements

Synthesis involves building up a compound by reacting together elements ▪, or compounds with simple molecules. The elements or compounds link up to form a new compound. One example of synthesis is the reaction of oxygen with hydrogen to produce water. Synthesis also means producing substances such as drugs by chemical reactions, rather than by extracting them from natural sources, such as plants.

# Corrosion

A chemical reaction that breaks down materials

Rain can cause stone statues to break up, or **corrode**. This is because the rain may contain acid ▪, which reacts with compounds in the stone and changes them to new, powdery compounds, so that the stone crumbles away. Steel can corrode to form **rust**. This occurs when iron in the steel combines with oxygen and water from the air and rain. Rust has little strength and crumbles easily.

# Hydrolysis

A chemical reaction involving water

Water can react with many substances and change them into other substances. Hydrolysis occurs in digestion, when complex compounds in your food are broken down inside your body to produce simpler compounds and body heat.

# Thermochemistry

The study of the changes in heat energy that occur during chemical reactions

Chemical reactions that give out heat, such as burning, are **exothermic** reactions. Reactions that take in heat from their surroundings, such as cooking, are **endothermic**.

# Oxidation

A chemical reaction in which oxygen combines with a substance

Burning is oxidation. When a fuel burns, it combines with oxygen in the air and gives out heat. It also forms waste products, such as smoke. An **oxidizing agent** is a substance that provides the oxygen so that oxidation can occur. Oxidation also has a more general meaning: it is a reaction in which atoms of an element lose electrons. An oxidizing agent takes up the electrons, so it is also known as an **electron acceptor**.

*2 Silver crystals begin to form on the wire tree*

*Clear silver nitrate solution*

*3 The clear solution turns blue as copper nitrate forms*

### Silver-tree experiment

*When copper wire is placed in silver nitrate solution, the silver is precipitated out of the solution and forms beautiful crystals that cling to the copper wire. The solution turns blue as copper ions displace the silver ions, forming a solution of copper nitrate. The equation for this reaction is:*
$$Cu + 2AgNO_3 \rightarrow Cu(NO_3)_2 + 2Ag$$

# Displacement

A chemical reaction in which one element takes the place of another element in a compound

Adding copper to a solution of a silver compound displaces the silver from the compound. The copper dissolves to form a copper compound, and metallic silver is produced. This is also called a **substitution reaction**.

# Electrochemistry

When you listen to music on a personal stereo, you are using electrochemistry. Chemical reactions in the batteries generate electricity, while the wires contain pure metal produced by electrolysis.

**Chrome-plated plastic**
*These plastic machine parts have been electroplated with chromium metal.*

## Electrochemistry

The branch of chemistry that involves electricity

Electricity is important in chemistry, because many chemical compounds are made of electrically charged particles called ions ■. A battery ■ uses a chemical reaction to generate an electric current, while an electric current can be used to break up a chemical compound, as in electrolysis.

## Electrolysis

The use of an electric current to split up a substance

An ionic compound that is molten or in solution ■ contains ions of the elements ■ that make up the compound. The ions have either negative or positive electric charges. **Electrodes** pass an electric current through the molten compound or solution, which is called an **electrolyte**. The electrode with a negative charge is the **cathode**, and it attracts the positive ions. The electrode with a positive charge is the **anode**, and it attracts negative ions. Electrolysis can break down a compound into the elements it contains, because the ions lose their charge at the electrodes and usually become atoms of the elements. Electrolysis is used to extract pure metals from ores ■ and in electroplating.

*Chlorine gas collects in the test tube over the positive electrode*

*The copper chloride solution loses its blue color as the copper is deposited on the cathode*

*Deposits of pure copper form on the cathode*

*Electrolysis cell*

*The anode is the positively charged electrode*

*The cathode is the negatively charged electrode*

**Electrolysis**
*When electricity passes through copper chloride solution, the positively charged copper ions move toward the cathode, where they lose their charge and become copper atoms. The negative chloride ions move toward the anode, where they lose their charge and become chlorine atoms. Pairs of chlorine atoms link up to form molecules of chlorine gas.*

## Electroplating

Coating objects with a thin layer of metal by electrolysis

To electroplate a knife with silver, the knife is first placed in a solution of a silver compound. An electric current is then passed through the knife. Silver leaves the solution and is deposited in a thin, even layer on the knife. **Anodizing** uses electrolysis to put a protective layer of metal oxide, usually of aluminum, onto a metal object.

## Faraday's laws of electrolysis

The mass of an element produced by electrolysis is proportional to the quantity of electricity, and to the atomic mass of the element

The amount of an element produced by electrolysis depends on the quantity of electric charge (measured in coulombs ■) passed through the electrolyte. The quantity of 96,500 coulombs is called the **Faraday constant**, after the scientist Michael Faraday ■. This quantity, or multiples of it, produces one mole ■ of an element (the atomic mass in grams). The multiple depends on the number of electric charges on an element's ions. Twice the Faraday constant produces one mole of copper, because its ions have two charges.

### See also

Battery 108 • Coulomb 105
Element 132 • Faraday 107 • Ion 144
Mole 146 • Ore 150 • Solution 28

# Acids & bases

When you eat sugary foods, a weak acid forms in your mouth. This acid can dissolve the surface of your teeth and cause tooth decay. The opposite of an acid is a base. Your saliva is a weak base that neutralizes the acid in your mouth and protects your teeth. Strong acids and bases are dangerous.

## See also

Atom 34 • Compound 138
Ion 144 • Mineral 150

## Acid

A compound that forms hydrogen ions when it dissolves in water

Many metals dissolve in acid. The acid's hydrogen ions ▨ take electrons from the metal atoms ▨. A salt of the metal forms, and hydrogen gas is released. An acid reacts with a base to form a salt and water. An **acidic** substance is one that has the properties of an acid. Strong acids produced from minerals ▨ are called **mineral acids**. They include hydrochloric acid, nitric acid, and sulfuric acid.

## Salt

A compound formed by an acid and a base, or an acid and a metal

All salts are ionic compounds ▨. They contain positive ions (usually metal ions) linked to negative ions. Common salt is sodium chloride, a compound of positive sodium ions and negative chloride ions. A **double salt** is a compound of two salts. An **acid salt** is a salt that contains hydrogen and is acidic.

### pH testing
*These liquids are tested with universal indicator paper. Lemon juice is the most acidic and ammonia is the most alkaline.*

## Base

A compound that neutralizes an acid

A base contains hydroxyl ($OH^-$) ions with metal or other ions, as in sodium hydroxide (NaOH). An acid contains hydrogen ($H^+$) ions with nonmetal ions, as in nitric acid ($HNO_3$). When a base and acid react, the hydroxyl and hydrogen ions link up to form water ($H_2O$). The metal and nonmetal ions link up to form a salt, such as sodium nitrate ($NaNO_3$). A **basic** substance is one that has the properties of a base. An **alkali** is a base that dissolves in water. A substance is **alkaline** if it is soluble and basic. Strong alkalis are said to be **caustic**. An **amphoteric** substance can act as both an acid and a base.

## Neutral

Neither acidic nor basic

Your stomach produces acid to dissolve food. Too much acid gives you acid indigestion. The medicines you take to ease this pain contain bases that neutralize extra acid. Adding a base to an acid, or an acid to a base, gives a neutral solution of a salt.

## pH

A measure of acidity or alkalinity

The **pH scale** goes from 0 to 14. A neutral substance has a pH of 7, an acid is less than 7, and an alkali is more than 7. A strong acid has a low pH, and a strong alkali a high pH. **Indicators** change color in acids or alkalis. **Phenolphthalein** is colorless in acids and pink-purple in alkalis. **Litmus** is red in acids and blue in alkalis. **Universal indicator** undergoes several color changes over a wide pH range, showing how weak or strong an acid or base is.

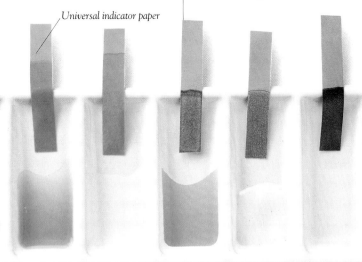

*Universal indicator paper*

| Lemon juice | Malt vinegar | Purified water | Disinfectant | Cleaning fluid | Ammonia |
|---|---|---|---|---|---|
| pH 2 | pH 3 | pH 7 | pH 9 | pH 10 | pH 11 |

# Inorganic chemistry

Chemistry is important because it brings us all kinds of materials that are vital to our lives. Apart from metals, most of these are compounds of elements. Inorganic chemistry studies the elements and the way they combine to form thousands of different compounds.

**See also**

Combining power 141 • Compound 138
Element 132 • Extraction 157
Ion 144 • Ionic bond 140
Metal 132 • Nonmetal 132
Organic compound 152 • Radical 145

Sulfur

*Pyrite is often called "fool's gold," because of its golden color*

Pyrite

## Inorganic compound

A substance in which atoms of two or more elements (except carbon) are combined together

Some compounds ▪ are called inorganic because they come from minerals and not living, or organic, things. Carbon compounds are present in all living things, and these are studied in organic ▪ chemistry. However, the element carbon itself, and a few simple carbon compounds are studied in inorganic chemistry. Inorganic compounds are made of metals ▪, or hydrogen combined with a non-metal ▪, or a group of non-metals. Inside these compounds, atoms or groups of atoms called radicals ▪ link together. These are mostly ions ▪ joined by ionic bonds ▪.

Iron nails

**Two elements, one compound**
*The mineral pyrite is made of iron(II) disulfide, an inorganic compound of the elements iron and sulfur.*

## Mineral

An element or inorganic compound that is naturally present in the ground or dissolved in sea water

A few minerals, such as gold, carbon, and sulfur, are pure elements ▪. Most other minerals contain a particular inorganic compound. The mineral bauxite is made of aluminum oxide, for example, and the mineral galena consists of lead sulfide. Such minerals are found in rocks, while salt occurs in the sea. An **ore** is a mineral from which a product, usually a metal, is extracted ▪. Bauxite is an aluminum ore.

## PRINCIPAL INORGANIC IONS AND RADICALS

| Name | Formula | Power | Name | Formula | Power |
|------|---------|-------|------|---------|-------|
| Aluminum | Al | 3+ | Nitrate | $NO_3$ | 1– |
| Ammonium | $NH_4$ | 1+ | Oxide | O | 2– |
| Bromide | Br | 1– | Peroxide | $O_2$ | 2– |
| Calcium | Ca | 2+ | Phosphate | $PO_4$ | 3– |
| Carbonate | $CO_3$ | 2– | Potassium | K | 1+ |
| Chlorate | $ClO_3$ | 1– | Silicate | $SiO_3$ | 2– |
| Chloride | Cl | 1– | Silver(I) (Argentous) | Ag | 1+ |
| Chromium | Cr | 3+ | Silver(II) (Argentic) | Ag | 2+ |
| Copper(I) (Cuprous) | Cu | 1+ | Sodium | Na | 1+ |
| Copper(II) (Cupric) | Cu | 2+ | Sulfate | $SO_4$ | 2– |
| Cyanide | CN | 1– | Sulfide | S | 2– |
| Fluoride | F | 1– | Sulfite | $SO_3$ | 2– |
| Gold(I) (Aurous) | Au | 1+ | Tin(II) (Stannous) | Sn | 2+ |
| Gold(III) (Auric) | Au | 3+ | Tin(IV) (Stannic) | Sn | 4+ |
| Hydrogen | H | 1+ | Zinc | Zn | 2+ |
| Hydrogen carbonate or bicarbonate | $HCO_3$ | 1– | | | |
| Hydroxide | OH | 1– | | | |
| Iodide | I | 1– | | | |
| Iron(II) (Ferrous) | Fe | 2+ | | | |
| Iron(III) (Ferric) | Fe | 3+ | | | |
| Lead(II) (Plumbous) | Pb | 2+ | | | |
| Lead(IV) (Plumbic) | Pb | 4+ | | | |
| Magnesium | Mg | 2+ | | | |

**Note** *Compounds form by the combination of positive and negative ions or radicals in proportions determined by the combining power. Some compounds have names in which the element is followed by its combining power in Roman numerals, such as copper(II) sulfate. Names in parenthesis ending in -ic and -ous are former names.*

**Background picture:** *stalactites are calcium carbonate columns that form on cave roofs*

# PRINCIPAL INORGANIC COMPOUNDS

| Chemical name | Common name | Formula | Uses |
|---|---|---|---|
| Aluminum oxide | Alumina | $Al_2O_3$ | Abrasive |
| Aluminum potassium sulfate | Alum | $KAl(SO_4)_2.12H_2O$ | Mordant |
| Aluminum sulfate | | $Al_2(SO_4)_3$ | Water purification |
| Ammonia | | $NH_3$ | Refrigerant |
| Ammonium chloride | Sal ammoniac | $NH_4Cl$ | Dry cells |
| Ammonium nitrate | | $NH_4NO_3$ | Explosives, fertilizer |
| Ammonium phosphate | | $(NH_4)_2HPO_4$ | Fertilizer |
| Ammonium sulfate | | $(NH_4)_2SO_4$ | Fertilizer |
| Barium sulfate | | $BaSO_4$ | X-ray pictures |
| Calcium carbonate | | $CaCO_3$ | Cement, toothpaste |
| Calcium hydroxide | Slaked lime | $Ca(OH)_2$ | Mortar, plaster |
| Calcium oxide | Lime, quicklime | $CaO$ | Manufacture of glass |
| Calcium sulfate | | $CaSO_4$ | Plaster of Paris |
| Carbon dioxide | | $CO_2$ | Used in fire extinguishers |
| Carbon monoxide | | $CO$ | Reducing agent |
| Copper(II) sulfate | | $CuSO_4$ | Fungicide |
| Hydrochloric acid | | $HCl$ | Strong acid |
| Hydrogen cyanide | Prussic acid | $HCN$ | Poison |
| Hydrogen oxide | Water | $H_2O$ | Solvent |
| Hydrogen peroxide | | $H_2O_2$ | Bleach, disinfectant |
| Hydrogen sulphide | | $H_2S$ | Chemical analysis |
| Lead(II) oxide | Litharge | $PbO$ | Manufacture of glass |
| Magnesium hydroxide | | $Mg(OH)_2$ | Medicine (antacid) |
| Magnesium sulfate | Epsom salt | $MgSO_4$ | Medicine (laxative) |
| Manganese(IV) oxide | Manganese dioxide | $MnO_2$ | Dry cells |
| Nitric acid | | $HNO_3$ | Strong acid |
| Nitrogen dioxide | | $NO_2$ | Manufacture of nitric acid |
| Nitrogen monoxide | Nitric oxide | $NO$ | Manufacture of nitric acid |
| Nitrous oxide | Laughing gas | $N_2O$ | Anesthetic |
| Potassium carbonate | Potash | $K_2CO_3$ | Manufacture of glass & soap |
| Potassium hydroxide | Caustic potash | $KOH$ | Manufacture of soap |
| Potassium nitrate | Niter, saltpeter | $KNO_3$ | Explosives |
| Potassium permanganate | | $KMnO_4$ | Disinfectant |
| Silicon carbide | Carborundum | $SiC$ | Abrasive |
| Silicon(IV) oxide | Silica | $SiO_2$ | Manufacture of glass |
| Silver chloride | | $AgCl$ | Photography |
| Sodium carbonate | Washing soda, sal soda | $Na_2CO_3.10H_2O$ | Manufacture of glass & soap |
| Sodium chloride | Salt | $NaCl$ | Table salt |
| Sodium hydrogencarbonate | Sodium bicarbonate | $NaHCO_3$ | Baking powder |
| Sodium hydroxide | Caustic soda | $NaOH$ | Manufacture of soap |
| Sodium hypochlorite | | $NaOCl$ | Bleach |
| Sodium nitrate | Chile saltpeter | $NaNO_3$ | Fertilizer |
| Sodium sulfate | Glauber's salt | $Na_2SO_4.10H_2O$ | Used in detergents & dyes |
| Sodium tetraborate | Borax | $Na_2B_4O_7.10H_2O$ | Enamel & glass |
| Sodium thiosulfate | Hypo | $Na_2S_2O_3$ | Photography |
| Sulfuric acid | | $H_2SO_4$ | Car batteries |
| Sulfur(IV) oxide | Sulfur dioxide | $SO_2$ | Preservative |
| Titanium(IV) oxide | Titanium dioxide | $TiO_2$ | White pigment |
| Tungsten carbide | | $WC$ | Abrasives |
| Zinc oxide | | $ZnO$ | White pigment, cosmetics |

**Note** In the chemical formulas above, a dot (.) represents a bond with water of crystallization.

*Background picture: crystals of copper(II) sulfate*

# Organic chemistry

Plants, animals, and crude oil are composed mainly of compounds containing the element carbon. Organic chemistry studies these compounds and the materials – such as fuels, medicines, and plastics – that are made from them.

## Organic compound

A substance in which atoms of carbon and one or more other elements are combined

There are millions of carbon compounds ■ – more than all the compounds of the other elements ■ added together. This is because any number of carbon atoms ■ can join together inside a molecule ■ as chains or rings of carbon atoms. Atoms of hydrogen, nitrogen, oxygen, or other elements link to the chain or ring. These compounds are called organic because they make up living things. A few simple carbon compounds, such as carbon dioxide, are inorganic.

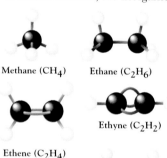

Methane (CH$_4$)     Ethane (C$_2$H$_6$)

Ethyne (C$_2$H$_2$)

Ethene (C$_2$H$_4$)

Benzene (C$_6$H$_6$)

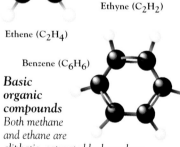

*Basic organic compounds*
*Both methane and ethane are aliphatic, saturated hydrocarbons. Ethene is an alkene, an unsaturated hydrocarbon with a double bond between its carbon atoms. Ethyne is an unsaturated hydrocarbon with carbon atoms linked by a triple bond. Benzene is an aromatic hydrocarbon with a ring of carbon atoms linked by single and double bonds.*

## Saturated compound

An organic compound that contains single bonds between its carbon atoms

The atoms in the molecules of an organic compound are joined by covalent bonds ■. Each carbon atom makes four bonds. In the molecule of a saturated compound, such as ethane (CH$_3$–CH$_3$), each carbon atom uses one of its four bonds to link to the next carbon atom. The remaining three bonds link with other atoms. An **unsaturated compound** has molecules in which a pair of carbon atoms each use two or three bonds to join together, creating double or triple bonds. Ethene (CH$_2$=CH$_2$) is an unsaturated compound containing a double bond.

## Aromatic compound

An organic compound that contains a ring of carbon atoms

The molecules of an aromatic compound usually contain a ring of six carbon atoms. This ring may be linked to other rings or chains of atoms. The carbon atoms in the ring are joined together by single and double bonds. In a structural formula ■, a ring of six carbon atoms is represented by a hexagon. Aromatic compounds include benzene and phenol. They are called aromatic because many have a strong smell.

## Aliphatic compound

An organic compound that contains a chain of carbon atoms

Aliphatic compounds and aromatic compounds are the two main classes of organic compounds. The carbon atoms in an aliphatic compound form a straight chain, or a chain with side branches. Ethane and ethanol are aliphatic compounds, and so is methane, although it only contains one carbon atom.

*Fuels such as gasoline and the butane in this burner are organic compounds*

*Plastic gas can*

*Soap is made from either plant or animal oils*   *Plastics are made from crude oil*   *Natural sponges are living sea creatures*

*Organic compounds*
*The everyday items labeled above contain organic compounds. All are made of the elements carbon and hydrogen, usually combined with oxygen, and sometimes another element or two. The difference between them depends mainly on the number of carbon atoms in each molecule and on how they are arranged. All of these products are derived either from living things (plants or animals) or from crude oil.*

# Alkane

An aliphatic hydrocarbon with carbon atoms linked by single bonds

Alkanes are a group of saturated hydrocarbons. An alkane molecule contains a chain of carbon atoms linked by single bonds. Alkanes are also called **paraffins**. Their names end in -ane, and they include methane, ethane, and butane.

# Alkyl group

A group of atoms present in many organic compounds

Alkyl groups are alkane molecules that have lost one hydrogen atom. They include methyl ($CH_3-$) and ethyl ($C_2H_5-$) groups, which form from methane and ethane molecules. **Aryl groups** are aromatic hydrocarbons that have lost one hydrogen atom. They include phenyl groups ($C_6H_5-$), which form from benzene molecules. Many compounds have alkyl or aryl groups linked to other atoms or groups. Linking a methyl group to an atom of chlorine, for example, gives a compound called chloromethane ($CH_3Cl$). The chlorine atom takes the place of the hydrogen atom missing from the methane molecule.

*Aerosol spray*
*Scientists have discovered that CFCs damage the ozone layer in the Earth's atmosphere. Less harmful gases are now being used in aerosol sprays.*

# Chlorofluorocarbon (CFC)

A compound that contains carbon, chlorine, and fluorine

CFCs and **fluorocarbons** are like hydrocarbons, but the hydrogen atoms are replaced by chlorine or fluorine atoms. They were widely used in refrigerators and aerosol sprays, but it is now known that they harm the Earth's atmosphere.

# Alkene

An aliphatic hydrocarbon with a double bond

The alkenes are a group of unsaturated hydrocarbons. Each has a chain of carbon atoms in which two carbon atoms are linked by a double bond. They are also called **olefins**, meaning "oil formers," because they react with halogen ▪ gases to give oily products. They include ethene. The **alkynes**, or **acetylenes**, are unsaturated hydrocarbons with carbon atoms linked by a triple bond, as in an ethyne molecule.

*Milk from cows*

*Rice breakfast cereal*

*Flowering poinsettia plant*

*Sugar made from sugar cane plants*

*This shirt is made of fibers from cotton plants*

# Hydrocarbon

An organic compound containing only carbon and hydrogen

Hydrocarbons are either saturated or unsaturated compounds. Each molecule has a chain or ring of carbon atoms to which hydrogen atoms are linked. Hydrocarbons with just a few carbon atoms in their molecules are gases. Those with several or many carbon atoms are liquids or waxy solids. Fuels such as natural gas, gasoline, and coal contain hydrocarbons.

# Isomer

A compound that has the same number and type of atoms in its molecules as another compound

Ethanol, an alcohol ▪, and methoxymethane, an ether ▪, are isomers. The molecules of both compounds contain two carbon atoms, six hydrogen atoms, and one oxygen atom. But inside the compounds the atoms link together in different ways. Their structural formulas show the difference. Ethanol is $CH_3CH_2OH$, and methoxymethane is $CH_3OCH_3$.

## See also

Alcohol 154 • Atom 34 • Compound 138
Covalent bond 140 • Element 132
Ether 154 • Halogens 137
Molecule 138 • Structural formula 139

*Continued on next page* ➤

# Carbohydrate

A compound of carbon, hydrogen, and oxygen, in which there are two hydrogen atoms for every oxygen atom

Carbohydrates contain hydrogen and oxygen combined in the ratio of 2 to 1, the same proportions as in water. They are an important part of our diet, as they provide us with energy to live. Sweet, soluble carbohydrates, such as glucose and sucrose, are called **sugars**. Many sugars have molecules with six or twelve carbon atoms. **Starch** is a carbohydrate that occurs in cereals and potatoes. **Cellulose** is a carbohydrate that makes up the stems of plants. Starch and cellulose are polymers ▪ composed of many sugar molecules linked together. Plants use sunlight to form carbohydrates and oxygen from carbon dioxide and water. This is called photosynthesis.

Grape juice contains the sugar glucose, a carbohydrate

***From grape juice to wine vinegar***
*Grape juice contains the carbohydrate glucose ($C_6H_{12}O_6$). In wine making, the glucose in the grape juice breaks down into ethanol and carbon dioxide gas ($2C_2H_5OH + 2CO_2$). When ethanol combines with oxygen, it forms ethanoic acid and water, or wine vinegar ($C_2H_5OH + O_2 \rightarrow CH_3COOH + H_2O$).*

## See also

Acid 149 • Alkyl group 153 • Base 149
Fermentation 145 • Hydrocarbon 153
Polymer 146 • Salt 149 • Solvent 28

# Ether

An organic compound that contains an oxygen atom

An ether contains two alkyl groups ▪ linked to an atom of oxygen. The most important is ethoxyethane, or diethyl ether, in which two ethyl groups link to an oxygen atom. It is used as a solvent ▪ and as an anesthetic.

# Alcohol

An organic compound that contains a pair of oxygen and hydrogen atoms

An alcohol is like a hydrocarbon ▪, except that a hydroxyl (–OH) group has replaced a hydrogen atom. When this happens to the hydrocarbon ethane ($C_2H_6$), for example, it becomes the alcohol ethanol ($C_2H_5OH$). Ethanol is present in alcoholic drinks and is also used as a solvent and a fuel.

When wine is made from grape juice, the glucose breaks down to form ethanol, an alcohol

# Ester

A compound made from an organic acid and alcohol

A carboxylic acid reacts with an alcohol to form an ester plus water. In a similar way, an inorganic acid and base ▪ form a salt ▪ and water. Ethanol and ethanoic acid form ethyl ethanoate, a liquid with a fruity smell used as a solvent and in nail polish. Fats and oils made from plants and animals, such as margarine and butter, are esters.

# Carboxylic acid

An organic acid

Organic compounds that contain a carboxyl group (–COOH) are weak acids ▪. This is because the carboxyl group can lose its hydrogen atom easily. When carboxylic acids combine with alcohols, they form esters. **Fatty acids** are like hydrocarbons, except that a carboxyl group has replaced an atom of hydrogen. The most important fatty acid is ethanoic acid, or acetic acid, which gives vinegar its sharp taste. **Amino acids** are carboxylic acids that also contain an amino group (–$NH_2$). Amino acids are very important to human beings, because they can link up to form proteins. Proteins give us energy and help our bodies grow.

*When wine vinegar is made from wine, the ethanol combines with oxygen to form ethanoic acid, a carboxylic acid*

## ORGANIC GROUPS

| Name | Formula |
| --- | --- |
| Amino | –$NH_2$ |
| Butyl | $C_4H_9$– |
| Carbonyl | =CO |
| Carboxyl | –COOH |
| Ethyl | $C_2H_5$– |
| Methyl | $CH_3$– |
| Nitro | –$NO_2$ |
| Pentyl | $C_5H_{11}$– |
| Phenyl | $C_6H_5$– |
| Propyl | $C_3H_7$– |
| Vinyl | $CH_2$=CH– |

***Background picture:*** *a vinyl record*

◄ *Continued from previous page*

# PRINCIPAL ORGANIC COMPOUNDS

| Name | Formula | Uses |
|------|---------|------|
| Benzene | $C_6H_6$ | Solvent, plastics |
| Butadiene | $CH_2:CH.CH:CH_2$ | Synthetic rubber |
| Butane | $C_4H_{10}$ | Fuel |
| Citric acid | $C_3H_5O(COOH)_3$ | Flavoring, health salts |
| CS gas | $C_6H_4ClCH:C(CN)_2$ | Tear gas |
| Dichlorodiethyl sulfide, mustard gas | $(CH_2ClCH_2)_2S$ | Poison gas |
| Ethanal, acetaldehyde | $CH_3CHO$ | Industrial chemicals |
| Ethane | $C_2H_6$ | Fuel |
| Ethane-1,2-diol, ethylene glycol, glycol | $(CH_2OH)_2$ | Antifreeze, plastics |
| Ethanoic acid, acetic acid | $CH_3COOH$ | Vinegar, chemicals |
| Ethanol, ethyl alcohol | $C_2H_5OH$ | Alcoholic drinks, fuel, solvent |
| Ethene, ethylene | $H_2C:CH_2$ | Polythene, chemicals |
| Ethoxyethane, diethyl ether, ether | $C_2H_5OC_2H_5$ | Anesthetic, solvent |
| Ethyl ethanoate, ethyl acetate | $CH_3COOC_2H_5$ | Solvent, flavoring, cosmetics |
| Ethyne, acetylene | $C_2H_2$ | Oxyacetylene welding |
| Fluorescein | $C_{20}H_{12}O_5$ | Fluorescent dye |
| Fructose, levulose | $C_6H_{12}O_6$ | Honey, fruit juice |
| Glucose, dextrose | $C_6H_{12}O_6$ | Honey, jam, candy, beer |
| Glycerol, glycerine | $CH_2OH.CHOH.CH_2OH$ | Plastics, explosives, medicines |
| Lactic acid | $CH_3CHOHCOOH$ | Food & textile industries |
| Lactose, milk sugar | $C_{12}H_{22}O_{11}$ | Occurs in milk |
| Methanal, formaldehyde, formalin | $HCHO$ | Disinfectant, preservative |
| Methane, firedamp, marsh gas | $CH_4$ | Natural gas, chemicals |
| Methanoic acid, formic acid | $HCOOH$ | Textile industry |
| Methanol, methyl alcohol | $CH_3OH$ | Solvent |
| Methylbenzene, toluene | $C_6H_5CH_3$ | Explosives, chemicals |
| Methylnitrobenzene, trinitrotoluene (TNT) | $C_6H_2CH_3(NO_2)_3$ | Explosive |
| Naphthalene | $C_{10}H_8$ | Plastics, dyes |
| Nitroglycerin(e) | $C_3H_5(ONO_2)_3$ | Explosive (dynamite) |
| Octane | $C_8H_{18}$ | Fuel |
| Phenol, carbolic acid, hydroxybenzene | $C_6H_5OH$ | Disinfectant, dyes, plastics |
| Propane | $C_3H_8$ | Fuel |
| Propanone, acetone | $CH_3COCH_3$ | Solvent, chemicals |
| Sucrose | $C_{12}H_{22}O_{11}$ | Cane sugar, beet sugar |
| Tartaric acid, dihydroxysuccinic acid | $HOOC(CHOH)_2COOH$ | Health salts, dyes |
| Tetrachloromethane, carbon tetrachloride | $CCl_4$ | Dry cleaning, fire extinguishers |
| Tetraethyllead | $(C_2H_5)_4Pb$ | Additive in leaded gasoline |
| Trichloromethane, chloroform | $CHCl_3$ | Solvent, former anesthetic |
| Urea, carbamide | $CO(NH_2)_2$ | Fertilizer, medicines, plastics |
| Warfarin | $C_{19}H_{16}O_4$ | Rat poison, anticoagulant |

**Note** In the chemical formulas above, bonds between carbon atoms are shown by dots. A single dot (.) is a single bond, and a pair of dots (:) a double bond.

*Background picture: a cloud of smoke and flames created by an explosion*

# Chemical analysis

Given a mystery substance, how could you find out its identity? The best way would be by chemical analysis. Scientists use chemical analysis to check the purity of foods and medicines.

*Flame tests*
*From left to right: strontium (red), calcium (orange/red), potassium (violet) and barium (yellow/green).*

## Chemical analysis

A method of finding the composition of a substance or a mixture of substances

**Analytical chemistry** is the branch of chemistry that deals with chemical analysis. There are two main kinds of chemical analysis, called qualitative analysis and quantitative analysis.

## Qualitative analysis

Testing a substance or mixture to find out which elements or compounds it contains

Adding different reagents to a substance or mixture produces chemical reactions ▪ that show which elements ▪ or compounds ▪ are present. The flame test, mass spectroscopy ▪, chromatography, and spectroscopy ▪ are also used.

*Paper chromatography*
*Simple paper chromatography separates out pigments from a mixture of colored flower petals and a solvent, such as nail polish remover.*

## Chromatography

A method of analysing a mixture by separating the substances present

In simple chromatography, a solution of the mixture passes through paper that absorbs the dissolved substances. Some of the substances are taken up faster than others, so the substances separate out. They can be identified by, for example, their color or how well they conduct heat. In **thin layer chromatography**, a porous film is used to separate a mixture. In **gas chromatography**, the mixture is vaporized and then mixed with a gas that carries it through a column of absorbent material.

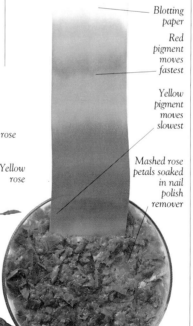

Blotting paper

Red pigment moves fastest

Yellow pigment moves slowest

Red rose

Yellow rose

Mashed rose petals soaked in nail polish remover

## Flame test

A test for certain metallic elements

A small amount of the compound to be tested is placed on the end of a platinum wire and held in a gas flame. Each element gives the flame a particular color. Sodium compounds color the flame yellow, and potassium compounds violet. **Flame photometry** examines the light produced by the flame to measure the amount of an element that is present.

## Quantitative analysis

Testing a substance or mixture to measure the amounts of elements present

Spectroscopy can be used to measure the concentrations of different elements in a substance or mixture, as well as to identify them. Two other methods of quantitative analysis use chemical reactions. **Volumetric analysis** measures how much of a particular reagent ▪ is needed to react with an element present in a substance or mixture. **Gravimetric analysis** uses a chemical reaction to form a compound of an element that can then be weighed.

### See also

Chemical reaction 144 • Compound 138
Element 132 • Mass spectroscopy 35
Reagent 144 • Spectroscopy 81

# Chemical industry

Chemistry is put to work on a gigantic scale by the chemical industry. Every day, we use many of its products. These include materials such as plastics and paints, and pure chemical compounds, which go into medicines, for example.

**Chemical plant**
*This factory uses the contact process to produce large amounts of sulfuric acid for use in industry.*

## Chemical engineering

Designing, building, and operating factories and machines that make chemical products

Chemical engineers in factories control machines that use chemical processes to make useful materials and products. **Raw materials** are substances used as the starting point of these processes. Most raw materials occur naturally. They include air, oil, coal, ores ▪, limestone, and plants. Nitrogen from the air, for example, goes to make a chemical compound called ammonia. Ammonia is then used to manufacture fertilizers.

## Chemical process

A chemical reaction used to make a particular product

The chemical industry has several standard processes to make basic chemical compounds. The **contact process** makes sulfuric acid from sulfur and oxygen by bringing them in contact with a catalyst ▪. The **Haber process** produces ammonia by reacting ▪ nitrogen with hydrogen. The **Solvay process** manufactures sodium carbonate by reacting ammonia, salt (sodium chloride), and carbon dioxide made from limestone.

*Ammonia*   *Salt*
*Coal*   *Limestone*

**Raw materials**

*Sodium carbonate*

**Product**

*Soaps*   **Materials from product**   *Glassware*

**The Solvay process**
*The raw materials of ammonia, water, salt, and limestone are heated by coal, another raw material. The main product of the reaction is sodium carbonate (washing soda, or soda ash), which is important in the manufacture of soap and glass.*

**New from old**
*Compressed waste metal is collected for recycling.*

## Recycling

Using waste products to make new products

Unwanted metal cans, glass bottles, newspapers, and plastic articles can be recycled to make new products. Recycling helps to save raw materials. It reduces pollution, too, because the waste does not have to be destroyed or dumped.

## Extraction

Obtaining a useful substance from a raw material

Several processes are used in extraction. **Flotation** separates ores from rock by grinding the rock and then adding it to water so that the ore particles float and the rock particles sink. **Leaching** involves treating a material with a solvent ▪, often water, to dissolve a soluble substance in it. Leaching is used to extract sugar from plants, and metals from ores. Gold, for example, is obtained from ore by treating the ore with a solution of sodium cyanide. The metal dissolves out of the ore, and can later be separated from the solution. The substances produced by extraction may need **refining**. This removes impurities to give a very pure substance. Smelting ▪ and electrolysis ▪ are used to refine metals.

## By-product

A substance obtained during the manufacture of another substance

Making one product may also produce a second product that is useful. For example, some gold is obtained as a by-product when copper and silver are refined.

# Natural products

Many of the products we use today, such as paper and glass, are made from naturally occurring materials, such as wood and sand. These are changed or processed by methods that are based on those that have been used for hundreds of years.

### Lubricating oil
*Oils are used to make machinery run smoothly and quietly.*

## Oil

A thick, viscous liquid obtained from plants and animals

The kind of oil that is used to make fuels and lubricating oils is crude oil or petroleum ▧, which is found in the ground. It is formed from the buried and compressed remains of long-dead organisms. Other oils come from plants and animals. Plant oils include olive oil, which is made by pressing olives, and sunflower oil, which is made from sunflower seeds. **Linseed oil** is made from flax seeds, and is used in putty. Animal oils include fish oil, which is a source of vitamins. Oils do not mix with water, but become soluble if chemicals are added.

## Margarine

A substitute for butter made with vegetable oils or animal fats

Margarine is made by treating oils such as palm oil with hydrogen. The oil thickens to produce a fatty solid that spreads easily. Margarine was invented in the 1860s by a French chemist, Hippolyte Mège-Mouriés. Almost any vegetable, animal, or fish oil can be made into margarine.

## Paper

Material made of natural fibers pressed together as a thin sheet

Paper is produced from a pulp made by breaking down timber or cotton into a mixture of fibers and water. This is done either by grinding the timber or cotton, or by cooking it with caustic soda or other chemicals. Glues are often added to the pulp to improve the quality of the paper. The pulp is spread in a thin layer on a long mesh belt, where it dries, and is pressed to form paper.

*1 First the raw material must be broken down into its basic fibers. In the case of wood, this means beating wood chips and sawdust with water until it is thoroughly pulped.*

*Layers of paper between absorbent material*

### Paper making
*Fine hand-made paper is still made by traditional methods. Although it is usually made from pulped soft wood, cotten rags and linen are also used, particularly in Europe and the United States. The Chinese probably invented paper making in about AD 105, and this simple process has changed very little.*

### Concrete
*Concrete is poured into molds and then sets hard to form blocks of any size or shape for use in building.*

## Cement

A material used in building to stick bricks or stone blocks together

Cement is made by heating crushed limestone and clay. It is mixed with sand and water for use in building. The compounds in the cement react with water and set hard. **Mortar** is a similar building material made by mixing slaked lime (calcium hydroxide) with sand and water. The lime sets hard by reacting with carbon dioxide in the air to form calcium carbonate. **Concrete** is a mixture of cement, stones, sand, and water. **Reinforced concrete** contains steel rods to strengthen it.

*The final consistency of the pulp should be 0.5% fiber to 99.5% water*

*Pressing board*

*3 When drained, the thin layer of paper from the mold is laid on a piece of absorbent material. Successive layers of the material and paper are laid on top. When a stack of paper is ready, it is pressed between two boards.*

# Glass

A transparent material made from sand

Glass, such as that used to make bottles, is made by heating sand, soda, and lime. These melt together and set hard to give a transparent brittle material that can be molded into any shape. Other substances may be added to glass to improve its strength, heat resistance, and optical qualities. **Glass fibers** are glass threads used in fiberoptics ■ and to make insulating materials. When plastic ■ is reinforced with glass fibers, **fiberglass** is formed. This is strong, resists corrosion, and is used to make the hulls of boats. **Enamel** is a thin layer of glass fixed to a metal object. It gives a protective coating, and is also used in jewelry.

Mold                                   Deckle

**2** A mold and deckle are lowered into a container of pulp. When they are just covered by the liquid, a layer of pulp will be resting on the mold, its edges contained by the deckle. The mold is then lifted out, and tilted to get rid of surplus water.

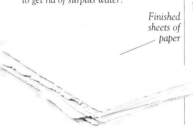

Finished sheets of paper

Raw clay    Shaped clay    Finished, glazed pot

**Making pots**
Clay pots are first molded and then fired in a kiln. They may also be covered with a glaze and fired again, to give the pot a glassy, protective surface.

# Ceramics

Hard and strong materials made from clay or minerals

Earthenware is a ceramic used for pots, tiles, and pipes. It is made by molding or pressing moist clay into shape, and then heating it to a high temperature in an oven called a **kiln**. Fine tableware is made of **porcelain**, a ceramic produced from china clay (kaolin), quartz, and feldspar. Ceramics are also made of metal oxides such as alumina. Ceramics resist corrosion, heat, and electricity. They are used in insulators, the spark plugs of car engines, parts of spacecraft, and **refractories**, which are heat-resistant materials for lining the insides of furnaces.

# Turpentine

A liquid obtained from pine trees

Turpentine is used in the mixing of paints, varnishes, and polishes. It is a colorless liquid with a strong, pinelike smell and is made by distilling the resin of pine trees.

**4** After two hours, the sheets of paper are separated from the absorbent material. The sheets are then laid out separately to dry for a further 2–4 hours, before they are pressed again for 2–3 days.

## See also
Dye 161 • Fiber optics 85
Hydrocarbon 153 • Petroleum 164
Plastic 162 • Polymer 146

# Cosmetics

Substances that people use to improve their appearance

Cosmetics include creams, lotions, and powders for cleaning, moistening, softening, and decorating the skin and hair. Most cosmetics are made of natural substances obtained from plants, petroleum, and minerals, but synthetic compounds such as dyes ■ may also be included. **Perfume** has a pleasant odor, and is used on its own or in cosmetics. Most perfumes are made from plant oils, but some contain animal products or synthetic products.

**Making up**
Most cosmetics contain oils and scents extracted from plants and minerals.

# Rubber

A tough elastic material made from the latex of rubber trees

Natural rubber is made from latex, a liquid taken from rubber trees. It is a natural polymer ■ of a hydrocarbon ■. Treating rubber with sulfur to harden it is called **vulcanizing**. Both natural rubber and synthetic rubber (which is made by polymerizing hydrocarbons) are used to make tires and many other products.

# Textiles

The clothes we put on each day, and the curtains, carpets, and furniture coverings that decorate our homes are all textiles. They are made of tiny fibers linked together. The fibers either come from plants and animals or are made by chemical processes.

**Weaving**
*A weaver at work on his loom in Mexico. Many textiles are woven in factories on machine-powered looms.*

## Weaving

Making a fabric by lacing threads

Cloth is woven on a **loom**. A set of parallel threads, called the **warp**, is held tightly by the loom. The loom moves another set of threads, called the **weft**, over and under the threads in the warp. This laces the weft and the warp together. Using threads of different colors gives a patterned cloth. Patterns can also be printed onto fabrics.

*Undyed fleece*

*Reels of spun wool*

## See also

Compound 138

Chemical process 157 • Polymer 146

## Textile

A fabric made of fibers

Many textiles are made of **natural fibers** obtained from plants and animals. The fibers can be stuck together to produce textiles such as **felt**, but mostly they are made into thread, which is then woven or knitted together to produce a fabric. **Wool** comes from sheep. When a fleece is cut off a sheep, the fibers in the fleece can be spun into woolen thread. The hair of other animals, such as goats, rabbits, and camels, is also used to make textiles. **Cotton** is a fine thread obtained from the fibers of cotton seed pods, or bolls. **Linen** thread is made of fibers from the stalks of flax plants. **Silk** is made from the cocoons of silkworms. The long fibers of the cocoons are unwound and spun into thread. Synthetic fibers, such as polyester, are also used to make textiles. Many textiles are a mix of natural fibers and synthetic fibers.

*Woven rug*

**From a fleece to a woven rug**
*The fleece of a sheep is a mass of long or curly fibers. The fleece is cut off, and the fibers are spun into thread. The thread is dyed and woven into a rug on a loom.*

***Making nylon***
*Nylon is formed when solutions of special organic chemicals react together. In this experiment, one solution is poured onto the other. Nylon forms where the solutions meet.*

*Nylon fiber is pulled out*

*Solution of hexanedioic acid*

*1,6-diaminohexane solution*

## Synthetic fiber

A fiber made by a chemical process

Textiles such as polyester, nylon, rayon, acetate, and acrylic are made of synthetic fibers. These textiles are better than natural fibers in some ways, being strong and crease resistant, for example. Synthetic fibers can be made by treating wood to extract cellulose or by making chemical compounds ▥ react together to produce polymers ▥. The cellulose and polymers are then either dissolved in solvents or melted. The resulting liquid is forced through tiny holes to form long fibers that are spun into thread to make textiles. They are often mixed with natural fibers to produce a textile that has the best properties of several types of fiber.

## Spinning

The production of thread

Machines first separate, clean, and line up the natural fibers in cotton and wool. Synthetic fibers may be added to the natural fibers at this point. Spinning machines then twist the fibers together to form a continuous thread, or **yarn**, which is wound to produce reels of cotton and wool. Thread can also be made entirely of synthetic fibers spun together.

# Synthetic products

Many products that were once made only of natural materials, such as dyes, have been much improved by using chemical processes. Synthetic dyes, for example, can be made in a much greater range of colors than natural dyes.

**See also**

Acid 149 • Alkali 149
Chemical reaction 144 • Molecule 138
Oil 158 • Oxidation 147 • Salt 149

## Paint

A mixture of pigment and liquid used to color or protect a surface

The colored pigment is suspended in a natural or synthetic oil, which may form an emulsion with water or may be dissolved in a solvent. When paint dries on a surface, the oil either reacts with oxygen in the air or it loses water or solvent by evaporation. This forms a hard layer of paint on the surface.

## Adhesive

A substance that sticks surfaces firmly together

As an adhesive or **glue** sets, it either reacts with oxygen in the air or loses water or a solvent by evaporation. When the adhesive hardens, powerful bonds form between the molecules in the adhesive and the surfaces, holding them together. Some strong adhesives are made of two liquids. When mixed together, a chemical reaction ■ occurs between them.

## Soap

A cleaning agent

Soap is made by boiling fats and oils ■ with a strong alkali ■, such as sodium hydroxide or potassium hydroxide. Soap contains sodium or potassium salts ■ of organic acids ■ with long molecules ■. Soap cleans in water because its molecules surround particles of greasy dirt on the surface of soiled skin or cloth. The molecules carry the particles away from the surface and into the water. Washing liquids and powders contain **detergents**, which are made of chemicals obtained from petroleum. They have similar molecules to soap and clean in the same way.

### Soap molecule

Soap contains sodium stearate ($C_{17}H_{35}$ COONa). This loses its sodium atom in solution, to become an ion with a long hydrocarbon tail fixed to a COO head.

Hydrogen

Carbon

Oxygen

Sodium

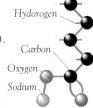

## Explosive

A substance that can suddenly burst apart with great power

Heat or a sudden shock sets off an explosive. A very fast chemical reaction occurs that changes the explosive into gases. A destructive wave of high-pressure gas moves out as it explodes, breaking up rocks in quarrying, for example. **Gunpowder** is an explosive mixture of potassium nitrate, carbon, and sulfur. **Dynamite** and **gelignite** both contain nitroglycerine.

## Bleaching

Removing color

Bleaching removes stains and whitens or lightens materials. Chlorine, oxygen, hydrogen peroxide, and sulfur dioxide all bleach materials. They oxidize ■ colored substances, causing them to lose color. Household bleach often contains sodium hypochlorite, which produces chlorine.

## Dye

A substance that colors material

Synthetic dyes are made of stable compounds, so they do not fade. They attach firmly to fibers in cloth and to other surfaces. The surface may absorb the dye, or a chemical reaction between the dye and the surface may bind the dye. A **mordant** is a substance that fixes dyes to material.

### Soap molecules in water
The tails of the soap molecules stick into greasy dirt. Attraction between the heads of the molecules and water lifts the dirt.

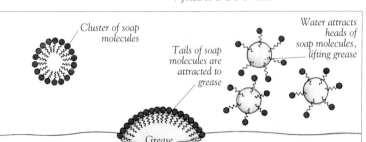

Cluster of soap molecules

Tails of soap molecules are attracted to grease

Water attracts heads of soap molecules, lifting grease

Cloth

Grease

Cloth

# Plastics

Clothes, boxes, bottles, bags, computers, furniture – almost anything can be made using plastics. They are unlike traditional materials, such as wood. Plastics are made to have special properties, such as a particular strength or flexibility.

## See also

Adhesive 161 • Compound 138
Extrusion 166 • Molecule 138
Polymer 146

## Plastic

A synthetic material that can be easily shaped to form an object

Plastics are made from chemical compounds ■ obtained from plants, animals, coal, and petroleum. They are soft or liquid when first made and can be molded into shape under heat or pressure before they harden.

## Synthetic resin

The material of which a plastic is made

Chemical compounds react to form synthetic resins, which are then shaped to make plastic objects. The compounds form polymers ■, which is why the names of many plastics begin with poly-. Polymers have very long molecules ■, and the structure of these molecules gives plastics different properties, making them hard or flexible. An **epoxy resin**, for example, sets very hard and is used to make strong parts and adhesives ■. **Acrylic resins** give rigid and transparent plastics that are used in lenses.

## Thermoplastic

A material that softens when heated and hardens when cooled

Thermoplastics are very useful, because they can be molded into any shape. Some thermoplastics, such as polythene, can also be extruded ■ to make pipes and tubes. Plastics that set hard when heated and remain hard are **thermosetting plastics**. They are used in electrical fittings, such as plugs and sockets, where it is important that the plastic does not melt if there is an electrical fault.

## Injection molding

A method of making plastic objects

Many plastic objects, such as combs, cooking equipment, and toothbrushes, are made by injection molding. Hot, soft plastic is first injected into a mold. Thermoplastics are then cooled so the plastic hardens. Thermosetting plastics set hard while still hot. The mold is then opened, and the object is removed.

## Biodegradability

The capacity of a material to rot away after use

**Biodegradable** plastics begin to break down after a few months or years. Bacteria can attack the plastics so that they rot away. Bags and containers are often made of biodegradable plastics so they do not litter the environment long after being thrown away.

Hydrogen
Carbon

**Ethene molecules**

**Polythene molecule**

*Making polymers*
*Carbon and hydrogen atoms join to make short molecules of ethene (or ethylene). Hundreds of ethene molecules may join together as a chain to form one long molecule of the polymer polythene (polyethylene).*

*Materials of many uses*
*There is a vast range of plastic products available for use in business, in industry, and in the home. The capacity of plastics to be formed into any shape desired makes them versatile manufacturing materials.*

## PRINCIPAL PLASTICS

| Name | Made from | Uses |
|---|---|---|
| Acrylic | Derivatives of acrylic acid | Synthetic fibers, paints |
| Bakelite | Phenol, formaldehyde | Electrical fittings |
| Butyl rubber | Methylpropene, methylbutadiene | Inner tubes |
| Celluloid | Cellulose nitrate, camphor | Early plastic once used for photographic film |
| Kevlar | Phenylenediamine, terephthalyl chloride | High-strength materials |
| Neoprene | Chlorobutadiene | Synthetic rubber |
| Nylon | Hexanedioic acid | Synthetic fibers |
| Polyester | Organic acids and alcohols | Synthetic fibers |
| Polyethylene, polythene | Ethene | Film, bags, pipes, containers |
| Polymethyl methacrylate, Plexiglas, Lucite | Methyl methacrylate | Substitute for glass |
| Polystyrene | Styrene (phenylethene) | Plastic foam |
| Polytetrafluoroethene (PTFE), Teflon | Tetrafluoroethene | Nonstick pans, body parts |
| Polyurethane | Isocyanates, organic alcohols | Plastic foam, adhesives |
| Polyvinyl acetate (PVA) | Vinyl acetate | Adhesives |
| Polyvinyl chloride (PVC) | Vinyl chloride (chloroethene) | Electrical insulation, waterproof clothing |
| Rayon | Cellulose | Synthetic fibers |

**Background picture:** *a Bakelite radio*

## Silicone

A plastic made with the element silicon

The molecules of most plastics contain long chains of carbon atoms. Silicones have large molecules containing chains or rings of alternate silicon and oxygen atoms. They are liquids, plastics, or rubbery materials that resist heat, corrosion, and electricity. Silicones are used as lubricants and to make electrical insulators, paints, and coatings.

## Plasticizer

A substance added to a plastic to improve its properties

A plasticizer may be added to a synthetic resin during the manufacture of a plastic. It makes the plastic less brittle and easier to shape.

### Reinforced bike
*The 1992 Olympic winner of the 4,000-meter cycle sprint, Chris Boardman, rode a revolutionary Lotus bike to victory. The bike has a lightweight carbon-fiber frame, molded from a single piece of material, and carbon-fiber wheels.*

## Laminate

Thin layers of plastics and other materials sealed together

When thin layers of materials such as plastic and wood are glued together, they can be very strong. If layers of glass are bonded with clear plastic, they form a tough laminate. Car windshields may be made of this laminated glass. **Composites** are very strong, light materials made up of several layers of different materials, especially reinforced plastics. They can easily be made in curved shapes.

## Reinforced plastics

Plastics filled with fibers

Reinforced plastics contain thin fibers, especially fibers of glass or carbon, which are hard to break. They are very tough materials that resist corrosion. Burning synthetic fibers produces long **carbon fibers**. Plastics reinforced with these fibers are very strong yet very light, as well as heat resistant.

# Coal and oil

Our supply of energy depends greatly on coal and crude oil, which we burn in power stations and use to make fuels. Coal and oil are also a rich source of chemicals, from which we make plastics, dyes, and other synthetic products that we use every day.

## Fossil fuel

A material that can be burned and that comes from the fossil remains of animals and plants

Coal, natural gas, and fuels that are obtained from petroleum are called fossil fuels. They are the products of the decay of plants and animals that lived millions of years ago. In a few centuries, all the deposits of fossil fuels are likely to be used up, so it is important to reduce the use of fossil fuels by using less gasoline and electricity.

## Natural gas

A gas found underground and used as a fuel

Natural gas is mostly methane. It is often found in petroleum deposits. The gas is piped up from huge underground deposits, and then channelled to cities and towns. There, the gas is used as a fuel for cooking and heating. Natural gas is also a source of propane and butane, which are stored in cylinders for use as fuel. It also contains helium, a light gas used to fill balloons and airships. Chemicals such as methanol are obtained from natural gas and used to make many synthetic products.

## Coal

A solid fuel found underground

Coal is the remains of thick forests that covered the land millions of years ago. The trees and undergrowth were buried, and heat and pressure slowly changed them into coal. Some power stations burn coal to produce electricity. Heating coal without air gives **coke**, a form of carbon used in blast furnaces ▒ to make iron. The heating also yields **coal gas**, a mixture of hydrogen and methane once used as a fuel, and **coal tar**, a black liquid that contains benzene, phenol, and other chemicals. **Pitch**, a black, sticky substance used to surface roads, is obtained from coal tar.

*Coal mining*
At this open-pit mine in Germany, the coal is mined by digging from above. Most coal lies deep below the ground, and tunnels have to be bored to reach the rich seams.

## Petroleum

A dark liquid found in large underground deposits

Petroleum is also called **crude oil** or simply oil. It is a fossil fuel formed from plants and marine animals that became buried millions of years ago. Heat and pressure slowly changed them into petroleum, which is a mixture of many different hydrocarbons ▒. Oil rigs bring petroleum to the surface, and it is then transported to oil refineries to make products such as fuels. **Petrochemicals** are chemicals obtained from petroleum. They are used to make synthetic products such as plastics ▒ and detergents ▒.

*Drilling at sea*
Today, much of the world's oil and natural gas is taken from oilfields in the sea bed. The drilling rigs burn off, or flare, unwanted gas.

## Producer gas

A fuel gas made from coke

Blowing air over burning coke gives producer gas, which contains carbon monoxide. Using steam instead of air gives **water gas**, which contains hydrogen as well as carbon monoxide. Both gases are used as fuels in industry and in the production of chemicals.

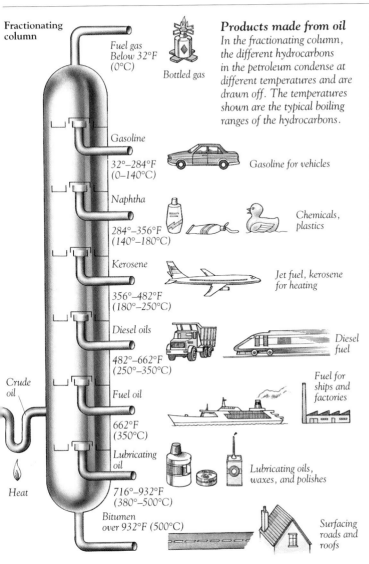

**Fractionating column**

Fuel gas
Below 32°F
(0°C)

*Bottled gas*

Gasoline

32°–284°F
(0–140°C)

*Gasoline for vehicles*

Naphtha

284°–356°F
(140°–180°C)

*Chemicals, plastics*

Kerosene

356°–482°F
(180°–250°C)

*Jet fuel, kerosene for heating*

Diesel oils

482°–662°F
(250°–350°C)

*Diesel fuel*

Fuel oil

662°F
(350°C)

*Fuel for ships and factories*

Lubricating oil

716°–932°F
(380°–500°C)

*Lubricating oils, waxes, and polishes*

Bitumen
over 932°F (500°C)

*Surfacing roads and roofs*

Crude oil

Heat

### Products made from oil

*In the fractionating column, the different hydrocarbons in the petroleum condense at different temperatures and are drawn off. The temperatures shown are the typical boiling ranges of the hydrocarbons.*

# Oil refinery

A factory that makes gasoline and other products from petroleum or crude oil

Crude oil is made up of many different hydrocarbon molecules ▦. In an oil refinery, hydrocarbons are separated into gasoline and other products by a process called fractional distillation ▦. The oil is heated to turn part of it into vapor, which is passed into a fractionating column. There, the vapor rises towards the top and begins to cool. The different hydrocarbons in the oil vapor condense at different heights and are withdrawn. Those with long molecules and high boiling points condense first, but hydrocarbons with shorter molecules and lower boiling points condense higher up. Light products such as **gasoline** are withdrawn from near the top of the column and heavier products like **diesel oil** and fuel oil are taken lower down. The heaviest hydrocarbons, such as **bitumen**, are left at the bottom.

# Cracking

A process used in oil refining to produce lighter hydrocarbons

An oil refinery can get more gasoline from petroleum by cracking. Cracking involves heating the oils to a very high temperature or treating them with a catalyst ▦. The heaviest hydrocarbons – made up of long molecules – are broken up or "cracked" to give gasoline, which has shorter molecules and is less dense.

# Charcoal

A form of carbon

Heating wood without air gives charcoal, which is almost all carbon. It makes a good fuel for cooking food on barbecues.

# Creosote

A dark brown liquid used to preserve timber

Creosote is obtained from coal tar, or from gases produced by heating wood without air. It contains phenol and cresol (methylphenol).

# Mineral spirits

A liquid used as a solvent

Mineral spirits is a mixture of hydrocarbons obtained from petroleum. It is used to make paints and varnishes, and to clean paint brushes after use.

# Denatured alcohol

A solvent and fuel

Denatured alcohol, or **methylated spirit**, is mostly ethanol mixed with methanol. Sometimes colored with dye, it can be burned in lamps with wicks.

# Metals

From early times, metals have played an important part in the development of civilization, providing useful tools and, later, machines. The extraction and working of metals is still a vital industry, because no other common materials are as strong or so easy to shape.

*Copper wire*

*Copper rod*

## Metallurgy

The study of metals

Metals ▦ are metallic elements ▦, such as iron and aluminum, which mostly occur in ores ▦. Metallurgy studies the extraction of metals from their ores, and the mixing of metals to make alloys. It also includes the treatment of metals and alloys to make them stronger. **Metal fatigue** is a weakness that may develop in a metal. Some metals weaken when they are subjected to repeated forces for a long time. The wings of aircraft, for example, are regularly checked for metal fatigue.

## Extrusion

Shaping a metal or other material by forcing it through a hole

In extrusion, hot metal is forced through a hole in a mold called a **die**. The emerging metal usually has the shape of a rod or tube. The hole's size determines the width of the rod or tube. **Wire** is a metal thread made by forcing a rod through smaller and smaller holes.

### See also

Blast furnace 168 • Electrolysis 148
Element 132 • Melting point 24
Metal 132 • Non-metal 132 • Ore 150

## Smelting

Heating an ore to obtain a metal

An ore is a mineral, a compound of a metal with one or more nonmetals ▦, such as oxygen or sulfur. Smelting removes the nonmetal from the ore. Lead ore, called galena, is made of the compound lead sulfide. Heating it makes the sulfur combine with oxygen in the air, leaving lead. Smelting often involves heating an ore with carbon, which removes oxygen. A blast furnace ▦ produces iron in this way. A **flux** is often added during smelting. It combines with impurities in the ore and removes them. Electrolysis ▦ can also be used to extract metals from ores.

## Welding

Joining metals by heating them

A welding torch heats the edges of two metal objects so that the metals melt and flow together. Extra metal may be added to the joint, which hardens as the metal cools. **Oxyacetylene welding** burns acetylene (ethyne) gas in oxygen to give a very hot flame. **Electric-arc welding** passes a strong electric current through the joint to heat the metals. **Soldering** uses solder, an alloy with a low melting point ▦, to join metal parts. The solder is placed at the joint and then heated. It melts and then sticks the parts together as it cools and hardens.

### Forged coins
*The shapes and designs of coins are produced by forging.*

## Forging

Beating or pressing metal into shape

A forging machine forces a block of red-hot metal into a mold called a die. The metal takes the shape of the die. Forged objects are usually very strong. They include engine parts.

## Alloy

A mixture of metals or a metal and nonmetal

Mixing a metal with other metals, or sometimes with a nonmetal such as carbon, gives an alloy with more useful properties than the metal alone. Alloying a metal may increase its hardness, strength, and resistance to corrosion, for example.

*Solder*

*Soldering iron*

### Soldering
*Solder is often used to join electrical components together. It is an alloy of the metals tin and lead.*

## Tempering

Treating a metal to strengthen it

A metal object may bend or break in use. If the metal is tempered before it is shaped into an object, it will be harder and stronger. Tempering involves heating the metal and rapidly cooling it in oil or water. The metal is then heated again and slowly cooled. **Annealing** is another treatment in which a metal is heated and cooled slowly. It makes the metal tougher, yet easier to shape.

# Casting

## Molding a metal object

Shapes ranging from simple blocks to complex statues are made by casting. If a metal object is to be cast, a mold must first be made. Molten metal is poured into the mold, where it cools and solidifies. The object is then removed from the mold. **Continuous casting** forms a continuous metal strip by passing molten metal through a cooling chamber and pressing it between rollers. Casting is also used to shape glass and plastics.

*3 The metal is removed from the mold and the pieces of the statue are welded together.*

*2 Molten bronze is poured into ceramic molds made from the original plaster molds.*

*Bronze horse, polished and cleaned to remove any casting scars*

*1 A clay sculpture is made first. When this is dry, plaster molds are made of different parts of the horse.*

*Clay sculpture*

*Plaster mold*

### Casting a metal statue

*In its simplest form, casting involves making a mold and pouring in molten metal. Artists often use a more complex process, making several molds before they are ready to cast in metal.*

## PRINCIPAL ALLOYS

| Name | Main constituents | Properties | Uses |
|---|---|---|---|
| Alnico | Aluminum, nickel, cobalt, iron | Highly magnetic | Permanent magnets |
| Babbitt metal | Tin, copper, antimony | Hard & strong | Bearings |
| Bell metal | Copper, tin | Sonorous | Bells |
| Brass | Copper, zinc | Easy to shape | Musical instruments, screws & castings |
| Bronze | Copper, tin | Resists corrosion & wear | Statues, bearings |
| Chromium steel (stainless steel) | Iron, chromium, carbon | Resists corrosion | Cutlery, surgical & industrial parts |
| Constantan | Copper, nickel | Stable electrical resistance | Electrical parts |
| Cupronickel | Copper, nickel | Durable | Coinage |
| Duralumin | Copper, aluminum | Strong & light | Bicycles, aircraft |
| German silver | Copper, zinc, nickel | Silver color | Jewelry |
| Gun metal | Copper, tin, zinc | Tough & resists corrosion | Bearings, gears |
| Invar | Iron, nickel | Low expansion | Watches, thermostats |
| Magnalium | Aluminum, magnesium | Strong & light | Aircraft |
| Mischmetal | Cerium, iron, lanthanum | Catches fire | Lighters |
| Monel metal | Nickel, copper | Hard & durable | Chemical equipment |
| Nichrome | Nickel, chromium | Heat resistant | Electrical wiring |
| Ormolu | Copper, zinc, tin | Gold color | Furniture decoration |
| Osmiridium | Osmium, iridium | Resists corrosion | Pen nibs |
| Permalloy | Nickel, iron | Highly magnetic | Electrical machinery |
| Pewter | Tin, lead | Fairly soft | Tableware |
| Solder | Tin, lead | Low melting point | Joining metals |
| Sterling silver | Silver, copper | Harder than pure silver | Jewelry |
| Wood's metal | Bismuth, lead, tin, cadmium | Melts at 158°F (70°C) | Sprinkler systems |

**Background picture:** *an alloy car wheel*

# Iron & steel

Objects as big as ships and skyscrapers, or as small as pins and needles, are made of steel. Steel is an alloy of iron and carbon. It is a strong, hard metal with thousands of different uses.

## Steel

**An alloy of iron and carbon**

Iron is a strong metal. Adding carbon to iron in a proportion of 0.1% to 1.5% changes the iron into steel, which is harder. Heat treatment, such as tempering ■, further increases the metal's hardness and strength. Steel is used to make machines, tools, and large girders that support buildings and bridges. Other metals can be added. Adding chromium forms **stainless steel**, which does not rust.

### Inside a blast furnace

*Iron ore, coke, and limestone are mixed and treated to make lumps called sinter, which the conveyor belt carries to the top of the furnace.*

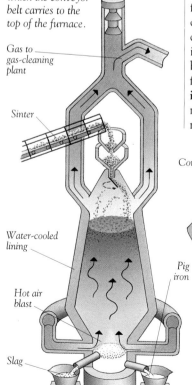

Gas to gas-cleaning plant

Sinter

Water-cooled lining

Hot air blast

Slag

## Blast furnace

**A tall furnace that produces iron from iron ore**

Iron ore, coke ■, and limestone are fed into the top of a blast furnace. Hot air blasts up through the furnace and heats the materials as they descend. The heat causes carbon in the coke to combine with the oxygen in the ore and give carbon dioxide. This escapes, leaving molten iron to flow from the base of the furnace. The limestone combines with impurities in the ore to form **slag**, which floats on the molten iron and is removed. A blast furnace produces **pig iron**, which contains a high proportion of carbon. Adding scrap steel to pig iron gives **cast iron**, which is brittle. Removing the carbon from pig iron gives **wrought iron**, a pure form of iron used to make ornamental gates and railings.

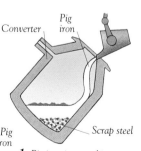

Converter

Pig iron

Pig iron

Scrap steel

**1** *Pig iron is poured into the converter*

### Making steel

*Basic oxygen converters take a charge of up to 385 tons (350 tonnes) of "hot metal" at a time and convert it into steel in about 40 minutes or less.*

## Steel converter

**A large furnace that produces steel**

Pig iron from a blast furnace goes to a steel converter. This heats the pig iron so that some of the carbon in it burns away, leaving the correct proportion of carbon required to make steel. Waste steel can be recycled by adding it to the converter. A **basic oxygen converter** is a huge container of molten pig iron onto which oxygen is blown to remove carbon. A **Bessemer converter** blows air through the pig iron. An **open-hearth furnace** blows air over a charge of pig iron. An **electric-arc furnace** makes steel by electrically heating scrap steel.

## Galvanizing

**The process of coating iron or steel with zinc to stop it rusting**

A coating of zinc prevents the corrosion of an iron or steel object. This is because the oxygen in the air reacts with the zinc rather than with the iron and forms a protecting layer of zinc compounds. Galvanizing is done either by dipping the iron or steel first in acid and then into a bath of molten zinc or by electrolysis ■.

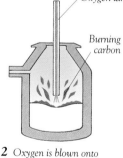

Oxygen lance

Burning carbon

**2** *Oxygen is blown onto the metal at high pressure*

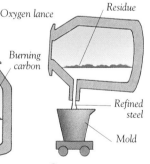

Residue

Refined steel

Mold

**3** *The refined steel is poured off*

### See also

Coke 164 • Electrolysis 148
Tempering 166

# Mathematics

The various branches of mathematics teach us how to understand shapes and handle numbers. We can apply mathematics, making measurements and calculations to give us machines that work and structures that are safe. Computers rely on mathematics to perform tasks.

## MATHEMATICAL SYMBOLS

| Symbol | Meaning | Example |
|---|---|---|
| = | equals | $7 = 4 + 3$ |
| ≠ | is not equal to | $7 \neq 4 + 2$ |
| + | plus (add) | $8 + 6 = 14$ |
| − | minus (subtract) | $9 - 6 = 3$ |
| - | negative (minus numbers) | $4 - 6 = -2$ |
| X | times (multiplied by) | $3 \times 5 = 15$ |
| ÷ | divided by | $8 \div 2 = 4$ |
| < | is less than | $5 < 9$ |
| ≤ | is less than or equal to | $9 \leq 9$ and $11 \leq 13$ |
| > | is more than | $8 > 3$ |
| ≥ | is more than or equal to | $3 \geq 3$ and $9 \geq 5$ |
| $x^2$ | squared | $4^2 = 16$ |
| √ | square root of | $\sqrt{16} = 4$ |
| α | is proportional to | $x \alpha y$ (if x = 1, 2, 3... and y = 3, 6, 9... ) |
| ∞ | infinity | *Background picture: an abacus* |

## Calculator

A machine that makes mathematical calculations

You operate the number keys of a calculator to feed in numbers, and then press other keys to do a calculation, such as addition or multiplication. The answer appears on the display. Inside the calculator is an integrated circuit that does the calculation faster than you could on paper. Some electronic calculators can be programmed like a computer to do advanced calculations. An **abacus** is a simple calculator invented about 5,000 years ago and is still used in some countries today. It consists of beads strung on rows of wires or rods to represent units, tens, hundreds, and so on. You make calculations by moving the beads along the rows.

## Protractor

A device for measuring angles

To measure an angle, you place a protractor over two lines that meet at the angle, with the base of the protractor on one of the lines. The center of the protractor must be on the meeting point of the lines. The angle is then read from a scale.

## Compass

A device for drawing a circle

You can set a compass to draw a circle of a particular size. Place the point and pencil on paper against a ruler. Then move the pencil away from the point until the distance between them is equal to the radius of the circle you want to draw. Now press firmly on the point, and rotate the pencil end to draw the circle.

## Triangle

A device for drawing simple shapes

You can draw along the sides of a triangle to form shapes containing the same angles as the set square. These include squares, rectangles, and triangles.

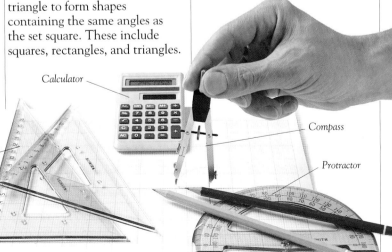

Calculator

Triangle

Compass

Protractor

**Using math tools**
*You can use a compass to draw circles, and a set square to draw rectangles and triangles.*

# Numbers

The way we count quantities and write numbers is important. Our decimal number system helps us to make calculations and handle money, while computers use a code based on the binary system.

## Number

How many things exist in any quantity of things

A written number consists of **digits** or **numerals**, which are symbols such as 5, 0, 2, and 7. The number 313 has three digits, for example. A **positive number** is any number greater than zero, such as 6. A **negative number** is less than zero, such as –6. A whole number is called an **integer**. A whole number greater than 1 that can be divided only by 1 and by itself is a **prime number**, such as 2, 3, 5, 7, 11, 13, 17, 19, 23, and so on. A **base** is a number on which an entire number system is based. The decimal system uses 10 as a base. The binary system uses 2 as a base.

## Binary number

A number made of the digits 0 and 1

The binary number 1101 means one eight, one four, no two, and one one. Each digit has twice the value of the digit to its right.

| 1 | 1 | 0 | 1 |
| 1 | 0 | 1 | 1 |

*The binary system*
*The light bulbs represent, from left to right, eight, four, two and one. The binary number 1101 is 13 (8 + 4 + 0 + 1), and 1011 is 11 in decimal numbers (8 + 0 + 2 + 1).*

## Decimal number

A number made of the ten digits from 0 to 9

The number 24.06 means two tens, four ones, no tenths, and six hundredths. Each digit in a number has ten times the value of the digit to its right. The **decimal point** is a dot that shows which digits represent values greater than 1 and which represent values less than 1. The digits after the dot are called **decimal places**. A **recurring decimal** has one or more digits that repeat for ever, as in 0.1666666... (one sixth). A **rounded number** is an approximate number, so 0.1666666... can be rounded to 0.167, and 231,543 to 230,000.

## Fraction

A number expressed as one number divided by another

Two-thirds ($\frac{2}{3}$ or 2/3) is a fraction. The top number (2) is the **numerator**, and the bottom number (3) is the **denominator**. The numerator is less than the denominator in a **proper fraction**, and more in an **improper fraction**, such as 22/7. A **mixed number** contains a whole number and a fraction, such as $2\frac{1}{2}$.

## Rational number

A whole number or a fraction

125, –6, 24/88, and –33/5 are all rational numbers. An **irrational number** is one that is not equal to one integer divided by another. If written as a decimal number, the digits never stop. For example, the square root of 2 is 1.414213... .

## Square

A number multiplied by itself

The square of 5, or 5 squared ($5^2$), is 5 x 5, or 25. The **square root** ($\sqrt{}$) of a number is the number that, when squared, gives the first number. The square root of 36 is 6.

*The cube*
*Each edge of this cube has three blocks, so it contains 3 cubed (3 x 3 x 3), or 27, blocks in all.*

## Cube

A number multiplied by itself twice

The cube of 2, or 2 cubed ($2^3$), is 2 x 2 x 2, or 8. The **cube root** ($\sqrt[3]{}$) of a number is the number that, when cubed, gives the first number. The cube root of 27 is 3.

## Power

How many times a number is multiplied by itself

10 raised to the sixth power is 10 x 10 x 10 x 10 x 10 x 10, making 1,000,000 or $10^6$. The **index**, or **exponent**, is the number of the power (in this case, 6). **Standard form**, or **scientific notation**, shows a large or small number as a number between 1 and 10 multiplied by a power of 10, so 434,000 is 4.34 x $10^5$. Small numbers have negative powers, so 4.34 x $10^{-5}$ = 0.0000434.

## Reciprocal

The result of dividing a number into 1

The reciprocal of 7 is 1/7. The reciprocal of a fraction is the fraction turned upside down, so the reciprocal of 1/7 is 7/1, or 7.

## Infinity

A number that is too big to count

An **infinite** quantity is endless and cannot be measured. An **infinitesimal** object is too small to be measured.

# Arithmetic & algebra

You use arithmetic whenever you count money or make calculations. Algebra is very useful in science because it enables us to write formulas, for example, and to write computer programs.

## Arithmetic

The addition, subtraction, multiplication, and division of numbers

A **sum** of several numbers is their total when added together. For example, 15 is the sum of 7 and 8. A **product** is the result of multiplying numbers, so 15 is the product of 3 and 5. **Multiples** are numbers given by multiplying one number by others. The numbers 8, 12, and 16 are multiples of 4 (4 x 2 = 8; 4 x 3 = 12; 4 x 4 = 16). A **quotient** is the whole number result of a division, and the **remainder** is any amount left over. When 7 is divided by 3, it gives a quotient of 2 and a remainder of 1.

## Sequence

A set of numbers that have a particular relationship

The numbers 2, 4, 6, 8, 10, and so on, form a sequence of even numbers, because all are multiples of 2. A sequence is also called a **series**. An **arithmetic progression** is a series in which you add or subtract the same number each time to get the next number, such as: 4, 7, 10, 13, 16, and so on (start at 4 and add 3 each time). In a **geometric progression**, you multiply or divide by the same number each time to get the next number, such as: 2, 4, 8, 16, 32, and so on (start at 2 and multiply by 2 each time). In the **Fibonacci series**, each number is the result of adding together the two previous numbers, such as: 1, 1, 2, 3, 5, 8, 13, 21, 34, 55, and so on.

## Magic square

A square array of numbers in which the columns, rows, and diagonals each add up to the same total

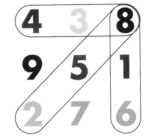

**Magic square**
*In this magic square, any three numbers in a straight line add up to 15.*

## Parentheses

The symbols ( and )

Parentheses surround any operation in arithmetic, such as adding or multiplying, that must be carried out first. So 3 + (4 x 2) = 3 + 8 = 11, but (3 + 4) x 2 = 7 x 2 = 14.

## Calculus

The use of algebra to calculate changing quantities

Calculus deals with quantities such as curving lines. It can, for example, calculate the slope of the line at any point and the area under any part of a curve.

## Probability

The degree of chance that something might happen

Probability ranges from 0 (will not happen) to 1 (will happen). Throwing a die to get 5 has a probability of 1/6, as this is one result out of six possible results.

## Percentage

A fraction given as a number that you have to divide by 100

$\frac{3}{4}$ is equal to 75 ÷ 100, so 3/4 is often shown as 75 per cent (75%).

## Ratio

A comparison between two numbers or amounts

The masses of two objects of 10 kilograms and 2 kilograms are in the ratio 5:1 (5 to 1). You divide two numbers or amounts to get their ratio. Two amounts that vary are **proportional** if they always have the same ratio.

## Algebra

The use of letters to represent quantities in calculations

The area of a rectangle is the length multiplied by the width. If we call the length $l$ and the width $w$, the area of any rectangle is $l$ x $w$, or $lw$. The letters $l$ and $w$ stand for numbers – in this case, the actual length of either side in units such as inches. $l$ and $w$ are **variables**, meaning that they can take any value. A calculation using variables, such as $lw$, is called an **expression**. Algebra often uses $x$ and $y$ as variables.

## Equation

A mathematical statement that two quantities or expressions are equal

In your pocket are nine coins marked 10 and 5. If the total value is 65, how many of each kind are there? You can calculate the answer using an equation. Let the number of "10" coins be $x$. Their value is $10x$. The number of "5" coins is $9–x$, and their value is $5(9–x)$. As the values total 65, this gives us the equation: $65 = 10x + 5(9–x)$. Solving this equation shows that $x = 4$, so there must be four coins marked 10 and five coins marked 5.

# Trigonometry

It is possible to find out how far away you are from something, or how high mountains and buildings are, without actually measuring these things. Trigonometry uses triangles to solve such problems.

## Trigonometry

The branch of mathematics that studies triangles

A triangle has three sides and three angles where each pair of sides meets. If you know the size of any three of these sides and angles, you can work out the others using trigonometry. You make calculations using the length of one side and a trigonometrical ratio.

## Angle

The space between two lines that meet or cross

The angle formed where two lines meet or cross is expressed as the amount of rotation needed to move one of the lines to the position of the other line. This movement is measured in degrees (°) or radians. An angle of 0° is a **null** or **zero angle**. Where the lines make a square corner, the angle is 90° and is called a **right angle**. An **acute angle** is less than 90°, and an angle that is between 90° and 180° is an **obtuse angle**. A **reflex angle** is between 180° and 360°, while an angle of 360° is a **round angle**. A **solid angle** is the amount by which a cone spreads from its point, or **vertex**.

### See also

Reciprocal 170

## Degree (°)

A unit used to measure angles

A degree can be divided into 60 units called **minutes** ('), while a minute is made up of 60 smaller units called **seconds** ("). A **radian** (rad) is another unit of angle equal to 57.296°, or 180°/pi (pi = 3.14159). The word degree also refers to other small units, such as degrees of temperature.

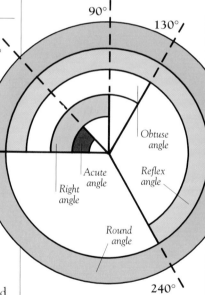

*Rotation and angles*
*Two lines lying on top of each other have an angle of 0°. If one line rotates about one end, the angle between the lines increases. An angle of 45° is an acute angle. A right angle is formed when the line makes a quarter turn and rotates 90°, while an angle of 130° is an obtuse angle. Any angle formed by a rotation of more than 180°, such as 240°, is a reflex angle. The line makes a complete rotation in 360° and returns to its original position, giving a round angle.*

## Pythagoras

Greek philosopher
(c.580–c.500 BC)

Pythagoras proposed that everything is governed by relationships of numbers. He is best known for the **Pythagorean theorem**. This states that the square of the length of the hypotenuse of a right-angled triangle (side C in the diagram below) is equal to the sum of the squares of the lengths of the other two sides $(C^2 = A^2 + B^2)$.

## Trigonometrical ratio

The ratio of the lengths of two sides of a right-angled triangle

One angle of a right-angled triangle is 90°. Either of the other two angles has six trigonometrical ratios. The **sine** (sin) of the angle is the length of the side opposite the angle divided by the hypotenuse (the side opposite the right angle). The **cosine** (cos) of the angle is the length of the adjacent side (next to the angle) divided by the hypotenuse. The **tangent** (tan) is the length of the opposite side divided by the adjacent side. Calculators can give these ratios. The **cosecant** (cosec), **secant** (sec), and **cotangent** (cot) are the reciprocals of the sine, cosine, and tangent respectively.

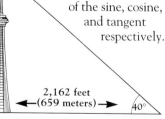

2,162 feet
◄—(659 meters)—► 40°

*Making use of trigonometry*
*The height of the tower equals the distance (2,162 feet) multiplied by the tangent of 40° (0.839) = 1,814 feet (553 meters).*

# Geometry

Whenever engineers design machines, architects plan buildings, or navigators plot their routes, they use geometry. Geometry tells us what points, lines, and shapes are like and how to make use of them.

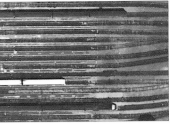

**Railroad tracks**
*This overhead view shows how each pair of rails are always the same distance apart.*

## Geometry

The branch of mathematics that studies points, lines, and shapes

A point is a position in space . It has no size and no dimensions, which are length, width, and height. A line connects two or more points. A straight line has only one dimension, which is length. Plane geometry studies lines and flat shapes, such as circles and squares, which occupy a flat surface called a **plane** and have two dimensions – length and width. Solid geometry studies **solids**, which are solid shapes, such as spheres and cubes, with three dimensions.

**Natural symmetry**
*We consider symmetrical patterns and shapes that occur in nature, such as this snow crystal, to possess great beauty.*

## Convex

Curving outward

The top of a dome is convex. The inside of the dome is **concave**, and curves inward. Convex and concave lenses and mirrors are used in optical instruments.

| Convex lens | Concave lens |
|---|---|

**Concave and convex lenses**
*A convex lens makes light rays come together, or converge. A concave lens makes light rays spread apart, or diverge. (For more on lenses, see pages 84–89.)*

## See also

## Symmetrical

Made of matching parts

The letters H, M, O, and X are symmetrical. Imagine a vertical line cutting each letter down the center. Each half then becomes a mirror image of the other half. A line that is a center of symmetry is called an **axis**. Crystals form symmetrical shapes.

## Perpendicular

A line that meets another line at a right angle

When you draw two lines to write a capital T, each line is perpendicular to the other. A perpendicular is also a line that is at a right angle to a flat surface. An upright flag pole is perpendicular to the ground.

**Perpendicular letter**
*If you draw a capital T correctly, the two lines will meet at a 90° angle.*

## Parallel

Everywhere the same distance apart

Lines and surfaces can be parallel. The two rails of a railroad track form parallel lines, while the floors of a building form parallel surfaces. Parallel lines can also be curved. For example, two circles drawn with the same center, but with different radii, are parallel.

## Tangent

A straight line that touches a curve but continues on without crossing it

A **normal** is a straight line that is perpendicular to a tangent where it meets a curve. A normal is also a line that is perpendicular to a surface.

**Perpendicular in space**
*A straight line from the Space Shuttle to the nearest point on the ground is the normal to the Earth's surface at that point. The line also is at right angles to a tangent at that point – that is, any straight line that only touches the surface at the same place as the normal.*

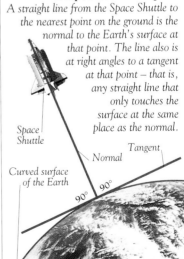

Space Shuttle

Normal

Tangent

Curved surface of the Earth

90°  90°

Continued on next page ➤

## Topology

The study of the properties of flat and solid shapes that are unchanged by squeezing, stretching, or twisting

Topology looks at the basic shapes of objects. If you can bend, stretch, or mold one shape to form another shape without breaking it or making holes in it, both shapes are topologically the same. A sphere is the same as a cube, for example, but it is not the same as a torus (a doughnut shape), because a sphere and a torus cannot be molded into each other. Unlike normal geometry, topology is not concerned with angles, distances, or whether lines are straight or parallel, because all these things change when one shape is molded into another. An unusual shape is the **Möbius strip** or **Moebius strip**, which has only one edge and one surface.

*The strip is given a half twist and the ends are glued together*

*One side is red, the other white*

*Paper strip*

**A shape with one surface**
*You can make a Möbius strip by taking a strip of paper, twisting one end of the paper through 180°, and sticking it to the other end. Using paper with a different color on each side will help you to see how the shape is formed.*

## Area

The size of a surface

The surface may be that of a flat shape, such as a circle. A **surface area** is the area of the surface all around a solid shape, such as a sphere. Area is measured in square length units, such as **square inches** (in²). You can work out an area by using a formula. This often includes the **base** of a shape, which is the length of its lowest side, and the **height**, which is the distance from the base to the top of the shape.

## Volume

The amount of space inside a solid shape

Volume is measured in cubic length units, such as **cubic inches** (in³). Another unit of volume is the **liter** (l), which is the volume of 1 kg of water at 4°C. It is equal to 1,000 cm³. A **milliliter** (ml) is a thousandth of a liter, or 1 cm³. A **quart** is an imperial unit of volume equal to 1.057 liters.

**Cross section of an orange**
*An orange is sphere shaped. If you cut an orange straight across, each cut surface has the shape of a circle.*

## Cross section

A plane shape obtained by cutting through a solid shape at right angles to its length or height

If you cut a sphere, the cut surface of each half is a cross-section. It has the shape of a circle. A **prism** has the same cross section when cut in two anywhere along its length or height. Cutting a cone in four different directions gives four curves called **conics** or **conic sections**. These curves are a **circle**, an **ellipse**, a **parabola**, and a **hyperbola**.

### GEOMETRIC FORMULAS

#### Formulas for area

| | |
|---|---|
| Square | l² |
| Rectangle | bh |
| Triangle | bh/2 |
| Circle | πr² |
| Sphere | 4πr² |
| Cylinder | πdh (excluding ends) |

| | |
|---|---|
| l = length |
| b = base |
| h = height |
| r = radius |
| d = diameter |
| π = pi (3.14159) |

#### Formulas for volume

| | |
|---|---|
| Cube | l³ |
| Brick | lbh |
| Sphere | 4/3πr³ |
| Cylinder | πr²h |

*Diameter 1.7 inches (18 centimeters)*

*The radius of the can is half the diameter*

*Height 9.1 inches (23 centimeters)*

**Using formulas**
*The can's volume is 3.14159 x 3.65² x 9.1 = 360 cubic inches (5,853 cubic centimeters). The curved surface area is πdh, or 3.14159 x 3.65 x 9.1 = 203 square inches (1,301 square centimeters). The complete surface area includes the circles at the top and base.*

◄ Continued from previous page

# Locus

The line traced by a moving point

The moving point follows a certain rule and may trace a curve. The locus of a point which moves so that it is always the same distance from a second point is a circle. The second point is the center of the circle.

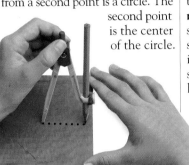

**Drawing a locus**
*A circle with a radius of 2 inches (5 centimeters) gives a locus of all points that are 2 inches (5 centimeters) from the point that forms the center of the circle.*

# Transformation

A change in the shape of a flat or solid shape

You can move, enlarge, reduce, or reflect a shape to produce another shape that is a transformation of the first. A **reflection** is a mirror image of a shape drawn on the opposite side of a mirror line. A **rotation** is a transformation in which a shape turns around a point or a line. A **translation** is a movement in which the shape moves in a straight line. An **enlargement** is an increase in size of a shape, in which all the dimensions of the two shapes are in the same ratio. A shape enlarged in different directions by different amounts is a transformation called a **stretch**.

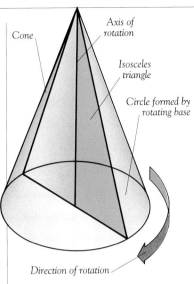

**From a triangle to a cone**
*Rotating an isosceles triangle (one that has two equal sides) around a line from the top to the center of the base produces a cone. This type of transformation is called a rotation.*

---

# CIRCLES AND CURVES

## Ellipse
An oval curve

## Radius
(plural: radii)
The distance from the center of a circle to the circumference

## Diameter
A line from one side of a circle that passes through the center to the other side

## Parabola
A type of open curve

## Hyperbola
A type of open curve with two branches

## Circle
A curve on which all points are equally distant from a center and the shape enclosed by this curve

## Semicircle
A shape that is half a circle

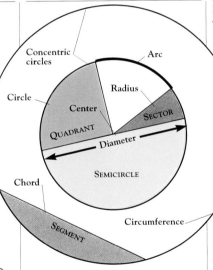

## Sector
A slice of a circle formed by two radii

## Center
The point at the middle of a shape or a solid. The center of a circle is equally distant from all points on it.

## Segment
The part of a circle between a chord and the circumference

## Concentric
Having the same center as another curve or shape

## Quadrant
A quarter of a circle

## Arc
A part of a curve

## Circumference
The distance around a circle

## Chord
A straight line joining any two points on the circumference of a circle

## Pi (π)
A number equal to the length of the circumference of any circle divided by the diameter. The value of pi is approximately 3.14159.

*Continued on next page ▶*

# PLANE AND SOLID SHAPES

## Plane Shapes

### Polygon
A flat shape with three or more straight sides

### Regular polygon
A polygon with sides of equal length

### Diagonal
A line between any two corners of a polygon that are not adjacent to each other

### Triangle
A polygon with three sides

### Equilateral triangle
A triangle with three equal sides

### Isosceles triangle
A triangle with two equal sides

### Right-angled triangle
A triangle in which the angle between two sides is a right angle

### Hypotenuse
The longest side of a right-angled triangle

*Diagonal*

### Quadrilateral
A polygon with four sides

### Square
A polygon with four equal sides that all meet at right angles

### Rhombus
A polygon with four equal sides that do not meet at right angles

### Octagon
A polygon with eight sides

### Rectangle
A quadrilateral with opposite sides of equal length that all meet at right angles

### Parallelogram
A quadrilateral with opposite sides of equal length that do not meet at right angles

### Trapezium
A quadrilateral with one pair of parallel sides

### Pentagon
A polygon with five sides

### Hexagon
A polygon with six sides

## Solid Shapes

### Polyhedron
A solid shape that has polygons as faces

### Regular polyhedron
A polyhedron in which all the edges are the same length

### Tetrahedron
A polyhedron that has four equal triangles as faces

### Cube
A polyhedron that has six equal squares as faces and in which every angle is a right angle

### Octahedron
A polyhedron having eight triangles as faces

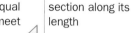

### Pyramid
A polyhedron with a polygon for a base and triangular sides that meet at the top

### Prism
A polyhedron with the same cross-section along its length

### Net
A flat shape that can be folded to form a polyhedron

*Net of a cube*

### Sphere
A round shape like a globe

### Hemisphere
Half a sphere

### Spheroid
An egg shape

### Cylinder
A shape like a tube or rod

### Cone
A shape with a circle for a base and one other rounded face that comes to a point at the top

### Torus
A shape like a doughnut

### Helix
A shape like a coiled spring

◄ *Continued from previous page*

# Abbreviations

Many terms and phrases in mathematics and science are shortened to make them easier to use. This table gives a selection of abbreviations, some of which have more than one meaning.

| | |
|---|---|
| A | Ampere |
| AC | Alternating current |
| Ag | Silver |
| AI | Artificial intelligence |
| AM | Amplitude modulation |
| aq | Aqueous solution |
| ASCII | American standard code for information interchange |
| atm | Atmosphere |
| Au | Gold |
| b | Base |
| BASIC | Beginners all-purpose symbolic instruction code |
| bp | Boiling point |
| Bq | Becquerel |
| c | Speed of light |
| C | Carbon |
| C | Celsius/Centigrade |
| C | Coulomb |
| Cal | Calorie |
| cc | Cubic centimeter |
| cd | Candela |
| Cd | Cadmium |
| CD | Compact disc |
| CFC | Chlorofluorocarbon |
| cm | Centimeter |
| CO | Carbon monoxide |
| $CO_2$ | Carbon dioxide |
| COBOL | Common business-oriented language |
| cos | Cosine |
| cosec | Cosecant |
| cot | Cotangent |
| CPU | Central processing unit |
| CRO | Cathode ray oscilloscope |
| CRT | Cathode ray tube |
| d | Diameter |
| DAT | Digital audio tape |
| dB | Decibel |
| DC | Direct current |
| DCC | Digital compact cassette |
| DDT | Dichlorodiphenyl-trichloroethane |
| DNA | Deoxyribonucleic acid |
| DOS | Disk operating system |
| DRAM | Dynamic random-access memory |
| DTP | Desktop publishing |
| emf | Electromotive force |
| EPROM | Erasable programmable read-only memory |
| eV | Electronvolt |
| F | Fahrenheit |
| F | Farad |
| F | Fluorine |
| Fe | Iron |

| | |
|---|---|
| FM | Frequency modulation |
| fp | Freezing point |
| ft. | Foot |
| g | Gas |
| g | Gram |
| g | Gravity |
| gal. | Gallon |
| h | Height |
| H | Hydrogen |
| Hg | Mercury |
| hp | Horsepower |
| hr | Hour |
| Hz | Hertz |
| IC | Integrated circuit |
| in. | Inch |
| IR | Infrared |
| J | Joule |
| K | Kelvin |
| K/Kb/KB | Kilobyte |
| K | Potassium |
| kcal | Kilocalorie |
| KE | Kinetic energy |
| kg | Kilogram |
| kHz | Kilohertz |
| kJ | Kilojoule |
| km | Kilometer |
| kW | Kilowatt |
| kWh | Kilowatt-hour |
| l | Length |
| l | Liquid |
| l | Liter |
| lb. | Pound |
| LCD | Liquid-crystal display |
| LED | Light-emitting diode |
| lm | Lumen |
| lx | Lux |
| m | Mass |
| m | Meter |
| M/Mb/MB | Megabyte |
| mA | Milliampere |
| mb | Millibar |
| mg | Milligram |
| MHD | Magnetohydrodynamics |
| MHz | Megahertz |
| mi. | Mile |
| ml | Milliliter |
| mm | Millimeter |
| mmHg | Millimeter of mercury |
| mol | Mole |
| mV | Millivolt |
| MV | Megavolt |
| MW | Megawatt |
| N | Newton |
| N | Nitrogen |
| Na | Sodium |
| nm | Nanometer |

| | |
|---|---|
| n-p-n | Negative-positive-negative |
| NTP | Normal temperature and pressure |
| NTSC | National Television Systems Committee |
| O | Oxygen |
| OCR | Optical character recognition |
| OOP | Object-oriented programming |
| oz. | Ounce |
| Pa | Pascal |
| PAL | Phase alteration line |
| Pb | Lead |
| PC | Personal computer |
| PD | Potential difference |
| PE | Potential energy |
| p-n-p | Positive-negative-positive |
| PROM | Programmable read-only memory |
| pt. | Pint |
| PTFE | Polytetrafluoroethene |
| PVA | Polyvinyl acetate |
| PVC | Polyvinyl chloride |
| PWR | Pressurized-water reactor |
| r | Radius |
| rad | Radian |
| radar | Radio detection and ranging |
| RAM | Random-access memory |
| RAM | Relative atomic mass |
| rd | Relative density |
| RMM | Relative molecular mass |
| RMS | Root mean square |
| ROM | Read-only memory |
| s | Second |
| s | Solid |
| S | Sulfur |
| SCR | Silicon-controlled rectifier |
| sec | Secant |
| SHM | Simple harmonic motion |
| SI | *Système International* |
| sin | Sine |
| SLR | Single-lens reflex |
| Sn | Tin |
| sonar | Sound navigation ranging |
| Sr | Strontium |
| SRAM | Static random-access memory |
| SSC | Superconducting super collider |
| STP | Standard temperature and pressure |
| Sv | Sievert |
| tan | Tangent |
| TNT | Trinitrotoluene |
| U–235 | Uranium 235 |
| UHF | Ultra-high frequency |
| USCS | United States Customary Systems |
| UV | Ultraviolet |
| V | Vanadium |
| V | Volt |
| VCR | Video cassette recorder |
| VDU | Visual display unit |
| VHF | Very high frequency |
| W | Tungsten |
| W | Watt |
| yd. | Yard |

# Pioneers of science, technology, and maths

**Maria Agnesi**
Italian mathematician (1718–99)
Studied and wrote extensively on
algebra and geometry.

**Alhazen**
Egyptian physicist (c.965–c.1038)
Realized that light comes from
outside the eye, explained how
lenses work, and made
parabolic mirrors.

**al-Khwarizmi**
Arab mathematician (c.800–c.850)
Introduced the Indian decimal
system of numbers and the use of
zero into Arab mathematics.

**André Marie Ampère**
French physicist (1775–1836)
Studied electromagnetism. Made the
distinction between electric current
and voltage. The ampere (A), the SI
unit of current, is named after him.

**Anders Ångström**
Swedish spectroscopist (1814–74)
Worked out that hot gas emits
light rays at the same wavelengths
as it absorbs them when cooler.
The angstrom (Å), a unit of
wavelength of light, is named
after him.

**Archimedes** (*See page 51*)

**Aristotle**
Greek philosopher (384–322 BC)
Advocated science based on
observation, thus providing the basic
philosophy of science.

**Arrhenius, Svante**
Swedish chemist (1859–1927)
Discovered that molecules may split
up into ions, and suggested that
carbon dioxide causes global warming.

**Amedeo Avogadro**
Italian physicist (1776–1856)
Realized that equal volumes of
gas contain equal numbers of
particles. Made the crucial
distinction between molecules
and atoms.

**Charles Babbage** (*See page 119*)

**Leo Baekeland**
Belgian-American chemist (1863–1944)
Developed Bakelite, the first widely
used synthetic plastic.

**John Bardeen**
American physicist (1908–91)
Invented the transistor with his
fellow American physicists **Walter
Brattain** (1902–1987) and **William
Shockley** (*see page 116*).

**Antoine Henri Becquerel**
(*See page 45*)

**Alexander Graham Bell**
(*See page 128*)

**Daniel Bernoulli**
Swiss physicist (1700–82)
Discovered that pressure in a fluid
decreases as its velocity increases.
Pioneer of hydrodynamics.

**Jöns Berzelius** (*See page 135*)

**Henry Bessemer**
English engineer (1813–98)
Developed a process for making
cheap steel (the Bessemer process).
**William Kelly** (1811–88), an
American engineer, invented a
similar process at about the same time.

**Bhaksara II**
Indian mathematician (c.1114–85)
Wrote extensively on arithmetic and
algebra. Designed a wheel that he
hoped would give perpetual motion.

**Joseph Black**
Scottish physicist (1728–99)
Identified carbon dioxide and
discovered latent heat.

**Niels Bohr** (*See page 45*)

**George Boole**
English mathematician (1815–64)
Applied algebra to logic, developing
sytems now used in computing.

**Robert Boyle** (*See page 135*)

**William Henry Bragg &
William Lawrence Bragg**
(*See page 143*)

**Robert Wilhelm Bunsen**
German chemist (1811–99)
Pioneered spectroscopy for analyzing
the light emitted by elements.

**Nicolas Carnot**
French physicist (1796–1832)
Founded thermodynamics by
establishing the theory of heat engines.

**Wallace Carothers**
American chemist (1896–1937)
Invented synthetic rubber and nylon.

**Henry Cavendish** (*See page 135*)

**Anders Celsius**
Swedish astronomer (1701–44)
Devised a temperature scale, taking
the freezing point of water as 0°C
and the boiling point as 100°C.
It was named the Celsius or
Centigrade scale.

**James Chadwick** (*See page 45*)

**Jacques Alexandre Charles**
French physicist (1746–1823)
Discovered Charles' law, which
states that when pressure remains
constant, gases expand as temperature
rises. Built the first gas-filled balloon.

**John Douglas Cockcroft**
English physicist (1867–1967)
With the Irish physicist **Ernest
Walton** (born 1903), he built a
particle accelerator to give the first
artificial nuclear reaction.

**Christopher Cockerell**
English inventor (born 1910)
Invented the hovercraft.

**Arthur Compton**
American physicist (1892–1962)
First found evidence of the existence
of photons.

**Nicolaus Copernicus**
Polish astronomer (1473–1543)
Proposed that the Earth moves around
the Sun, not the Sun around the Earth.

**Charles Augustin de Coulomb**
French physicist (1736–1806)
Discovered how friction varies with
pressure and how electrostatic
force varies with distance. The SI
unit of electric charge, the coulomb
(C), is named after him.

**Marie Curie & Pierre Curie**
(*See page 135*)

**Louis Daguerre**
French inventor (1789–1851)
Used silver compounds to develop
the first practical method of producing
photographs. They were single
pictures that could not be copied.

**Gottlieb Daimler** (*See page 97*)

**John Dalton** (*See page 45*)

**Abraham Darby**
English engineer (1678–1717)
First person to smelt iron successfully
using coke instead of charcoal.

**Humphry Davy** (*See page 135*)

**Louis-Victor de Broglie**
French physicist (1892–1987)
Developed the theory that elementary
particles behave like waves.

**Democritus** (*See page 45*)

**René Descartes**
French philosopher & mathematician
(1596–1650)
Developed a system of coordinates
applying algebra to geometry
(Cartesian coordinates). Worked on
optics and developed a theory of the
structure of the Solar System.

**Paul Dirac**
English physicist (1902–84)
Developed quantum theory, linking
it to relativity. Predicted the
existence of antiparticles – that
every particle has its opposite.

**George Eastman**
American inventor (1854–1932)
Popularized photography by inventing
roll film and an easy-to-use camera.

**Thomas Alva Edison** (*See page 127*)

**Albert Einstein** (*See page 47*)

**Leo Esaki**
Japanese physicist (born 1925)
Invented a diode, which was
smaller, worked faster, and needed
less power than existing diodes.
This "tunnel diode" was an
important development in
semiconductor electronics.

**Euclid**
Greek mathematician (c.300 BC)
Developed Euclidean geometry
which held sway until the 1800s,
when other kinds were found.

**Daniel Fahrenheit**
German physicist (1686–1736)
Made the first mercury thermometers,
and invented the Fahrenheit scale of
temperature.

**Michael Faraday** (*See page 107*)

**Philo T. Farnsworth** (*See page 130*)

**Enrico Fermi** (*See page 45*)

**Reginald Fessenden** (*See page 129*)

**Richard Feynman**
American physicist (1918–88)
Contributed to quantum
electrodynamics. Developed
Feynman diagrams, a system of
notation for particle collisions.

**Fibonacci (Leonardo of Pisa)**
Italian mathematician (c.1170–c.1250)
Established the use of decimal
numbers in Europe. Also
discovered the Fibonacci series.

**John Fleming** (*See page 116*)

**Jean Foucault**
French physicist (1819–68)
Made the first accurate
measurement of the speed of light.
Demonstrated the Earth's rotation
with a long pendulum. Invented
the gyroscope.

**Benjamin Franklin** (*See page 107*)

**Rosalind Franklin** (*See page 143*)

**Augustin Jean Fresnel**
French physicist (1788–1827)
Developed the wave theory of light.
Invented the Fresnel lens, which
consists of a series of glass rings. It
concentrates light into a strong
beam and is used in car headlights,
searchlights, and lighthouses.

**Dennis Gabor**
Hungarian–British physicist (1900–79)
Invented holography long before
the development of the laser.

**Galileo Galilei** (*See page 54*)

**Luigi Galvani** (*See page 107*)

**Johann Karl Friedrich Gauss**
German mathematician (1777–1855)
Contributed to all areas of
mathematics. Founder of modern
number theory.

**Joseph Gay-Lussac**
French chemist (1778–1850)
Like Charles, he researched how
pressure and temperature affect
gases. Discovered that volumes of
gases combine in simple ratios.

**Hans Geiger**
German physicist (1882–1945)
With Ernest Rutherford, he
developed a counter for detecting
ionizing radiation.

**Murray Gell-Mann** (*See page 45*)

**Sophie Germain**
French mathematician (1776–1831)
Studied number theory and the
resonant vibration of elastic bodies.

**William Gilbert**
English physicist (1544–1603)
Studied static electricity and
magnetism, discovering that the
Earth has a magnetic field.

**Robert Goddard**
American engineer (1882–1945)
Built and flew the first liquid-fuelled
rocket engine.

**Maria Goeppert-Mayer**
German–American mathematical
physicist (1906–72)
Suggested that protons and neutrons
are arranged in shells within the
nucleus of an atom.

**Fritz Haber**
German physical chemist (1868–1934)
Devised the Haber process, which
uses nitrogen from the air to make
ammonia.

**Otto Hahn** (*See page 45*)

**John Harrison**
English instrument maker (1693–1776)
Invented the ship's chronometer –
essential for accurate navigation.

**Stephen Hawking**
English physicist (born 1942)
Made important advances in the
theory of space-time and "space-time
singularities" (points of infinite
density) such as black holes.

**Werner Heisenberg**
German physicist (1901–76)
Pioneer in quantum mechanics.
Showed it is impossible to be sure of
both a particle's speed and its position
– Heisenberg's uncertainty principle.

*Continued on next page* ➤

**Hermann von Helmholtz**
German physicist (1821–94)
Established the law of conservation of energy. Advanced knowledge of sound and color.

**Joseph Henry** (*See page 107*)

**Hero of Alexandria** (*See page 97*)

**Heinrich Hertz** (*See page 75*)

**Dorothy Hodgkin** (*See page 143*)

**Robert Hooke**
English physicist (1635–1703)
Studied elasticity and discovered Hooke's law, which states that an elastic material changes size in proportion to the amount of force applied to it.

**Grace Hopper**
American mathematician (1906–92)
Developed the concept of automatic programming for computers.

**Christiaan Huygens**
Dutch physicist & astronomer (1629–95)
Improved lenses for telescopes. Put forward the wave theory of light. Built the first pendulum clock.

**Hypatia of Alexandria**
Greek philosopher & mathematician (c.370–c.415)
Early authority on algebra and geometry. She designed scientific apparatus, including a hydrometer and equipment for distilling water.

**Frédéric Joliot-Curie & Irène Joliot-Curie**
French nuclear physicists (Frédéric 1900–58; Irène 1897-1956)
Discovered how to make radioactivity artificially.

**James Prescott Joule** (*See page 70*)

**Lord Kelvin** (*See page 93*)

**Gustav Robert Kirchhoff**
German physicist (1824–87)
Invented spectroscopy, and discovered the elements cesium and rubidium.

**Koupho**
Chinese physicist (c.300)
Linked magnetism and electrostatics, stating: "Like poles repel; so do like charges."

**Sonya (Sofya) Kovalevskaya**
Russian astronomer & mathematician (1850–91)
Pioneer of differential equations.

**Stephanie Kwolek**
American chemist (born 1923)
Developed the synthetic fiber Kevlar (a type of plastic), which is five times stronger than steel yet very light.

**Paul Langevin**
French physicist (1872–1946)
Established the modern theory of magnetism, investigated ultrasound, and invented sonar.

**Marie Lavoisier**
French chemist (1758–1836)
With her husband **Antoine Lavoisier** (*see page 135*), she investigated the nature of elements. Made scientific drawings of their experiments.

**Antony van Leeuwenhoek**
Dutch microscopist (1632–1723)
Developed microscopes and used them to observe blood cells, bacteria, and many other things.

**Gottfried Wilhelm Leibniz**
German mathematician (1646–1716)
Invented calculus, and a calculator that could subtract, add, multiply, divide, and find square roots.

**Jean Lenoir**
Belgian engineer (1822–1900)
Invented the first practical internal combustion engine, using coal gas as a fuel.

**Justus von Liebig**
German chemist (1803–73)
Pioneer of organic chemistry, finding a quick way of assessing the carbon and hydrogen content of compounds.

**Kathleen Lonsdale**
Irish crystallographer (1903–71)
Pioneer in X-ray crystallography. Developed the work of William Henry and William Lawrence Bragg. Worked on organic crystals.

**Ada Lovelace** (*See page 119*)

**Auguste Lumière & Louis Lumière**
French scientists (Auguste 1862–1954; Louis 1864–1948)
Invented the *Cinématographe*, a combined motion-picture camera and projector, which recorded images on a celluloid strip.

**Theodore Maiman**
American physicist (born 1927)
Made the first laser, which produced red light from a ruby cylinder.

**Guglielmo Marconi** (*See page 129*)

**Maria the Jewess**
Egyptian alchemist (c.70)
Her theories formed the basis of western alchemy and so influenced the development of modern chemistry. She designed scientific instruments for distillation and sublimation.

**James Clerk Maxwell**
Scottish physicist (1831–79)
Identified light as electromagnetic radiation. Introduced the idea of the electromagnetic field and the kinetic theory of gases. Took the first color photograph.

**Lise Meitner** (*See page 45*)

**Dmitri Mendeleyev** (*See page 135*)

**Samuel Morse**
American engineer (1791–1872)
Built the first telegraph line (with Joseph Henry) and invented Morse code for sending messages by telegraph.

**John von Neumann** (*See page 119*)

**Thomas Newcomen**
English engineer (1663–1729)
Invented the first practical steam engine.

**Isaac Newton** (*See page 55*)

**Joseph Nicéphore Niepce**
French inventor (1765–1833)
Took the world's first photograph, which took eight hours to expose.

**Alfred Nobel**
Swedish chemist (1833–96)
Invented dynamite and founded Nobel prizes.

**Ida Noddack**
German chemist (born 1896)
Discovered rhenium with husband **Walter Noddack** (1893–1960). She was the first to suggest nuclear fission.

**Amelie Noether**
German mathematician (1882–1935)
Leading figure in the development of abstract algebra.

◀ *Continued from previous page*

**Hans Oersted** (*See page 107*)

**Georg Ohm**
German physicist (1789–1854)
Found relationship between current and voltage (Ohm's Law). The unit of electrical resistance, the ohm (Ω), is named after him.

**Blaise Pascal** (*See page 52*)

**Linus Pauling**
American chemist (born 1901)
Studied the forces holding atoms together and calculated the exact size and shape of complex organic molecules.

**Marguerite Perey**
French physicist (1909–75)
Discovered the naturally radioactive element francium.

**Max Planck** (*See page 45*)

**Joseph Priestley**
English–American chemist (1733–1804)
Discovered oxygen and several other gases.

**Ptolemy**
Egyptian–Greek astronomer (c.90–c.168)
Developed trigonometry. Wrote on optics and put forward a theory of the structure of the Universe.

**Pythagoras** (*See page 172*)

**Chandrasekhara Venkata Raman**
Indian physicist (1888–1970)
Showed the effects of molecules in scattering light (the Raman effect).

**William Ramsay**
Scottish chemist (1852–1916)
Discovered the elements neon, argon, xenon, and krypton. Realized that with helium they form a distinctive group of elements, now known as the noble gases.

**Wilhelm Roentgen** (*See page 75*)

**Count Rumford**
American physicist (1753–1814)
Realized that heat is a form of energy.

**Ernst Ruska**
German physicist (1906–88)
Pioneer of the electron microscope.

**Ernest Rutherford** (*See page 45*)

**Abdus Salam**
Pakistani physicist (born 1926)
Showed how the weak nuclear force and electromagnetic force are linked.

**Karl Scheele** (*See page 135*)

**Erwin Schrödinger**
Austrian physicist (1887–1961)
Developed the ideas of de Broglie and founded wave mechanics.

**Glenn Seaborg**
American physicist (born 1912)
Was a member of, and later led, a team that discovered plutonium and several other artificial elements.

**William Shockley** (*See page 116*)

**Frederick Soddy**
English radiochemist (1877–1956)
Discovered isotopes and, with Rutherford, explained radioactive decay.

**Joseph Swan** (*See page 127*)

**William Fox Talbot**
British inventor (1800–77)
Invented the process of developing a photograph to produce a negative from which many prints can be made.

**Nikola Tesla** (*See page 107*)

**Thales** (*See page 107*)

**Joseph John Thomson** (*See page 45*)

**Evangelista Torricelli**
Italian physicist (1608–47)
Discovered atmospheric pressure and invented the mercury barometer.

**Alan Turing** (*See page 119*)

**John Venn**
English mathematician (1834–1923)
Inventor of Venn diagrams, widely used in mathematics and logic.

**Pierre Vernier**
French mathematician and engineer (1580–1638)
Devised a precision measuring scale.

**Alessandro Volta** (*See page 107*)

**James Watt** (*See page 97*)

**George Westinghouse** (*See page 107*)

**Frank Whittle** (*See page 97*)

**Charles Wilson**
Scottish physicist (1869–1959)
Invented the Wilson cloud chamber, which was used to detect subatomic particles.

**Orville Wright & Wilbur Wright**
American aviators (Orville 1871–1948; Wilbur 1867–1912)
Designed, built, and flew the first powered aeroplane.

**Chien-Shiung Wu**
Chinese-American physicist (born 1912)
She developed the study of radioactive decay and made important discoveries about the way in which beta particles are emitted during decay.

**Xie Xide**
Chinese physicist (born 1921)
She made important advances in the study of semiconductors, solid-state physics, and compression in gases.

**Rosalyn (Sussman) Yalow**
American nuclear physicist (born 1921)
Expert on radioisotopes. Developed a way of using radioisotopes to detect hormones in the blood.

**Chen Ning Yang**
Chinese–American physicist (born 1922)
Made major advances in the study of nuclear physics, especially in relation to the weak nuclear force.

**Thomas Young**
English physicist (1773–1829)
Developed Huygens' wave theory of light. Also extended Hooke's work on elasticity and gave his name to the constant in Hooke's law – Young's modulus.

**Hideki Yukawa**
Japanese physicist (1907–81)
First proposed the strong nuclear force.

**Chongzi Zu**
Chinese mathematician & astronomer (429–500)
Computed pi (π) accurately and the length of a year as 365.2429 days.

**Vladimir Zworykin** (*See page 130*)

# Index

The index gives the page number of every entry and subentry in this book. For a subentry, the main entry under which it appears is given in parenthses ( ). Tables and table entries are shown by the italic word *table*.

# Acknowledgments

**Dorling Kindersley and
Neil Ardley would like to thank:**
Colin Walton, Chris Legee, Jane Tetzlaff,
and Robin Hunter for their design help;
Esther Labi, Simon Adams, John Farndon,
Graham Tomkinson, and Jenny Vaughan
for their editorial assistance. Photography:
Andy Crawford and Steve Gorton (DK
Studio), and Justin Scobie. Models: Silpa
Haria, Danny O'Sullivan, and Vicky
Watling. Thanks also to: Alpine Sports;
British Aerospace; British Coal; British
Nuclear Fuels; British Petroleum; British
Steel; L. Cornellissen & Sons Ltd.; Cotswold
Woollen Weavers; Covent Garden
Cycles; Door 'o' matic Ltd.; The Electricity
Association; EM Models; Keith Rookledge
of G. Farley & Sons Ltd.; Griffin &
George Ltd.; Hunt & O'Byrne; Chris
Saussman and Eric Matthews (Chemistry),
and Geoff Green (Physics) of Imperial
College, London; Keith Johnson & Pelling
Ltd.; Le Blanc Fine Art; National Power
(Didcot); "Quicks" Archery Specialists;
Southern Boat Center; Peter Leighton
(Chemistry) of University College,
London; Peter Vivian; Sid Wells.

### PICTURE CREDITS
t=top b=bottom c=center l=left r=right
**Aerofilms:** p 173 tr
**Ardea:** p 26 bl (Ron and Valerie Taylor)
**Associated Press Ltd.:** p 130 tl
**Paul Brierley:** pp 134, 173 bl
**Bruce Coleman:** pp 30 br (Keith
Gunnar), 38 bl (NASA), 78 b (Michael
P. Price), 83 tr (Kim Taylor)
**Colorific!:** p 89 tr
**E T Archive:** p 163 t

**ETSU/Dept of Trade and Industry:** p 71 t
**Mary Evans Picture Library:** pp 21 tr,
75 tr, 107 bl, 135 tl
**Yaël Freudmann:** p 125 br
**Robert Harding:** p 150 b
**Stuart Hildred:** p 148 tr
**Christopher Howson:** pp 87 tl, tc, tr
**Hulton Deutsch Collection:** pp 45 bc,
70 tr, 143 tl
**Image Bank:** pp 10 l, 11 tr,
(Harald Sund), 12 l (Bill Varie), 29 t
(Andy Caulfield), 83 bc (Eric Meola),
157 tr (Flip Chalfont), 158 tr (Colin
Molyneux), 164 rc (Co Rentmeester)
**NASA:** p 173 br
**National Maritime Museum:** p 51 b
**NHPA:** pp 16-17 (Peter Johnson)
**Ontario Science Centre:** p 103 bl
**Osram Limited:** p 83 br
**Oxford Scientific Films:** p 160 tl
(Miriam Austerman)
**Pictor Uniphoto:** pp 33 bl, 57 tr
**Planet Earth:** p 25 br (Georgette
Douwma)
**Rex Features:** pp 39 tr, 57 tl (Rick Falco)
**Science Photo Library:** pp 19 bl (Gregory
Sams), 20 tr (Lawrence Livermore
National Laboratory, University of
California), 34 l (Philippe Plailly),
35 tr (Geof Tompkinson), 40 bl
(Ressmayer/Starlight), 42 bl (Philippe
Plailly), 43 b (David Parker), 45 br (Los
Alamos National Laboratory), 46 t (Prof
Harold Edgerton), 47 t (Library of
Congress), 55 t (Dr. Jeremy Burgess), 61 t
(Simon Fraser, Newcastle University
Robotics Group), 63 br (NASA), 77 tr
(Sinclair Stammers), 88 br, 91 b
(Williams and Metcalf), 97 br, 99 tr
(CNRI), 113 bl (Alex Bartel), 117 tl
(David Parker), 117 tr (Dale
Boyer/NASA), 117 b (James King-

Holmes), 126 br (Dr. Jeremy Burgess), 129
tr, 135 rc (National Library of Medicine),
151 (Martin Dohrn), 157 tl (Martin
Bond), 164 b (Tony Craddock), 164 rc
(Co Rentmeester), 173 tc (Claude
Nuridsany and Marie Perennou)
**Frank Spooner Pictures:** p 109 tr
(Mitsuhiro Wada)
**Sporting Pictures (UK) Ltd:** p 163 br
**Stockphotos:** p 64 tl (Jon Davison)
**H R Wallingford Group:** pp 72 bl, 73 br
**Zefa:** pp 85 tr, 136 tr, 155

### ARTWORK CREDITS
**Karen Cochrane:** pp 27 tr, 33 tr, 53 tl,
106 bl
**Yaël Freudmann:** p 73 bl
**Andrew Green:** pp 15 t, 16, 17, 18 r, 22,
32 tr, 37 tc, 46–47, 49 bc, 59 b, 60, 61,
79 l, 79 br, 84 bl, 85 bl, 86 c, 98 b, 101 t,
103 tr, 129 c, 161 b
**Andrew Green / Janos Marffy:** pp 41 t,
74–75, 87 br, 88 t, 99 c
**Christopher Howson:** pp 171 c, 173 bc, br
**Judith Maguire:** pp 170 t, 172 c, br
**Janos Marffy:** pp 29 r, 66
**Janos Marffy / John Woodcock:** pp 165 t,
92–93
**Colin Salmon:** pp 24 l, 62 tr, lc, 63 bl,
64 tr, 65 b, 81 tr, 82 r, 95 c, 96 tl, b, 97 b,
110–111, 114 bc, 115 tr, 116 b, 120 b, 125
t, 130–131 b, 143 r, 168 b, 175 bl, bc, 176
**Colin Salmon / Judith Maguire:** pp 157 b,
175 tr
**Patrizio Semproni:** pp 35, 36, 38, 39, 42,
44 tr, 136 l, 138, 139, 140–141, 144, 152 l,
161 c, 162 cl, 162–163 b
**Salvatore Tomaselli:** pp 24, 25, 26
**Salvatore Tomaselli / Patrizio Semproni:**
pp 34–35
**Richard Ward:** p 104 cr
**John Woodcock:** pp 68-69, 92–93